CONTENTS

ACKNOWLEDGEMENTS

Stan Maklan has contributed his knowledge of how to lay the foundations of a customer-centric organization (Chapters 8, 9 and 10). Chapter 8 is about the implications of becoming customer-centric for an organization's value proposition and the business case and it will make firms reassess what becoming 'customer-centric' means. Chapter 10 on CRM failure is required reading for those embarking on a CRM journey.

An important theme of this book is the consideration of how different firms create value. Part 2 on the CRM agenda could not have been written without the contribution of Computer Sciences Corporation (CSC) Researchers Richard Pawson and Francis Hayden, who provided the initial spark for many of the ideas.

A number of CSC's CRM consultants have used their extensive experience, gained over years of consulting, to contribute in their area of specialization. Ian Thornhill prepared Chapter 15 on customer intelligence; Duncan Reid Chapter 16 on campaign management and Jim Mackay Chapter 13 on creating the customer-centric enterprise.

Myself, my colleagues and our contacts at Wolff-Olins, a leading brand agency, have become more convinced that the chasm between many organizations' brands and their CRM activities needs bridging. We have worked with Charlie Stott of Wolff-Olins to try to drive brand through into organizational behaviours.

In Part 6 we have leant heavily on CSC Research Services – CSC's network of researchers into the technology future. Linda Wooldridge and Piet Opperman prepared Chapter 20 on the internet generation. Chapter 21 on customer managed relationships expands on work from CSC's Howard Smith, Lynette Ryals and Doug Neal.

The construction of a book is a logistical problem, and Ian Thornhill maintained the work on track and dealt with the management of communications across the global organization that contributed to the book.

Sarah Taylor, of the Management Consultancies Association, and Fiona Czerniawska, the series editor, contributed regular feedback and comments. Hodder Headline and Liz Ross, the editor, helped us through the complexities of the publishing process.

If the words make sense that is due to Anne Pappenheim who edited the book and eliminated the obscure, the mixed metaphors, the hanging sentences, the over-inflated prose and the inappropriate sexual innuendos.

My wife, Elizabeth, listened to the work as it was being read out loud and helped guide the book towards the general business reader rather than the CRM specialist intent on further CRM navel-gazing.

CRM is a controversial subject. It was my responsibility to write those elements not contributed by others, and to weave other contributors' thinking into the story. If, in so doing, I have corrupted their message I apologize. All the errors of fact or interpretation that remain are, of course, my own.

Patrick Molineux, Bramley, May 2002.

CONTRIBUTORS

Mary Crowe	Piet Opperman	Howard Smith
Francis Hayden	Donal O'Shea	Charlie Stott
Jim Mackey	Richard Pawson	Ian Thornhill
Stan Maklan	Duncan Reid	Linda Wooldridge
Doug Neal	Lynette Ryals	

INTRODUCTION

BACKGROUND

Customer relationships have been with us since Neanderthals first sold spare mammoth skins to their friends. Then, it was the geographical proximity of supplier and customer, rather than a scientific process of customer attraction and retention, that triggered the relationships. As people congregated in towns, urbanization extended the physical distance between supplier and customer, creating the need for intermediaries – merchants – who transferred products from supplier to customer, adding their own margin along the way. But Shylock and Marco Polo are beyond the scope of the science or art of Customer Relationship Management (CRM) as we understand it today.

Industrialization meant that customers could no longer know the source of the products they bought. The transport revolution that dug canals, paved roads and laid railways transformed firms' ability to connect with new markets. Simultaneously, automation imposed standard products. How could firms compete, at a distance, with products that were not tailored to customers' needs? They invested in building brand, advertising and mass marketing to influence ever more remote customers and compete for an ever larger share of the market. Mass production and standardization, strong universal brand and a deep understanding of the market enabled Henry Ford to succeed.

However, the pursuit of the market is not what CRM has come to mean. Ironically, it was the most automated revolution to date – computerization – that enabled large companies to understand customers' needs at an individual level. And it was only during the 1980s that firms began to understand how to connect with individual customers rather than with an amorphous market. The planned extraction of profit from individual customers, by delivering value to them, is the essence of Customer Relationship Management and the subject of this book.

Inevitably, people with a product to sell insisted that their interpretation of CRM was the truth. If an organization, by good luck or judgement, adopted a version of CRM that coincided with its business needs, the concept worked. But for many, it did not. From 1999 onwards, industry analysts quoted rising failure rates. Suspicion replaced enthusiasm. Those who say 'CRM doesn't work' may have rejected a model of CRM, but they should not reject the concept entirely. Customer Relationship Management is something that all firms do, not something that some firms buy. It is an underlying principle of business.

The many versions of the CRM truth do hold nuggets of wisdom. Research shows that not all customers have equal value to a business. Customer service can significantly impact customer retention. Selling to existing customers is cheaper than acquiring new customers. More precise marketing can reduce costs and dramatically improve profits. Customer loyalty is priceless (and difficult to achieve). Relying upon customer inertia to retain customers is increasingly risky. Competition is so fierce that mass marketing techniques are inadequate. Meanwhile, new technologies allow organizations to create and store an unparalleled wealth of customer data. All this and more is true. Yet many companies find that CRM fails to meet their expectations.

The villain and the hero is technology. The technology industry appropriated the acronym 'CRM' and sucked in customer-related ideas and technologies. By the end of the 1990s, the acronym both misrepresented its subject and (as acronyms are wont to do) imposed on it an undeserved shelf life. CRM became a fad.

It also became one of the big beasts in the technology jungle. Enterprise Resource Planning (ERP) vendors (such as SAP and Peoplesoft) extended their offerings by exhorting firms who had 'connected their enterprise' to 'connect with their customers'. Siebel Systems established itself as the leader in a software market that had not existed in 1993. Today, hundreds of software applications jockey for a share of a CRM services market that Gartner estimates to be larger than the gross domestic product (GDP) of many African countries. Major consulting firms make billions from designing, implementing and fixing CRM initiatives. Students can spend years researching the subject. Aficionados can join internet communities where theories and ideas are discussed, case studies publicised and software advertised. Managers can attend business schools where customer strategies are dissected.

This book treats CRM not as a fad, but as a corporate strategy that executives ignore at their peril. It suggests that the bloodied corpses of failed projects that litter boardrooms are the result of misunderstanding what CRM is and what it can do. It aims to put a stop to managers saying: 'We implemented CRM last year – we bought product X'.

WHO SHOULD READ THIS BOOK AND WHY

This book views corporate strategy through the lens of the organization's connections with its customers. It is appropriate for readers who want to understand how to integrate customer strategy with corporate strategy, and readers for whom CRM is already a strategic corporate focus. It seeks to place its subject in the context of how firms extract value from and create value for customers.

For readers who know little or nothing about CRM, this book will provide an introduction to the subject. It explains how and why different firms do, and could, approach CRM. It does not push a particular version of the truth, but helps newcomers determine which direction to take.

For the manager or consultant tasked with improving CRM within an organization, the book presents frameworks and practical ideas that help create a common view of the value the investment can bring. Readers will find suggestions of how to approach the construction and implementation of CRM strategies, and what those strategies should contain. The book will not provide a step-by-step guide to constructing a notional ideal strategy, nor to any aspect of CRM. A recurring theme is that every organization needs to arrive at its own approach to CRM strategy and implementation. This book seeks to provide the foundation upon which strategists can lay down their version of the truth.

The CRM expert will find much of the content familiar. Inevitably a book covering such a broad subject covers many topics briefly, and those seeking details about specific areas will be disappointed. However, the book offers new frameworks and interprets existing frameworks in different ways, which may give even an expert a new perspective on a familiar idea.

STRUCTURE

The book is divided into six parts, each of which contains several chapters.

Part 1 Understanding CRM

This section provides a foundation in the subject by exploring what CRM is and where it has come from.

Chapter 1, The origins of CRM, explains the background. CRM is unusual, for it grew from neither a specific technology (as did ERP) nor from an event (as did resolving the Year 2000 date problem). This chapter describes the ideas and technologies that created it.

Chapter 2, What is CRM?, extends the definition. It examines some of the key themes, such as customer value, loyalty and customer centricity.

Part 2 Defining the CRM agenda

Part 2 discusses the thesis that different businesses create value for customers and extract it from them in quite different ways. The airline, the retailer, the insurer and the pharmaceuticals firm all need to manage their customer relationships in different ways. We explore how the way that an organization creates value for its customers should shape its CRM agenda.

Chapter 3, Creating customer value, introduces two frameworks that help an organization to identify the most effective customer management agenda. This chapter introduces the value configuration and value discipline models, and explains how firms can use these to understand how they create customer value. After reading Chapter 3, you will be able to identify your business as a value chain, value shop, value network or value pool, or understand that your firm encompasses multiple configurations.

Value chains manufacture and distribute products. Chapter 4, Selling products, describes how chains benefit from deploying CRM to sell and service more products more effectively.

Value shops create value by understanding customer needs and using their resources to solve specific customer problems – as hospitals, insurance brokers, consulting firms and architects do. Chapter 5, Connecting knowledge, explains how such organizations utilize CRM primarily as a knowledge management tool – very different from chains.

Value networks create value by connecting customers with each other and with third parties through the management of an infrastructure. Examples include telecommunications companies, banks and utilities. Here, the customers' experience of using the network is key. Chapter 6, Delivering service, suggests that the CRM focus for such firms is different again and is focused upon convenience, experience and service, rather than products.

Chapter 7, Managing capacity, introduces a new value configuration, the value pool. Many firms, such as airlines, cinemas and hotels, operate an infrastructure. However, they create value, not by mediating between customers, but by leasing use of this infrastructure to customers. Their CRM agenda is dictated by the need to employ resources (seats, beds, cars and so on) as efficiently as possible. CRM becomes a tool of capacity and yield management.

Part 3 Laying the foundations

Successful CRM initiatives are built on the foundation of a clear CRM strategy. While the variety of CRM activities makes offering an 'out of the box' strategy unrealistic, the first three chapters of this section introduce the components that should form the foundation for any strategy.

How a company connects with its customers is defined in the unique proposition that it offers them. Chapter 8, Defining the value proposition, describes how to construct a value proposition unique to the organization in order to form a springboard for improving CRM.

Nevertheless, a value proposition is not sufficient justification for investment in CRM. CRM business cases are rarely constructed with financial rigour. Chapter 9, Building the business case, suggests how to construct a financially rigorous business case based on accepted financial theory.

It is widely reported, by industry analysts, magazines, and in publications, that CRM fails more often than it succeeds. Chapter 10, Where is the one-to-one future?, examines why CRM initiatives fail to live up to expectations.

The section concludes by looking at another of the foundations. In Chapter 11, Segmentation within corporate strategy, the role of strategic customer segmentation is examined, and how, by deconstructing their customer base, companies can build a customer strategy that differentiates between their diverse customer base.

Part 4 Creating the customer-centric organization

CRM is more about business change than technology implementation. Despite all of the evidence that CRM success or failure is primarily dictated by the extent to which an organization changes *how* it interacts with customers, organizational change remains a low priority. This section looks at how an organization needs to change in order to deliver the promise made by its brand to its customers.

Chapter 8 defined brand as the construction and delivery of a customer promise. Chapter 12, Driving brand into the organization, explores how the brand must be driven deep into the organization to allow the firm to deliver its promise.

Chapter 13 is called Creating the customer-centric enterprise. Implementing a program to change an organization's structure and culture is hard – usually harder than implementing a new technology. This chapter introduces a framework describing seven drivers of change. Whereas brand-driven CRM aims to enable a company to establish a vision of the experience its customers should receive, the drivers of change framework considers how to re-engineer the organization to achieve this goal.

Part 5 Delivering CRM

It is hard to put boundaries around what constitutes CRM – its potential scope is almost limitless. Similarly, there are many different ways to divide it up. This section describes the benefits and challenges of the technologies and projects that enable CRM to be divided into six delivery areas.

A single customer view is often the foundation and starting point of CRM. Chapter 14, Customer consolidation, suggests that there is more to a single customer view than meets the eye. This chapter examines the challenges and issues associated with consolidating customer knowledge.

Chapter 15, Customer intelligence, focuses upon customer analysis. Some of the largest cheques have been signed for technologies which enable firms to understand customer profitability, risk, propensity to die, buy or live.

At the heart of many CRM initiatives lies a need to improve the effectiveness of customer marketing. Chapter 16, Campaign management, looks at techniques, tools and technologies to improve marketing or to introduce new marketing media.

Increasingly, companies are operating through more media and channels. Chapter 17, Multi-channel customer care, explores the challenges of a multi-channel and multimedia world. It exposes some of the myths of multi-channel management and proposes a more comprehensive framework to understand multi-channel strategy.

Self-service was one of the driving forces behind massive investment in internet sites during the dot.com boom and bust. The dramatically lower transaction costs of selling and servicing customers over the web triggered an avalanche of investment. Then reality struck. Chapter 18, Sales and service self-care, examines the challenges of customers primarily managing themselves through self-service channels. How can you build a self-care strategy that works?

CRM was introduced to many companies through the subject of Chapter 19, Sales automation. If better marketing was one driver behind CRM, selling more is equally important. What is sales automation and how can an organization make most effective use of it?

Part 6 To infinity and beyond

Every CRM initiative should consider how customers may demand products and service in the future. This final part explores three technology-enabled trends that will profoundly alter the customer landscape by 2010.

The global telecoms sector lurched into recession because of mountainous debts arising from buying 3G mobile communications licences. Nonetheless, while shareholders run scared of the sector, its impact on customers will be profound. By 2010, digital devices that do not yet exist will offer services that we do not yet provide in ways that we cannot yet foresee. They will use bandwidth which is to WAP what a Ferrari is to a horse and cart.

By 2010, hundreds of millions of people will never have experienced life without the internet. This new generation will be buying your products and services – or someone else's. Chapter 20 is a call to wake up to the internet generation: when will it hit your business?

The customer is in control. This is more than a cliché. As the business-to-business and business-to-customer landscapes move closer to the nirvana of perfect markets, customers are increasingly in control of how, when and why they connect with whom. This introduces a new future in which firms must respond rapidly to customers, rather than stalk them with ever increasing precision. Technology is enabling this transformation – but probably not the technology you think. Chapter 21, Customer managed relationships, explains how such relationships will redefine the CRM landscape by compelling, but also enabling, firms to mass customize – everything.

PART 1

UNDERSTANDING CRM

For something on which so many billions have been spent, CRM is still extraordinarily ill-defined. We are all products of our birth and upbringing, and CRM is no exception. The problem is that many parents claim the CRM child. Mapping the origins of an ill-defined acronym is not easy, but it is of value to consider some of the thinkers, ideas and technologies that have focused on the 'customer thing'. Risking the wrath of CRM high priests around the world, we offer our perspective on the origins of CRM.

Almost as fraught, is the question 'What is CRM?'. We will introduce you to some of the key terms and concepts that crop up in CRM definitions – loyalty, value, profitability – and use these concepts to shape a definition that encompasses the best of CRM. Ultimately, we want to provide you with the information to construct your own definition. Managing your customers is a process and concept that is as unique to your organization as your organization is itself a unique combination of processes, organizational structures, locations, information, software applications and technologies. You must develop your own understanding of how CRM can help you. In this section we offer some building blocks on which to base your definition.

CHAPTER 1

THE ORIGINS
OF CRM

INTRODUCTION

CRM has embraced many ideas and technologies that have the common theme of managing customers rather than managing the market. This chapter reviews the people, initiatives and technologies that have shaped perceptions of why and how organizations could and should connect with their customers.

Such an analysis is inevitably selective. Psychologists may consider that Sigmund Freud and his followers were primary influences on the corporate/customer relationship because they explained the underlying psychological influences on customer behaviour. The focus in this chapter is on the people who have contributed to corporate understanding of individual customers within the market, rather than how the market as a whole behaves.

THE GURUS

Many thinkers have provided frameworks and ideas that have helped firms to connect with their customers. Almost every CRM expert will award honours to different thinkers, but most will recognize this pantheon.

Wunderman

It is difficult to see the name Lester Wunderman without the label 'the father or grandfather of direct marketing'. Widely regarded as having created direct marketing in the mid-twentieth century, Wunderman was the first to think through the implications of connecting marketing initiatives as precisely as possible with the customers most likely to be receptive, using the marketing tools most appropriate to the product and the customers. This challenged the mass marketing concepts that had held sway since industrialization. By delivering more accurate marketing directly to customers, Wunderman laid the foundations for a more specific corporate focus on how to unlock the customer's wallet.

Porter and his successors

In 1985, Michael Porter[1] introduced the value chain. His model identified the sets of activities that all businesses perform to generate value for customers. According to Porter:

'Competitive advantage cannot be understood by looking at a firm as a whole. Advantage stems from the many discrete activities a firm performs – designing, producing, marketing, delivering and supporting products. Each of these activities can contribute to a firm's relative cost position and create a basis for differentiation.'

By deconstructing its activities, a firm could understand how it created value for its customers. Although by no means a CRM analysis, Porter's deconstruction enabled firms to consider which of their activities created customer value, and how.

The value chain was developed further in 1998. Many firms, including banks, consulting firms, airlines and telecommunications companies, found it difficult to apply the model of the chain. Øystein Fjeldstad and Charles Stabell of the Norwegian School of Management researched the model's limitations with respect to service industries[2]. In their view, the chain did not sufficiently capture the value-creation logic of such industries. They developed two further models to describe better the range of activities in which firms could engage to create customer value. Value shops – workshops not retail shops – focus on problem solving. They construct individual solutions through repeated fact finding. Value networks – of customers not necessarily companies – mediate between customers by supplying an infrastructure to which customers subscribe. Banks, utilities, telecommunications companies and Internet Service Providers are all networks. Neither shops nor networks execute the sequential process described for chains.

The three models of value chain, value shops and value networks were christened 'value configurations' because they described how firms are structured (or configured) to create value. This analysis, which has significant implications for our subject, is a central theme of this book.

Peppers and Rogers

The golden year of Customer Relationship Management was 1993. Then, Don Peppers and Martha Rogers released *The One to One Future*[3], which was followed by a series of books that further developed the theme.

The one-to-one movement described a fundamental shift from mass marketing (targeting share of market) to customer marketing (targeting share of customer). It called upon firms to rethink their approach to marketing products and services. Customer relationships would be based upon knowledge of individual customers, gained through interactions with them. This knowledge would be stored in technologies that enabled marketers to target individual customers with customized offerings.

The Peppers and Rogers process for establishing and managing customer relationships was:

1   Identify customers so that they can be uniquely separated as individuals from other customers.

2   Differentiate each customer by their value to the company and their needs.

3   Interact with them both effectively and cost-efficiently.

4   Customize some part of the company's behaviour towards each customer, based if possible on the interaction with that customer.

[1] Michael Porter, *Competitive Advantage: Creating and Sustaining Superior Business Performance*, The Free Press, 1985.
[2] C B Stabell and Ø D Fjeldstad, 'Configuring Value For Competitive Advantage: On Chains, Shops, and Networks', *Strategic Management Journal*, Vol. 19, 1998.
[3] Don Peppers and Martha Rogers, *The One to One Future*, Currency/Doubleday, 1993.

These four stages (IDIC) are a cycle. When a company customizes its behaviour, it learns more about that individual's needs. As with so many influential frameworks, the IDIC cycle works because it is a codification of common sense. Prior to industrialization, the only business model was one in which suppliers (butchers, bakers, candlestick makers) knew their customers personally and customized products accordingly. Industrialization severed that link, but now software has enabled it to be recreated.

Whether CRM is the same as one-to-one, or whether one-to-one is an aspect of CRM, is an unprofitable debate. When you buy a burger at McDonald's, you engage in a brief connection with a specific employee, but there is no corporate memory of that connection. Many retailers have implemented loyalty schemes to transform these brief connections by uniquely identifying individual customers. One-to-one is founded upon a unique identification of each customer to begin the cyclical process of IDIC. By using CRM techniques, mass marketers can become customer marketers.

Davis and Pine

Traditionally, customization of any product or service, from car to insurance policy, was incompatible with low cost. Stan Davis introduced the concept of mass customization, which was later developed by Joseph Pine in 1993[4]. Davis and Pine explored a shift from mass production (in which the same product is produced repeatedly to a consistent standard) to mass customization (in which the product is adapted to customer needs but still at a low cost by transforming a company's deployment of technology). Using technology, firms could take advantage of the benefits of customization at mass production prices.

In a mass produced world, all goods and services are much the same and the customers' emphasis is on price. The more customized the product, the more difficult it is for customers to make price comparisons and their focus shifts to relevance. However, because the mass customizer builds at mass production prices, the relevance of the product at a competitive price means that customers still perceive good value. The virtuous circle is reinforced by a learning effect: as companies gain experience customizing similar products, they understand better what base products the customers want.

A mass customizer fragments the market through economies of scope, in contrast to the mass producer who reduces choice through economies of scale. The ultimate expression of the mass producer is Henry Ford's famous offer for the Model T: 'You can have any colour as long as it's black'. If Ford is the icon of the mass producer, Michael Dell is the icon of the mass customizer – building PCs to customer-defined specifications.

Hammer and Champy

Also in 1993, Michael Hammer and James Champy released *Reengineering the Corporation*[5]. Although Hammer had introduced re-engineering in his earlier work in 1990[6], the 1993 work took the business world by storm. Although not directly related to CRM, re-engineering had a profound influence upon customer relationships, primarily in the automation of customer experience. Re-engineering focused upon obliterating processes that did not add value to customers. Early projects found that customer value was produced by less than 10 per cent of processes. The majority of work was checking, coordinating, and handing off within and between departments. Each step took time and introduced errors needing correction and revalidation. Re-engineering was a call to restructure what and how work was done for customers.

[4] B Joseph Pine II, *Mass Customisation – The New Frontier in Business Competition*, Harvard Business School Press, 1993.
[5] Michael Hammer and James Champy, *Reengineering the Corporation*, Harper Business, 1993.
[6] Michael Hammer, 'Reengineering Work: Don't Automate, Obliterate', *Harvard Business Review*, July–Aug 1990.

However, many re-engineering efforts failed when the focus upon internal process and cost resulted in the automation rather than the optimization of the customer experience. This was a misunderstanding of re-engineering. The focus should be upon the elimination of activities that do not add value to customers. Perhaps the problem was that some firms equated customer value to price.

Reichheld

Customer retention, and a focus upon existing customers, is a foundation of CRM belief. In 1996, Frederick Reichheld released *The Loyalty Effect*[7] and was the first to demonstrate widely how building the loyalty of customers could deliver shareholder value. Investment in customers was economically justified. Reichheld showed that for many firms, a 5 per cent increase in customer retention could deliver a 25–100 per cent increase in profits. Reichheld offered the appealing analogy that fixing customer retention is like fixing a hole in your bucket: you can pour new customers into your bucket but if the existing customers are leaking out of the bottom, then you can only grow if you pour customers in faster. That becomes harder to do in increasingly saturated markets with a static population. Fix the leak and customer numbers build incrementally. By demonstrating the economics of retention, Reichheld built customer loyalty into the CRM debate.

Treacy and Wiersema

In 1995, Michael Treacy and Fred Wiersema[8] introduced the value discipline model. This offered a simple framework that codified how leading firms achieve results. Their research found that market leaders achieve success by delivering superior customer value in line with one of three value disciplines, while meeting industry standards in the other two (Table 1.1).

THE THREE VALUE DISCIPLINES

OPERATIONAL EXCELLENCE	Provide customers with reliable products or services at competitive prices and deliver them with minimal difficulty and inconvenience to the customer.
PRODUCT LEADERSHIP	Offer leading products and services that consistently enhance the customer's use or application of the product, thereby making rivals' goods obsolete.
CUSTOMER INTIMACY	Segment and target markets precisely, and then tailor the offerings to exactly match the demands of those niches.

TABLE 1.1: The three value disciplines

The correlation between CRM and customer intimacy appears clear. Arguably, the more customer-intimate an organization aspires to be, the greater its investment in CRM. However, the statement by some firms that they wish to be 'customer-intimate' or 'customer-centric' is often mistaken for a woolly intention to start treating customers better in order to drive cross-sell, referral and retention. Customer intimacy, while perhaps demanding improvements in customer service, is not necessarily about being nicer to people; it is about making products and services relevant to the explicit or calculated needs of individual customers. By providing a framework for firms to measure the extent to which they would allow customers to drive their business, the value discipline model also claimed a place in the CRM pantheon.

[7] Frederick Reichheld, *The Loyalty Effect*, Harvard Business School Press, 1996.
[8] Michael Treacy and Fred Wiersema, *The Discipline of Market Leaders*, Addison-Wesley, 1995.

In different ways, these thinkers showed how organizations could gain competitive advantage by identifying what customers value and by meeting their needs. Consolidating this thinking offers valuable insight.

Wunderman began the process of focusing more precisely on how to place the right proposition directly in front of the right customer. One-to-one talked about the migration from share of market to share of customer, and the need to understand a customer's unique requirements and to differentiate products and services accordingly. Reichheld demonstrated the value of loyalty and retention. Customer intimacy suggested that some market leaders should prioritize their corporate resources for customizing product and service. Mass customization offers a shift away from mass production to achieve leading, customized products at mass production prices. Re-engineering talked about the need to focus processes upon the creation of customer value – although customer value was often lost in the rush to automation. Finally, value configurations offered a framework to understand how firms were organized to create customer value.

CRM encompasses, or is encompassed by, all of these ideas. The ideas, directly or indirectly, changed how companies perceived they could extract value from CRM, and deliver it to, their customers.

CORPORATE INITIATIVES

From the 1980s, many firms embarked on initiatives that also influenced CRM thinking. Two programs in particular are worth highlighting.

☐ Some firms invested in customer care programs. They trained staff in techniques of customer care, for example, answering telephones, handling complaints, understanding and reacting appropriately to different customer behaviours. British Airways instituted one of the best known of these programs called 'Putting people first'. Such programs offered something different to CRM. They highlighted a growing realization that customer service could be a competitive differentiator.

☐ In a highly competitive market, airlines needed to recognize and secure the loyalty of the minority of air travellers who travel frequently. High individual transaction costs (air tickets are expensive), combined with very tight margins (small differences in the number of filled seats make the difference between profitability and unprofitability), meant that the loyalty of valued customers was very hard to achieve, but was particularly critical. Airlines bound customers to them more tightly by rewarding frequent flyers and business or first class passengers with free flights, airport lounges, preferred standby status and quicker check-in. The loyalty program remains important to many CRM initiatives.

Customer care and loyalty programs show that customer service can be a differentiator and that, the more competitive the business environment, the more customer loyalty becomes a priceless asset.

TECHNOLOGIES

Purists may sniff at considering technology in a discussion of CRM origins. After all, as any expert will tell you before selling you a software licence, CRM is not about technology but enabled by it. While true, the development of CRM has been profoundly influenced by technology.

Codd

'A Relational Model of Data for Large Shared Data Banks' may not be a catchy title, but none of the achievements in CRM would be possible without the database that was born in this paper by Ted Codd (1970), an IBM researcher. Although not a technology program, CRM is typically a technology-enabled program and a database that stores customer data and releases views of that data to users, and underpins almost all CRM initiatives.

During the 1980s, information systems (IS) and marketing turned their attention to two major customer-related uses of the database:

1 Many firms invested in what we now call a single view of the customer or customer information system. The ability to separate data from the program code enabled organizations to store all information about each customer in one place. We discuss the twenty-first century single customer view in Chapter 14, because it remains an important concept.

2 Marketers' eyes lit up at database technology. Intuition-based marketing was replaced by database marketing, allowing marketers to analyze customer information and run direct mail campaigns to targeted customers. Such marketing has increased in sophistication over the years and remains important. We discuss campaign management in Chapter 16.

Siebel

Siebel Systems was founded in 1993 – the golden year of CRM. From its inception, Siebel saw extraordinary growth. In 2000, *Fortune Magazine* ranked Siebel Systems second among the '100 Fastest Growing Companies', while *Business Week* named it the most influential company in software. Estimates of Siebel's share of the market are impossible to quantify, but some analysts calculate that in 2001 Siebel-related expenditure constituted approximately one-third of total CRM spend. Siebel is discussed in this chapter not because it can – or does – claim to have started CRM, but because it has influenced the world's perception of CRM.

Siebel's original market was sales automation, although it did not create this technology. Since the advent of mobile computing, firms have used mobile technology to support salespeople. What Siebel achieved was to provide customer-oriented data that supported the salespeople (such as customer contact history), and tools that explained a customer's relationship with a company. As Siebel rapidly expanded its function across multiple channels and media, it offered firms a tool to create a customer-centric view of their business across all of the customer touchpoints. This, so the theory went, would create competitive advantage.

Siebel rapidly placed an equals sign between product and acronym. It established an effective partnership program with systems integrators. It developed powerful advertising and a highly motivated salesforce. Combine these attributes with rich CRM function and, at least initially, little competition, and Siebel's leadership was not surprising. The disadvantage of this dominance, which was not Siebel's fault, was that some companies thought: 'We've implemented Siebel so we've implemented CRM'. This was far from the case. As an enabling technology, Siebel has proved successful for many companies, but only where the software supports a reshaping of the corporate strategy.

Siebel Systems put CRM squarely upon the corporate agenda. Through its success, Siebel created a bandwagon for other players to jump on. Its advertising created an awareness of the potential benefits that would not have become evident if the subject had been left to the theoreticians. Moreover, its partnership program created an environment in which systems integrators wanted to play the CRM game.

SUMMARY

1 CRM is rooted in the work of gurus, in corporate initiatives, and in technologies. It was not born of an event or specific technology. Any attempt to trace a particular parent is futile and unnecessary. CRM grew organically from the need to consolidate a wide body of thought and innovation into a manageable term that inevitably became an acronym.

2 The influences of CRM affect how we should perceive it. It is not a specific definable concept, but a management principle which a firm can use to create value for its customers and extract value from them. CRM thus becomes a corporate discipline that all companies do, not that some companies buy.

3 The influences that shaped CRM share some common themes. They aim for a greater understanding of customer needs because that can, in turn, drive greater profitability. They focus upon gaining competitive advantage by looking at a business not just from the perspective of management and shareholders, but also from that of the customer.

CHAPTER 2

WHAT IS CRM?

INTRODUCTION

There are as many definitions of CRM as there are firms offering services to implement it. Nobody is right and nobody is wrong. To make things more difficult, CRM is probably not the best acronym for the theories, disciplines and technologies that organizations apply to customer management. 'Relationship' implies significant commitment between customer and supplier, but most customers do not want a relationship with their cat food supplier. The term 'management' suggests a degree of corporate control over customers that does not exist. Even the word 'customer' is not clear: does it include partners, employees, suppliers and distributors?

The way that an organization manages its customers must be as unique to that organization as its customer base. So, constructing your own definition is fundamental. Without it, you are planning a meal without knowing the ingredients. In this chapter, the key ingredients that are woven into most definitions are explored. You are offered a definition of CRM built from those ingredients, but you are urged not to accept this definition as 'right'. Instead, use the information in this chapter to build the definition that is right for your organization.

The ingredients

☐ **Loyalty** – Loyal customers make repeat purchases, forgive errors, recruit new customers, and teach you about their likes and dislikes. They are cheaper to sell to than new customers because they carry no cost of acquisition.

☐ **Value** – Value is increasingly replacing relationship in the CRM lexicon. Most of the CRM gurus described in Chapter 1 talked about the need to create value for customers.

☐ **Profitability** – CRM is the element of corporate strategy that aims to improve corporate profitability through understanding its customers.

☐ **Customer-centric** (or customer-intimate) – Being customer-centric is about understanding to what extent you will allow customers to drive your business. Will you impose your own product and service on them, or customize it to their needs? All firms must be customer-centric in some way unless they ignore their customers completely, but some are more customer-centric than others.

☐ **Customer process** – CRM is something firms do rather than buy. Customer management does not end with the implementation of technology, but it might begin there.

☐ **Segmentation** – The segmentation of customers into groups that share particular characteristics is fundamental to many CRM initiatives. Basing your strategy upon the individual needs of 100,000 customers is impossible. But by grouping customers based on characteristics that you deem important (such as their requirements from you or value to you) it becomes possible to drive strategy from the customer perspective.

CUSTOMER LOYALTY

Research suggests that in many sectors, such as hotels, restaurants, grocery stores and airlines, loyal customers outspend occasional customers by as much as ten or fifteen times. Regardless of whether a customer uses a single supermarket simply because it is geographically close, the fact remains that the regular customer is likely to be significantly more valuable than the occasional visitor. In this context, winning customer loyalty seems both an obvious and high priority strategy.

Harvard Business Review offers its CRM definition[1]: 'CRM aligns business processes with customer strategies to build customer loyalty and increase profits over time.'

Your definition of loyalty may be more complex. Many firms have loyal customers that they do not want – ask motor insurers about drivers with poor claims records. Customer analytics can help you identify and then destroy the loyalty of undesirable customers. Loyalty can be an active force, for instance when customers recruit new customers, and tell firms about their likes and dislikes. However, what looks like loyalty can be inertia. Regular surveys by the UK Consumers' Association of customer satisfaction with high street banks report high levels of customer retention combined with low levels of satisfaction. Loyalty to an airline may be dictated by the employer's corporate travel policy. Loyalty to a lender may be contracted by a legal agreement that punishes disloyalty. Loyalty may reflect a lack of effective competition.

Loyalty should be in your definition of CRM. But it should be a loyalty tempered with realism: a loyalty not confused with inertia, but one focused upon valued customers.

CUSTOMER VALUE

Customer value is often defined as the profit that can be extracted from customers. But this definition only works if the customers do not have a choice. Instead, think of customer value as what customers value. It may be price, but it is more likely to be a complex web of at least five factors, unique to your company, and probably different for each customer segment. All organizations must balance how they deliver these factors.

1   *Value for money* is usually important. This means more than price. For example, do customers pay so much for the function offered by a Gucci handbag, or for the brand name? Why do customers shopping for food select higher priced products when cheaper goods are available? Value for money is not simply about the price and function of the product, but the value that the customer perceives around it.

2   Increasingly, *convenience* may be critical. The value of time is key to the fast food industry. Internet banking is about convenience. The mobile ice cream van charges more than a shop. Convenience costs. How do you balance convenience with value for money?

[1] Darrell K Rigby, Frederick F Reichheld, Phil Schefter, *Avoid the Four Perils of CRM*, Harvard Business Review, February 2002.

3 Fifty years ago, customers bought food from numerous suppliers because no one supplier offered all types of food. Supermarkets are popular because of the *breadth* of their solution to their customers' needs – many offer photo processing, pharmacies, bakeries, flower shops, ATMs (Automatic Teller Machines), compact discs and clothes, as well as groceries. Customers may be willing to put up with more inconvenience, when more of their needs are answered.

4 Some customers will pay more for better *service*. Retail banks deploy self-care technology in order to offer the mass affluent personal banking services which were previously the domain of the very rich, at much lower cost. At a minimum, firms must offer competent service, but if customers are willing to pay for more, would it be worth your while delivering it?

5 Some customers pay premium prices for *customization*. They may have furniture made to order, a bank account with a wider range of options for debt repayment, a car with a choice of extras. Attempts to become customer-intimate may reflect a desire to create value by customizing the offering. But can customization be reconciled with required price?

Successful relationship management begins by understanding what customers value – a blindingly obvious but regularly neglected point. It is hard work to understand your 'value map' – the combination of these five factors and others relevant to your firm – and from it create a framework to drive the delivery of products and services. Nevertheless, it is fundamental to the success of any CRM initiative.

CUSTOMER PROFITABILITY

By any definition, the need to extract more money from customers is important. Except for a few organizations with loftier ambitions – the Roman Catholic Church may reasonably argue that souls matter more than cents – business is about money. But CRM can drive profitability in three ways:

1 Extracting more money from each customer.

2 Using knowledge gained from customers to deliver value to them more cost-effectively.

3 Pleasing customers sufficiently that they refer other customers to you.

Extracting economic value

The most obvious value that customers bring to a firm is profit over the duration of the relationship (sometimes called lifetime value). At its simplest, CRM can be seen as processes, tools and technologies to increase profitability – or even further, to sell additional offerings to existing customers ('cross-sell'). However, if we see CRM simply as a tool to sell more, then the business case may fall down. As we discuss in Chapter 9, cross-sell may fail to repay the capital investment required to implement customer-focused initiatives. For firms with little synergy between their offerings, cross-sell may not be realistic because the customer may not see how being good at one thing translates to being good in another unrelated area.

As well as helping to get more money from customers, CRM can also reduce the cost of servicing them. A single customer view can reduce costs by enabling transactions to be processed once across multiple systems. Implementing self-service media (such as a transactional website) can reduce per transaction costs – if you persuade enough customers to use it.

Learning and innovation

CRM can be used to learn about customer needs, with the potential to increase profitability in three further ways:

1 **Reduce waste** – If you understand your customers, you will not spend money developing, producing and marketing what customers will not buy. How much has your firm wasted on the development of product and service that proved to be unsuccessful? Would a better knowledge of your customer needs have prevented that waste?

2 **Focus operations better** – For example, by shifting some customer interaction to a call centre you may be able to reduce overheads while still satisfying customer needs, instead of trying to excel in ways that do not deliver value to your customers.

3 **Improve the marketing win rate** – If you understand what makes existing customers buy from you, it is easier to find new customers.

Referral and relationship effects

Satisfied customers may refer others. Very satisfied customers will almost certainly refer others. Ten years ago, referral was important but was limited to family, friends and word of mouth. Now, a combination of the internet and an influential consumer lobby enable satisfied customers to spread the word to an increasingly large global, virtual community. The converse is also true. Evidence of disgruntled customers publishing savage attacks on firms is easy to find. UK bank FirstDirect claims to obtain 33 per cent of new customers by word of mouth referral. In the saturated UK banking market and with rising acquisition costs, such an impact is important to the business case. Relationship effects may justify investment in the seemingly intangible – for example, improving customer service – when a business case purely based on cross-selling more to existing customers is insufficient.

CUSTOMER-CENTRIC

Customer-centricity is not about being nice to customers (although that is important, as Chapter 12 suggests). Nor is it an absolute. The 'ladder of customer-centricity' in Figure 2.1 shows the different degrees to which customer needs dictate business strategy.

Notice that these definitions do not mention customer service. Delivering outstanding service can be as applicable to product-centric as to customer-centric firms, and justifying investment on the grounds of needing to move from being product-centric to customer-centric misses the point. CRM is not necessarily about becoming more customer-centric, for that may not be the right ambition for your organization. The question to ask is how customer-centric your corporate strategy should be.

CUSTOMER PROCESSES

No matter how you define CRM, it is useful to see it as something that firms do as corporate processes. The relevant processes are:

1 **Managing customer information** – Acquiring and maintaining customer data is always a foundation of customer management. The quality of that information is critical. Its breadth will depend upon corporate ambition and customer needs focus. At its most basic, demographic information, such as gender and address, can be used to enable supply-driven

The truly customer-centric firm will partner with customers to understand their current and future needs and source appropriate offerings from wherever necessary. At this stage, the full array of customer management technologies may need to be deployed – or perhaps the service becomes so intimate that CRM technology becomes redundant because every solution becomes individual. The firm adapts its offerings to the customer, exists to serve that customer and is perceived to do so.

On the middle rung of the ladder we wobble briefly; firms are midway between customer and product-centric. They analyze customers needs and promote appropriate offerings. Customer needs determine *which* proposition is presented *when*, but offerings are not changed. Over and above a customer database, the firm needs technologies to predict customer needs. There is no restructuring of the business, but rather the deployment of predictive technologies to achieve more focused marketing. The customer remains a target of, rather than partner in, the business, but the firm at least understands the customers' needs and tries to match them.

A firm makes no attempt to identify individual customers. Corporate focus is upon acquiring more customers and increasing market share. In technology terms, independent product management engines manage a supply-driven business. The market is the target, rather than the customer. Such firms can still pursue customer intimacy by building product to order. But more likely they will seek to focus upon operational excellence (price) or product leadership (quality and innovation).

A firm starts to become customer-centric, it drives its offerings according to customer need. The customer becomes almost a partner in the process. The firm must be willing to learn from customers and adopt and adapt processes, organizational structures, facilities, applications software, information flows and technology infrastructure based on this learning. Sophisticated decision support tools become essential, as does software to manage *differentiated* interaction with customers. Sophisticated data management technologies (data marts or data warehouses) are necessary to store customer information. Marketing technologies need to be used that will deliver targeted, relevant offerings and enable corporate learning from the results.

A firm markets to individual customers. This demands their identification: name, address or telephone number. The minimum technology requirement is a database of uniquely identified customers and a campaign management tool. It remains a supply-driven model. Individual customer needs are not considered: the customer is identified by name but exists as a target at which the offering can be pushed. Individual customers are recognized, but as targets.

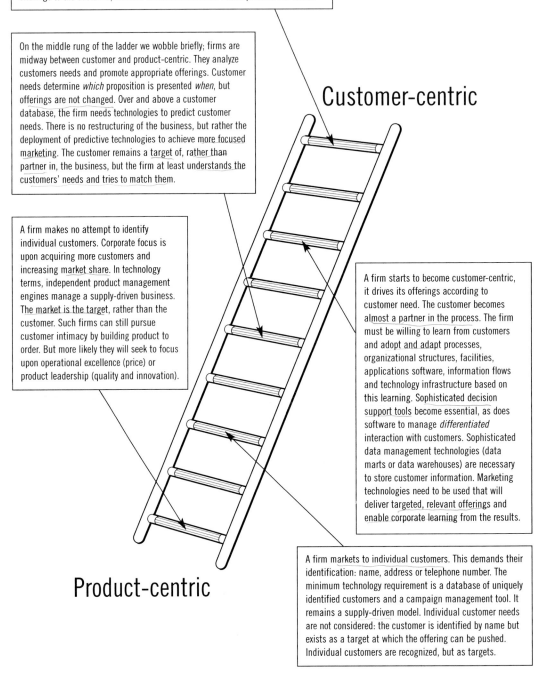

Customer-centric

Product-centric

FIGURE 2.1: Ladder of customer-centricity

cross-sell. However, firms may capture more sophisticated information about customers' relationships with other customers or prospects and their behaviours, for example, their use of different channels. Firms can derive further information about their customers, such as their propensity to buy, to die, and to defraud.

2 **Making decisions about customers** – Customer information is the fuel for most customer-oriented initiatives, but, like fuel, it achieves nothing unless used. Management information, OLAP (Online Analytical Processing) and data mining technologies (for example, regression analysis and neural networking tools) can be used to understand customer needs. Such technologies may be superfluous for a product-centric firm on the lowest rung of the ladder (see Figure 2.1). The challenge is to embed the information about customer needs into the customer interaction. Customer decision making can help firms to understand customer profitability, risk, and propensities. Effective customer analyses can drive corporate strategy – dictating corporate decisions, not just calculating cross-sell potential.

3 **Marketing to customers** – Technology has allowed marketing to become more sophisticated. Data analysis enabled blind mailings to lists of addresses to be replaced by sophisticated segment-driven marketing. The concept of timing – targeting at a relevant time for the customer – was introduced with event-driven marketing. Direct interaction between supplier and customer enabled the marketing to be integrated into customer interactions, based on customer responses over internet or telephone. Personalization technologies enable the marketing of offerings calculated to be relevant to individual customer needs.

4 **Interacting with customers** – Interaction involves more than 'being nice to customers'. It is about three Cs: contact, channel and content management. It is about managing customer contacts incrementally across different channels and media. It is about what the customer (or the intermediary) sees – making the content appropriate, relevant, and aligned.

We will return to these four processes in more detail throughout this book.

SEGMENTATION

The foundation, often the starting point, of CRM initiatives is the division of the customer base into customer segments. A pie can be sliced in any number of ways, and there is no right answer to segmentation. The only certainty is that segmentation will vary from firm to firm. Segmentation can be used for different purposes: to drive corporate strategy, to dictate specific marketing campaigns or to differentiate customer service.

How many segments? At a corporate strategic level, more than ten segments may be confusing, but fewer than five may yield insufficient granularity. For specific marketing campaigns, scores, even thousands, of different segments may be built using sophisticated marketing technology to make small differences in the marketing to different customers.

Traditional segmentation models were based on demographics (e.g. combinations of gender, age, address) or on current or anticipated profitability. The volume of data now available offers more sophistication. Behavioural segmentation involves grouping customers according to their behaviour (when they interact or what services they use, for instance). Organizations that seek to focus on customer intimacy may replace segmentation on customer profitability with segmentation based on customer needs from the business.

There is no easy answer to segmentation. Firms probably need different segmentation models in different areas of their business, involving a sophisticated mix of customer characteristics, and an iterative process of analysis and adaptation to change the segmentation models to be ever more accurate. A hair salon may find that the right segmentation model is one based on service (cut, colour, curl) or demographics (women under 30) or profitability (customers spending over a certain amount each month) or behaviour (frequency of visit). Most likely the answer is an amalgamation of them all. The only way to obtain the right answer is to experiment. This requires deep knowledge of the business – only the management team with that knowledge can shape the segmentation model that works.

A DEFINITION OF CRM

This definition of CRM is no better nor worse than any other, but it weaves together and highlights the six important concepts discussed in this chapter.

Customer Relationship Management is what organizations do both to understand their customers, usually by segmenting them, and to translate that understanding into improved corporate profitability. This is achieved by adapting relevant processes of the organization to build the active loyalty of valued customers through understanding what they value and delivering it to them. Ultimately, this represents a journey to understand how customer-centric the organization wants to be, and to realize that ambition.

Now throw this definition away and build your own, giving priority to the elements that you deem important.

SUMMARY

1   Consider how advanced your understanding is of your customers' loyalty. What percentage are active loyalists and what percentage inert? Do you differentiate your treatment of loyal customers? Do you understand what drives loyalty in your business and have a plan in place to convert ambivalent customers into loyal, valued customers?

2   Construct a customer value model for your business. Consider, possibly by segment, how your customers balance the relative importance of value for money and time, a customized solution, a total solution and excellent service. If you understand that value map, how well do you deliver against it?

3   How well do you understand customer profitability? Could you split your customers into ten categories according to their economic value to you? Consider calculating the variation in customer profitability – or at least estimating it. Do you learn from customers and do something different as a result? Do you ask customers for feedback and act on it? If not, why not? How do you justify ignoring the most valuable feedback your business can receive? How many of your customers refer other customers? Why? Why don't they?

4   Consider how customer-centric you want to be. Calculate whether this level of business ambition is aligned with your technology investment. Maybe you have invested too much or too little. Would your board agree how customer-centric you should be? If not, should you consider getting at least your executives, if not your staff, aligned?

5   Find or devise a definition of CRM for your organization. Factor into your search the key concepts described in this chapter which you deem to be relevant to your needs.

PART 2

DEFINING THE CRM AGENDA

In Part 2 we get more specific. There is a major flaw at the heart of much CRM thinking. For too long the CRM agenda has been product-led. For product companies, that is fine, but tens of millions of people do not work for product companies. They work in what we call the service industries, although 'service' seems the wrong word when companies view CRM as a tool to stalk customers. Marketers nod sagely at pronouncements like 'the customer is in control' before shouldering the marketing 12-bore and setting off in pursuit of a prospect list. This is not necessarily an agenda that will deliver your customers' loyalty.

Firms create value for their customers in different ways. In this section two important frameworks are used, value configurations and value disciplines, to suggest that you need to rethink your CRM agenda not in terms of the industry you are in, but in terms of how you create value for your customers. We suggest that many businesses are setting their CRM agenda incorrectly and this section shows how each organization can identify the best priorities for its CRM.

This section builds upon ideas by Richard Pawson and Francis Hayden of CSC that were developed into an understanding that there is a reason why CRM is failing to deliver for many firms: they are driving the right car down the wrong road. It is not CRM that is the problem. It is what organizations think that CRM can do for them.

23

CHAPTER 3

CREATING CUSTOMER VALUE

INTRODUCTION

As customers, we buy cars, groceries, train tickets, hospital procedures and insurance from different firms. The relationship with our bank is different from that with our car manufacturer or doctor. At work, we are customers of different firms again: they may provide cleaning or catering services, advertising campaigns or accountancy. All create value for us differently.

We have suggested that CRM is the component of corporate strategy that extracts value from, and delivers it to, customers. Therefore, the concept will also differ between different models of value creation. Imposing a single vision of what can be achieved across a number of industries does not make sense. Yet most analyses approach the subject as a single discipline flavoured by industry sector; significant differences in how firms create value become raspberry ripple in the vanilla ice cream. In this one-size-fits-all perception lie many problems and disappointments for CRM strategy and implementation.

An obvious approach is to attempt to differentiate CRM by industry sector. However, in most industries there are different models of value creation. GlaxoSmithKline creates value by a iterative research process to develop new drugs for customers. It also has a production business – manufacturing drugs to sell to customers. It may run drug trials and manage networks of patients with particular conditions. What is CRM for such a firm? It is relevant, but different, for each of those different processes. A conglomerate may run hotels that lease rooms to customers, a food product business that creates ready meals and a bespoke service offering individual catering solutions. Take almost any industry and apply a single CRM agenda, and you can only use that agenda for one aspect of that sector's value creating activities. This causes some firms, or business units, to disregard the concept entirely, rather than focusing upon a relevant agenda.

Nevertheless, not every CRM agenda is different. Firms across diverse industries create value in similar ways. We need a framework that describes how firms create customer value. In turn that framework can drive an understanding of where CRM can help different firms. We are fortunate; research has provided two frameworks that, in combination, offer a powerful tool to understand where to focus our CRM attention and what priority to give it. In this chapter, we introduce these two frameworks. In subsequent chapters we look in more detail at their implications for how firms shape their customer management agenda.

VALUE CONFIGURATIONS

All firms manage an infrastructure in the broadest sense of the term – physical, intellectual, electronic, financial. Some use that infrastructure to create products and services for customers, while others maintain the infrastructure for use by customers. All firms produce something. Yet some firms have products that they sell or rent to customers; the customer obtains value from the product. Other firms create value from the outcome of the customer relationship with the firm – not from the product. We obtain value from AT&T by connecting with our friends and family to have a conversation, not from the AT&T subscription; from HSBC by being able to pay for our groceries, not from owning a piece of plastic. We suggest that firms, or business units within firms, are structured to create customer value in one of four ways, called configurations, shown in Table 3.1.

	Value pools	**Value networks**
Infrastructure used by **customer** to obtain value from firm	Customer leases use of infrastructure from firm (e.g. airlines, car leasing companies).	Customer subscribes to firm for right to use an infrastructure (e.g. utilities telecommunications, retail banking).
	Value chains	**Value shops**
Infrastructure used by **firm** to create value for customer	Firm sells product to customer (e.g. car manufacturers, retailers).	Firm solves specific problem for customer (e.g. consultancies, hospitals, architects, insurance brokers).
	Customer obtains value from **product** (i.e. renting or buying).	Customer obtains value from **outcome** (i.e. connection is successful or problem is solved).

TABLE 3.1: Value configuration framework

Value chains

Volkswagen and General Motors, Nestlé and Cadbury's, Kodak and Apple, Sony and Bang & Olufsen, Amazon and Dell are product firms. They create value by identifying market needs and supplying relevant products. However customized the product, customer relationships are transactional and based upon the value that the customer obtains from using the firm's products.

Michael Porter[1] originally developed the framework to describe the sequential process to build products and called it the value chain. Chains gather inputs, turn them into finished products, distribute and then sell, market, and service those products. The product is the mechanism by which value is transferred from firm to customer. The firm adds value at each stage of the chain. This dictates a product-led agenda and, for such firms, CRM becomes a tool to sell more products more accurately to new and existing customers, typically through a range of channels and media. Chapter 4 will describe a set of CRM priorities for chains that revolve around selling more products.

[1] Michael Porter, *Competitive Advantage: Creating and Sustaining Superior Business Performance*, The Free Press, 1985.

Although applicable to firms that create value by supplying product, the chain did not describe sufficiently how all firms create value. The need to understand value creation in service industries drove the creation of two further models in 1998.

Value shops

McKinsey's and CSC's consulting arm, insurance brokers Heath Lambert Group and Hill House Hammond, Great Ormond Street Hospital and the Mayo Clinic do not build repeatable product but deploy corporate knowledge to solve individual customer problems. Customer relationships are driven by events not transactions. Relationships mean solving customer problems that demand a repetitive fact-finding exercise that may last hours, days, months or years.

Originally described by Øystein Fjeldstad and Charles Stabell[2], value shops (workshops, not retail shops) marshall resources around individual customer problems. The linear, sequential, incremental chain process does not apply. Shops find problems that their customers want them to solve. They cycle through a repeated fact-finding process to understand the problem, select an appropriate solution and then work to craft a solution to individual customer needs. There is an innate customer-centricity about shops lacking in chains. The shop must solve the problem the customer has, not build the product the chain wants to sell. The shop uses its corporate assets to understand how to solve the customer's problem: hospitals conduct tests; consultancies run consulting engagements; financial advisers complete assessments. Having diagnosed the problem, the shop has to choose the correct solution and methodology to solve it.

For value shops, a product-led CRM agenda is irrelevant. The value shop faces different challenges. It must connect a deep knowledge of its customers (often embedded in the heads of highly-trained staff) with its corporate knowledge of how to solve customer problems – its methodologies. Better product marketing becomes irrelevant. For value shops, CRM becomes the tool to connect the knowledge of customer with the knowledge of solution. Chapter 5 will suggest that value shops could reasonably abandon the CRM acronym and focus their attention upon a customer-oriented knowledge management agenda.

Shops still did not adequately describe all service firms. Fjeldstad and Stabell developed a third model: the value network (of customers, not necessarily of companies which is the other common use).

Value networks

Many service firms do not create value by selling physical product, or solving unique problems. They provide an infrastructure to which customers subscribe in order to enable them to connect, either directly or indirectly, with other people. The network then mediates between those customers. Networks seek to expand their network of customers and balance the contribution of customers to the network, and their consumptions of resources from it. AT&T is an obvious network, mediating conversations. But HSBC and Citicorp mediate customers' capital, enabling customers to make payments to, and borrow money from, each other – the bank is an intermediary. Insurers are also naturally networks: ING and Prudential mediate customer risk. So too are utilities and Internet Service Providers.

The CRM agenda for networks is different again from value chains or shops. As service companies, customers belong to networks for a connection service and to shops for a problem-solving service. All customers consume from networks (they borrow money, make claims,

---

[2] C B Stabell and Ø D Fjeldstad, 'Configuring Value For Competitive Advantage: On Chains, Shops, and Networks', *Strategic Management Journal*, Vol. 19, 1998.

switch on the oven) in return for contribution – primarily their subscription. Networks must use CRM to balance contribution and consumption to attract desirable customers to the network. Customer marketing and interaction is not about product, as it is for the chain, but about experience of the connection. The failure of CRM for many networks is that they have implemented the concept as a tool to sell more subscriptions (i.e. products) at the expense of experience. Chapter 6 calls for an overhaul of the thinking about Customer Relationship Management for such firms.

Value pools

Our research suggests that value chains, shops and networks still do not adequately cover the scope of value creation. In this book we introduce a fourth configuration. Cathay Pacific and British Airways, Hertz and Alamo, Meridien and Holiday Inn have been described as networks, but they create value, not by mediating between customers, but by mediating resources. They build and maintain an infrastructure that customers can rent for a defined period, rather than subscribe to. Whereas networks must, because of the way they create value, balance consumption from and contribution to the network, customers of firms such as Qantas have no direct impact on other customers. We have called this configuration the value pool.

Pools manage a fixed number of resources (expressed in seats, beds, cars, bodies). Shareholder value is created through optimizing the utilization of these units and extracting the maximum price. The CRM agenda for value pools is different again from chains, shops or networks and, as Chapter 7 will describe, it is focused upon maximizing yield from the available units. Pools can use the technologies to identify their best customers and develop schemes to reinforce the loyalty of those customers.

Just as all value chains share a common set of activities, processes and management issues, so do all shops, networks and pools. Where an organization has properties of more than one of the four configurations (and many do) then the CRM agenda for each configuration will be different. This is worth underlining. Although a particular firm may have only one enterprise CRM strategy, that strategy may need up to four distinct CRM agendas reflecting different models of value creation in the business.

VALUE DISCIPLINES

Configurations tell us how firms create value for customers, but on its own such a model is too blunt. Firms vary in the extent to which they seek to prioritize customer needs over aspects of their business such as operational efficiency – a highly customized individual solution will rarely be the cheapest. This prioritization is manifested in some firms' ambitions to change from being product to customer-centric, or developing mission statements emphasizing customer rather than market or product. In 1995, Treacy and Wiersima offered their value discipline framework that explored how market leaders, across any industry, prioritize their resources in pursuit of one of three disciplines while meeting industry standards in the other two disciplines.

Operational excellence

Operationally excellent firms minimize the customers' cost of doing business with them, not only in terms of price, but also in timeliness, and quality of service. The customer motivation is price and such firms will typically seek market share, and to dominate markets through price.

KWIK-FIT INSURANCE SERVICES, FREESERVE, EASYJET

Operational excellence can be illustrated through a firm representing each configuration. Our value shop, Kwik-Fit Insurance Services, a large UK insurance broker, seeks to find an individual solution to each customer's insurance needs by polling a range of different insurers for the cheapest solution; don't poll numerous insurers, one phone call to Kwik-Fit will suffice. Freeserve, a large UK ISP and our value network example, seeks to offer the best price and most reliable access to the internet. Finally, low-cost airline easyJet, the value pool, delivers the cheapest plane tickets over the internet without the frills that premium airline customers pay more for.

The operational excellence message? Why pay more when we can deliver the essence of what you want easily and cheaply?

Product leadership

Product – and for product read product and service – leaders gain a reputation amongst customers for the best offering through constant innovation. Quality and superiority draw their customers. Market share is again a priority but built on superiority rather than price. Product or service leaders seek to make other firms' offerings redundant.

BMW, WOLFF-OLINS, AOL, BRITISH AIRWAYS

Product leaders like to see themselves as 'simply the best'. Consider BMW – a value chain. BMW clearly competes on having the best cars and delivering a superior driving experience. Wolff-Olins, a leading branding consultancy and a value shop, competes by having the most innovative brand creation service available. Our value network example, AOL, tries to make other ISPs redundant by continually expanding its content to keep AOL customers within its immaculately-tended walled garden. The value pool example, British Airways, seeks to be the world's favourite airline – more destinations, good food, outstanding service.

Product or service leaders say to their customers 'How can you think of going anywhere else when we're so good at what we do?'

Customer intimacy

Customer-intimate firms know their customers better than anyone else, with a view to matching customers' needs as closely as possible. They may appear, whether they do or not, to address customers' individual needs. Customers are motivated by the relevance of the offering. For such firms, share of a customer's total spend (wallet share) rather than market share often becomes the primary measure.

> ## DELL, MCKINSEY'S, PRIVATE BANKING FIRMS, HOTEL IMPERIAL IN VIENNA
>
> Customer intimacy is again easy to identify among market leaders. While they stress the excellence of their product and service, the emphasis is upon the relevance of their offering to their individual customer needs. The priority is customization. Dell, the value chain, allows customers to configure their own PCs on the internet: they match PC to customer as precisely as possible. McKinsey's, the value shop, provides strategic advice to executives on many and varied topics. It adapts its service to the needs of its customers. Private banks as value networks, provide bespoke, individual, tailored banking services to their customers. The Hotel Imperial in Vienna offers an example of a customer intimate value pool; nothing is too much trouble and every individual customer need is catered for. However, note that the meaning of customer intimacy changes across the different configurations. We explore these differences further in subsequent chapters.

The leading examples of the disciplines across the configurations have been highlighted as recognizable benchmarks. Of course most firms neither need, nor should, tend to an extreme position. Consider customer intimacy or customer-centricity not as an on/off switch but as a scale where firms position themselves according to corporate priorities. The extent to which firms wish to emphasize customer intimacy becomes a CRM volume control.

While the correlation between CRM and customer intimacy may seem obvious, the concept is also relevant for firms pursuing the other disciplines. Product leaders must ensure that customers perceive their offerings as the best. By obtaining customer feedback, product leaders can improve their offerings. By servicing products effectively, they can ensure that their leadership is not compromised by ineffective support. However, CRM activities are more likely to be limited to measures to maintain superiority rather than focusing upon individual customer needs.

From the customer's perspective, operational excellence has a price and convenience focus that inevitably compromises individual customization. Such comparative insensitivity to customer's unique needs makes CRM less relevant but not redundant. Channel management is a high cost and the internet offers firms the capability to reduce distribution cost. However, which customers will use which channels? Effective CRM can enable the operationally excellent firm to balance price and accessibility on the one hand with quality and customization on the other.

THE CRM FRAMEWORK

In this book we suggest that your strategy should be driven by how you create value for customers, and by the extent to which you turn up or down the customer intimacy volume control. Table 3.2 summarizes how firms, and business units within complex firms, can start to consider their agenda. When the customer intimacy volume is turned up (the shaded horizontal cones), the CRM agenda begins to look different as individual customer needs are addressed.

Taken together, configurations and disciplines offer a framework that becomes central to understanding the complexity of CRM across different businesses and corporate priorities. Once it is clear which configurations you have within your organization you can define your agenda. If you can answer where CRM can help your business, and understand how high to turn the customer intimacy volume control appropriate to your corporate priorities, you have taken the most important step towards meeting your CRM ambitions and delivering against customer expectations.

	OPERATIONAL EXCELLENCE	PRODUCT LEADERSHIP	CUSTOMER INTIMACY	EXAMPLES OF CUSTOMER INTIMACY
Chains	Customers often not identified uniquely; little attempt to cross-sell; price and accessibility focus.	Customer product feedback loop integrated; emphasis on effective product support.	Product often customized to customer needs; customers uniquely identified; probably attempts to cross-sell to existing customers.	Manufacturer allows customers to configure products and builds to order.
Shops	Intimacy sacrificed to imposition of standard methods and solutions to deliver cheapest and most accessible solution.	Customer's solution is constrained by 'best practice' in the service specialization.	Customer needs dictate firm's solution and approach.	Consultancy works collaboratively to the customer's agenda without dictating approach or solution.
Network	Standard service imposed on customer – quality and relevance of experience compromised to low price.	Customer feedback used to enhance scope of network's service.	Customization of service and experience; marked differentiation in service treatment of different customers.	Bank allows customization of account options and delivers relevant differentiated experience.
Pools	One-size-fits-all and no frills service – customers 'rent' resource on price and availability.	Customer feedback used to expand breadth and quality of available resources.	High value customers differentiated and rewarded; high level of resource customization possible.	Hotel records valued customers' preferences and uses these to differentiate service across all hotels.

TABLE 3.2: CRM framework

SUMMARY

1   For value chains, the focus is upon product. CRM, even for the customer-intimate chain, is about customization of product; marketing of product and so on. A traditional CRM agenda of product cross-sell fits well with a chain.

2   All value shops are customer-intimate but shops can still emphasize different disciplines. The operationally excellent shop obtains the least from CRM because it enforces standardization of approach and solution. The product leader operates within constraints laid down by what it regards as best practice within its specialization. The truly customer-intimate shop does not impose standard approaches or best practice but plays to the customer's tune. For the shop, CRM is about knowledge management.

3   The value network establishes and manages an infrastructure for the customer to which the customer subscribes. CRM is about ensuring that the customer obtains incremental value the more the network is used, and CRM involves managing behaviour within the network – because behaviour is the primary determinant of customer value.

4   The value pool's focus is upon yield management and CRM is subordinate to this agenda. CRM must be used to identify the customers most likely to use the resources deployed by the pool most profitably, and CRM must identify customers that will fill unused capacity. Marketing is about optimizing resource usage.

CHAPTER 4

SELLING
PRODUCTS

INTRODUCTION

Chapter 3 introduced the value configurations – four fundamentally different ways in which firms are structured to create value for their customers: value chains, shops, networks and pools. The first of these, the value chain, describes firms that focus upon the manufacture and distribution of products. For example, Gucci and Marks & Spencer, Ford and Rolls Royce, Apple and Dell, Wal-Mart and Tesco all create value by transforming inputs into products and distributing them to customers. For such organizations CRM has a specific role: selling more products to new and existing customers. As the customer intimacy volume control is turned up, so value chains increasingly focus upon customizing their products, or delivery of products, to the individual needs of their customers.

> ## THE VALUE CHAIN'S AGENDA
>
> Product is the mechanism by which value is transferred from a chain to its customers. The value of CRM is in understanding what motivates customers to purchase product, and using that knowledge to acquire new customers more readily and to ensure that existing customers buy other products, purchase the same product again and recommend the products to others.

The value chain's agenda drives a four-stage CRM strategy, shown in Figure 4.1:

1 Acquiring data about customers to discover who is buying what and why.

2 Translating that data into an understanding of which customers are most valuable, and the potential of different customers to buy different products.

3 Using that insight to inform marketing. The marketer's job is to put the right product in front of the right customer at the right time and through the right medium.

4 When raising the level of customer intimacy, finding ways to customize products to customers' expressed needs and to deliver those products cost-effectively. This in turn delivers further data about customers.

This chapter looks at these four stages in detail, describing the CRM techniques that can help to deliver each strategy.

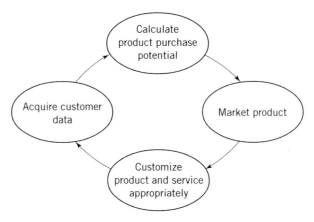

FIGURE 4.1: The value chain's CRM agenda

ACQUIRE CUSTOMER DATA

Chains that wish to migrate from a mass marketing, mass production model must base their CRM program on getting to know more about their customers. Many chains are unable to identify their customers uniquely. Customers of chains do not need to hand over personal data during the purchase or, if they do, the information is very limited. Therefore, value chains must start by acquiring customer data, which they can do in three ways:

1 Entice customers to complete registration forms, return warranties or take part in competitions.

2 Establish loyalty or account schemes to reward customers for delivering data each time they transact business.

3 Set up self-care schemes that uniquely identify customers when they sign in or log in.

Purchase schemes

The traditional data acquisition tools for chains that sell higher value items (such as white goods, computer software and cars) are warranty or registration schemes. Chains selling lower value items typically use competitions or market research data. For example, Bose manufactures and distributes high quality audio equipment – it is a value chain pursuing the value discipline of product leadership. As with similar chains, customers that purchase their Wave® CD Radio are invited to return a warranty that asks for customer data in return for protection over and above basic statutory rights. This provides Bose with uniquely identified customer data including information about customers' lifestyles. Such schemes are cheap and easy to implement but have severe limitations:

☐ The information that can be collected is limited, and so the conclusions that can be drawn from it are limited too. Customers buying stero equipment may find questions about family relationships intrusive and withhold that information. If the primary

33

determinant of purchase behaviour is the age of the children in the house, then no analysis will find the correlation.

☐ Opportunities to refresh data are limited. Even delighted new parents are unlikely to announce the birth of their new child to the firm that sold them furniture, let alone notify them of their new address. But out-of-date data means wasted marketing effort, and irritates the customers.

☐ However small the tick box that customers must tick to prevent unsolicited marketing, more customers are finding it. As concerns over data privacy rise, the chain may find itself collecting data that it cannot use. The UK Data Protection Act, the European Distance Selling Directive (which proposes a move to opt in customer communication rather than the current opt out model), the European Data Protection Directive and the US Unsolicited Electronic Commercial Mail Act 2001, together with discussion regarding a Federal Data Protection Act demonstrate the trend towards customer protection from corporate stalking.

☐ Customers do not want to cooperate. They need incentives. Software firms offer product fixes in return for registration; others run competitions which present lucky winners holidays in the sun. Nevertheless, the customer reward is usually insufficient to guarantee a response. The customers that do respond become a self-selecting sample which is unlikely to coincide with the most valuable customers.

Loyalty schemes

The construction of loyalty or account schemes is significantly more expensive than purchase schemes, but has greater potential because, as well as acquiring customer data, they can:

☐ Address the data refresh problem by enabling regular contact.

☐ Create a form of subscription in which the customer is rewarded for continuing loyalty.

Loyalty schemes turn a sequence of repeat purchases into mutually committed relationships where customers have an incentive to return. For example, UK retailer Tesco operates 'Clubcard' – a loyalty card scheme that, in return for using the card at point of sale, offers 1 per cent off subsequent purchases through a voucher scheme. By integrating point of sale technology with customer data, Tesco has the potential to draw remarkably precise conclusions about customer behaviours, profitability and preferences. However, these schemes also have disadvantages:

☐ They are costly to establish. By definition loyalty schemes must be rolled out across the business to allow customers to benefit wherever they interact with the firm.

☐ Realizing the benefits from the wealth of information that becomes available demands sophisticated data intelligence competence. Chapter 15 on customer intelligence explains the pitfalls of investing in analytical technologies.

☐ The rewards offered eat into increasingly tight margins. Simplistically, if customers are offered savings of 1 per cent and the firm's margin is 10 per cent, then the scheme only becomes worthwhile if it increases sales by 10 per cent.

Self-care schemes

Traditional chains may only know who their customers are through implementing registration or loyalty schemes. However, a chain using remote channels (telephone, internet, direct mail) can enforce a security process that provides customer identification data. In a number of sectors, value chains use the internet as their primary customer medium. Such 'e-chains' enable, and enforce, customer identification because customers must log in to complete secure financial transactions. Although www.amazon.com does not record detailed demographic information about its customers, it records detailed information about more important data for its proposition – purchase behaviours. The self-care model forces customers to register every time they buy. Over time, Amazon's technology builds up a sophisticated and accurate picture of its customers' tastes, which it translates into more precise customer marketing.

CALCULATE CROSS-SELL POTENTIAL

If you can identify each customer uniquely you have some customer data, perhaps only a name or address, but maybe more. Value chains can use this data with product data to decide on one of three customer decision-making priorities: cross-sell, re-sell and new sales. These are broadly covered by the term 'cross-sell' and use the same technologies.

1 **Cross-sell** – Involves selling additional (and ideally higher value) products, which may or may not be related to the original purchase, to existing customers. How much a chain should emphasize cross-sell in its CRM agenda can be expressed as:

> Potential sales frequency $\times$ breadth of product range = cross-sell potential

Product cross-sell to individual customers is unlikely to pay dividends for car manufacturers – the potential sales frequency is too low and the breadth of the product range is small. However, cross-sell is central to Amazon's strategy.

2 **Re-sell** – Particularly important for firms selling higher value products with defined lifespans (such as cars), but also for firms selling lower value products which seek to understand and nurture loyalty (e.g. to ensure customers keep buying Dove soap). Re-sell involves deploying the same technologies as cross-sell but asks three different questions of the data:

    1 How likely is it that this customer will purchase the same product again?

    2 What is the likelihood that they will seek a different product from the range?

    3 When are they likely to repurchase?

    For re-sellers, as opposed to cross-sellers, purchase timing becomes critical. Chapters 15 and 16 introduce some of the techniques for answering these questions.

3 **New sales** – An organization applying data mining technologies to its records of the purchasing behaviours of existing customers can discover the precise combination of data most likely to result in the sale of particular products. By integrating such models into the marketing process, it can focus customer acquisition activity more effectively, targeting prospects that have the same characteristics as valued customers. Such analyses are particularly important for firms focused upon gaining market share.

Customer analytics for the chain is simply about understanding who will buy what product when. The distinction between cross-sellers, re-sellers and new sellers is worth considering, not because it changes the technology used, but because the distinction fundamentally changes the answers that you seek from the data.

MARKETING THE PRODUCTS

There are four distinct strategies that support the chain's marketing objective of selling products, shown in Table 4.1. Any or all of these may be appropriate.

PRODUCT MARKETING	Market products directly to prospects as accurately as possible using the medium most likely to elicit a response.
AFFINITY MARKETING	Use prospects' affection for a third party – typically a community to which they belong such as a charity, university or football club – to market products.
PARTNERSHIP MARKETING	Broaden the overall customer proposition by combining products with complementary products or services from third parties.
COMMUNITY MARKETING	Facilitate a community of customers enthusiastic about the product and market indirectly through that club.

TABLE 4.1: The four customer marketing strategies

Product marketing

The CRM marketing agenda for the chain involves placing the right product in front of a receptive customer at the right time. Depending upon the value discipline pursued, the marketer attempts to woo the customer in different ways:

☐ Product leadership companies offer the best product (probably not the cheapest). The role of CRM is to deliver focused marketing messages convincing the customer that a particular product is superior. Direct marketing, for example, should emphasize innovative product features and how these differentiate the offering. After all, it is this differentiation that warrants the price premium.

☐ Operationally excellent companies promise the most cost-effective product for the purpose (probably amongst the cheapest or most accessible on the market). CRM, that is individual customer marketing, probably has a much less significant role because operationally excellent companies will tend to focus on mass marketing.

☐ Customer-intimate companies deliver the product that is best customized for customer needs (and probably more expensive). The role of CRM is to explain to individual customers why customization is important and how the product can be customized to their needs.

Aligning product marketing and value discipline is essential. A company like BMW, a product leader, must focus marketing messages upon superiority over the competition. The message is comparative. BUPA, a company which operates private hospitals, emphasizes customer intimacy and offers customer messages about how the service will be customized to the needs of the customer rather than overtly comparing their service to the National Health Service. The latter comparison would be the assertion of the product leader.

Affinity marketing

Affinity marketing is growing in importance. Many customers have an affinity to an organization that is almost a tribal identity. Sports teams are an obvious example, but so are charities, medical special interest groups, universities, hospitals, local towns, schools and so on. Affinity marketing involves creating a relationship with a third party organization as a platform to sell products to its supporters. This kind of scheme is particularly valuable because some of the customer's trust is transferred to your firm. Like most major football clubs, the London-based team West Ham United promotes affinity marketing schemes with a credit card provider, an online bookmaker and a football news service, as well as links to sponsors, on its website.

Partnership marketing

Many chains can identify related products or services provided by third parties that, if used in combination with their own products, can enhance the value of their offering. UK vehicle manufacturers now typically offer free subscriptions to third party breakdown services. Often, these partnership programs run in conjunction with loyalty programs, which are offered as one of the rewards for joining the scheme. There are a number of advantages to partnership marketing. It may be cheap and may even make a profit (if the partner offers you a discount, only some of which you pass on to the customer), at the same time as adding value to the customer. However, partners usually offer deep discounts only to leading firms. Siebel's CRM software is primarily implemented through its web of systems integration partners. Joint marketing, for example with IBM and Accenture, presents the sum of the whole – the systems integrators' implementation competence with the functional competence of the software. Since Siebel is a value chain and its partners value shops, there is no conflict in the partnerships.

Community marketing

The fourth marketing tool for the chain – forming communities of customers and then marketing to them – leads to the construction of a different value configuration altogether. Chains can form value networks. Community marketing may be particularly relevant for product leaders, but it is available to almost any chain that can develop a sense of shared community around its products. For example, Harley Davidson's Harley Owners Group® (HOG) claims 650,000 members and is a regularly cited example of community marketing. Such a network can transform the performance of a chain, yet the success of HOG has been in the creation of an experience for its members not as an overt product cross-sell tool.

Computer games companies are also leaders in community marketing. For example, www.throughtheages.com offers a community based around Microsoft's successful Ages of Empire game. Downloads, upgrades and discussions are facilitated and new associated products marketed through the website.

CUSTOMIZE PRODUCT

The end result of both customer intimacy and mass customization is that customers receive products that precisely match their needs. This shifts the customers' priority from price to relevance (and it is in any case difficult to do price comparisons for a customized product). The best example is Dell. Dell offers the classic case study of mass customization and customer intimacy. By enabling its customers to buy PCs to their own specification, Dell can compete on relevance rather than price. This is only possible because Dell identifies customers uniquely and captures information about their needs that it uses to build to order.

However, CRM is important to more firms than those seeking to customize product. For both product leaders and operationally excellent chains, customer interaction technologies offer three further opportunities:

1 Enables the customer to research products more effectively.

2 Reduces distribution costs using direct distribution models.

3 Obtains product feedback to improve the manufacture or distribution of products.

Provide accessible product information

Chain customers value the product more than how the product is delivered. Therefore the channel is often a delivery mechanism rather than an integral element of how value is created for customers. This contrasts with a network, where *how* service is delivered is more critical. Chains can reinforce loyalty to their products and attract new customers, by ensuring that they offer customers the necessary capabilities to find out about the products and provide help as efficiently as possible. The prospective washing machine owner may want to find out whether a machine requires hot or cold water supply or both. Most customers still have to phone a call centre or agent or visit outlets to find out the basic product information. An internet-based help function offers a more cost-effective product research tool.

It has been estimated that in 2001, over 4 trillion e-mails were sent in the US, primarily between businesses or between individuals. But to date relatively few firms, other than e-chains, have integrated e-mail connectivity between their business and customers into their operations. Doing so could save customers time and the firms money.

Reduce distribution costs

Particularly in operationally excellent firms, the distribution infrastructure is typically managed as a cost, rather than as an integral component of value delivery. Even though the internet has much lower operational costs than a branch infrastructure, capital investment costs are high. Many chains own their own distribution networks or influence distribution through franchisees. New media, such as the internet, offer the opportunity to distribute more cheaply to the customers willing to use them.

CRM offers chains access to lower cost direct distribution methods by revealing where these methods will be accepted. Chains should consider their distribution infrastructures and identify whether or not additional or replacement channels could be beneficial. Many chains that previously relied upon catalogues, such as clothing retailer Land's End, have successfully transferred significant business to the internet. The fundamental principles of distance selling remain the same although the medium has changed.

Whether investment in low cost distribution models makes sense depends upon the extent to which your products and services can be distributed at low cost. Domino's Pizza has built a successful international franchise on the back of lower infrastructure costs and home delivery of pizzas. However, in the luxury goods sector, firms such as Gucci use their outlets as the primary focus of sales activity and cost-effective distribution is less important.

Capture product feedback

All chains, particularly product leaders, must avoid creating products that nobody wants. CRM is an invaluable tool for obtaining customer feedback. Feedback buttons and e-mail links on the internet cost little yet provide valuable data to improve products. Acknowledging e-mails also has the secondary effect of strengthening the relatively weak bonds between chains and their customers.

However, although many websites offer 'Contact Us' buttons, few specifically request product feedback. Nokia does, and it increases the likelihood of customer contact. Contact centre and e-mail surveys offer another cost-effective means of obtaining feedback.

SUMMARY

1 Make acquisition of customer data a priority and consider the potential schemes for data acquisition. Balance cost of data acquisition against both your data analysis competence and potential value from that data.

2 Focus analytical CRM technologies upon identifying customers with potential for cross-sell, re-sell or new sell depending upon the nature of your business. Identify the potential for each.

3 Consider how effectively you use the four customer marketing strategies currently. If you use one or more consider whether you are using them effectively, and, if you are not, consider whether your organization could benefit from them.

4 Consider how you customize products for customers, and how precise that customization is. Can customers research your products as cost-effectively as possible, or is their research inconvenient to them and more costly to you? Do you make effective use of low cost distribution channels? Should you make better use of them? If you do not obtain product feedback from customers, why not? Customers may not want to provide feedback, but have you tried?

CHAPTER 5

CONNECTING KNOWLEDGE

INTRODUCTION

Organizations that fall into the second of the four value configurations introduced in Chapter 3 (value chains, shops, networks and pools) utilize their corporate knowledge to solve individual customer problems. The product-led CRM agenda suggested for value chains in the last chapter (identify customers, calculate cross-sell potential, market product, and service that product cost-effectively) is irrelevant for value shops. Try applying it to an architectural practice, consultancy or law firm, hospital or pharmaceutical research business. The fact that you cannot does not mean that CRM is irrelevant to these firms; it means that such firms have a different agenda.

Value shops produce individual solutions for their customers (often referred to as 'clients' or 'accounts') through an iterative process of understanding customers' needs. This implies a strong element of customer intimacy. Yet many shops struggle to understand the value of CRM, partly because they think it means the 'customer stalking' activities appropriate to a value chain. Whereas the value chain asks 'Who in the market will buy my product?', the value shop asks 'What does the customer in my market want?'

The insurance broker (a value shop) needs to understand why the customer needs insurance; cross-selling different products misses the point. The broker's objective is to understand and deliver the range of the customer's insurance needs. Cross-selling may be the right outcome (the broker wants to sell more) but the wrong objective (the broker has to sell the right product to solve the specific problems of the customer). If the broker sells a product that does not solve the customer's specific problem, then the customer will not return to that broker and is prone to tell friends, family and colleagues not to either. The 1980s and 1990s saw significant financial services mis-selling scandals of endowment and pension policies. These scandals resulted from industry structures that rewarded brokers for acting as chain product salespeople, rather than shop solution providers. The increasing trend, across Europe, towards salaried sales forces reflects a growing recognition that shops that act like chains ultimately destroy their own market by destroying customer trust.

The CRM agenda for value shops centres not on products but on customer-oriented knowledge management.

SOME ARE MORE INTIMATE THAN OTHERS

Value shops can pursue different value disciplines, although all shops are by definition customer-intimate. True customer intimacy, as practised by some top management consulting firms, means concentrating on a fixed customer base and being prepared to take on any problem that the customer has, no matter how tough, and to be paid by results.

Most large professional services firms (e.g. in the technology and legal sectors) take great pains to codify their approach to problem solving into standardized techniques, such as systems development methodologies. This is operational excellence, and is typically the only means by which large shops can achieve economies of scale. These firms struggle to reconcile their desire to be customer-intimate (which wins customers) with their need to achieve operational excellence (which generates profits). The more the consultancy must focus upon achieving profitability through standardization, the less flexibility it has to address any potential problem the customer may have, which in turn compromises its intimacy. This tension lies at the heart of any large shop.

Architects may specialize in high-tension canopies or law firms in high-technology start-ups. This is product leadership; customer value is created by specialization. Examples of such shops are Moorfields Eye Hospital and consultancies Hewson Group and Peppers & Rogers Group, who specialize in CRM consulting. Their CRM agendas are about improving their service – getting better at their specialization – and it would be more precise (if pedantic) to call them service leaders rather than product leaders.

The trade-off between the three disciplines of operational excellence, product leadership and customer intimacy is just as visible in shops as in chains. Attempts to pursue operational excellence within hospitals (no pun intended) for example, while welcomed by insurers and government, are often unpopular with patients who want to feel cared for as well as treated.

SHOP RELATIONSHIPS ARE EVENT-ORIENTED

The value shop's customer relationships are event-oriented. The customer needs a specific problem solved; the business needs a new computer system developed; the man with a broken leg needs it fixed; the newly-wed couple want the architect to build their house; grandparents want to set up a trust fund for their grandchildren. This is not a transactional relationship. It involves a highly intimate and repeated connection between customer and firm for hours, days, weeks, months or even years while the shop understands the customers' needs, and then pulls together the resources to solve the problem.

But once the customer's problem has been solved, the relationship with the shop may founder. The problem has been solved. Now, the shop's priority is to extend an already intimate connection into a longer-term relationship, so that the customer will bring their next problem to the shop.

The four CRM processes for the value shop shown in Figure 5.1 are related to, yet distinct from, the equivalent processes for the value chain.

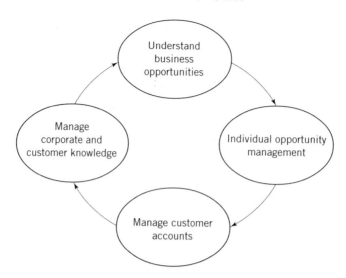

FIGURE 5.1: The value shop's CRM agenda

MANAGE CORPORATE AND CUSTOMER KNOWLEDGE

Shops have a different customer information problem to chains. Customer knowledge is gathered by (potentially) numerous staff over (potentially) an extended period. The knowledge is typically either scattered all over the organization or – even more difficult to integrate – in people's heads. Individual employees typically have enormous knowledge about their customers, but shops as corporate entities often have very little or the knowledge is highly dispersed. For example, like all consulting firms operating in a large account, McKinsey's may have multiple consultants working with a client. Customer knowledge is not acquired through a sequence of tightly defined transactions as it is for any chain, but through a complex, rolling, multifaceted relationship that stretches over weeks, months or years. How can McKinsey's hope to collect the knowledge about its customers that such relationships provide into something vaguely coherent? The answer is the same as that used by almost all significant consulting firms – a knowledge management environment that enables staff to connect the corporate knowledge, that is the heart of their value proposition, to their customers.

One of the most significant challenges any shop faces is to connect the knowledge of individual solutions – scattered amongst its specialists – with the customer-facing team or individual. The challenge increases with scale: in a five-person architect practice it is easy to share knowledge; the 50,000-person consultancy struggles to operate as if all 50,000 staff contribute to the customer's solution.

The amount of data adds to the information management problem. The frequentative fact-finding nature of the shop's interaction with the customer means that the shop's representatives are overwhelmed with customer data – think of a team of 20 information technology (IT) consultants developing a corporate strategy over six months, or hospital staff treating a cancer patient. What information needs to be shared, and what stored?

Nevertheless, whatever the size of the shop, much of the customer's perception of value is rooted in how the firm deploys its knowledge to solve the customer's problem. Clearly the shop needs structures and tools that enable it to collaborate effectively internally and bring its knowledge to the customer interface point.

If this sounds as if CRM for shops is knowledge management, it is. For the shop, the CRM agenda is a knowledge management agenda. Perhaps shops should not pursue CRM (with its chain-like connotations), but instead seek ways to merge their knowledge and customer management programs into a strategy to connect corporate knowledge of methodology (how) and solution (what) with customer (who).

If CRM and knowledge management remain separate strategies and, worse, separate technologies, shops will increasingly be unable to leverage scale as they grow.

Merging CRM with knowledge management is particularly appealing to the shops' customer-facing staff. It will help them win business through understanding and projecting a complete view of the firm's capabilities. Salespeople can cross-sell not by creating connections between products, but by applying corporate knowledge to the customer's issues.

The irony is that shops – although by definition always the most customer-intimate firms – may have least to gain from traditional CRM technologies. They are better served by knowledge management technologies that integrate knowledge of customer with knowledge of product and service at the point of customer connection.

As the shop grows bigger, a knowledge management program also eases the increasing difficulty of sharing customer information. Standard templates used across the organization also help. Most shops do this already, within corporate methodologies imposed across the business:

☐ Financial advisers use standard fact-finding forms to capture customer requirements. These may even be defined by regulation.

☐ Consultancies use standard methodologies such as CSC's Catalyst, which is a methodology to control business change.

☐ Architects use standard tools to capture designs.

However, shops most often use templates to capture internal methodologies and approaches in order to enforce a degree of standardization. It is rare to find shops adopting common templates to record customer events and their deep knowledge of customers. Shops need to focus upon what customer information is required and then construct and impose templates to capture and make that data available.

UNDERSTAND BUSINESS OPPORTUNITIES

Customer analytics for the chain are focused upon calculation of product cross-sell potential. For the shop, these technologies may be irrelevant. The term event is used here to differentiate from transactions. An event is an iterative and time-consuming exercise. It may be an afternoon with the financial adviser; a three-year systems implementation project; a six-hour operation followed by three weeks of patient recovery. It is both time-consuming and invariably important to the customer in a way that a transaction is not. The equation for assessing the value of analytics revolves around understanding events and the relationship between them.

☐ The number of events that the shop anticipates over a given period.

☐ Whether extrapolation between events is possible.

For example, consider two notional shops:

1 A group of 500 insurance brokers build financial services solutions for 50,000 customers. Each broker may have five events a day or 1000 a year. With 500,000 events a year, investment in analytical CRM software to identify prospects with specific opportunities may be useful. Given that opportunities can be extrapolated from known events (for instance, it is possible to identify reasonably accurately prospects likely to need retirement solutions), the investment seems even more attractive.

2 A consultancy with 10,000 staff delivering IT solutions to 250 customers. The average event may be worth $500,000 but there may be only 200 events per year. Since customer analytics is about finding patterns between numerous events, analytical CRM software is probably unnecessary.

There is likely to be a correlation between the outcome and the proportion of business-to-consumer (B2C) and business-to-business (B2B) relationships. A shop that operates in a business-to-business environment (such as an IT consultancy) is less likely to find analytical CRM tools useful. The number of events for a large shop in the business-to-consumer sector makes CRM analysis more relevant.

If analytical tools are appropriate, then their value in a shop is in identifying what opportunity to grasp with the customer and how.

The insurance broker could use analytics to try and cross-sell a pension product. However, this limits the ambition and fails to take advantage of the broader opportunity, which is to identify opportunities for retirement planning, not for selling pensions. This may appear a semantic argument. It isn't. If your data analysts are asked to construct patterns of pensions purchase, they will do so. A more sophisticated and relevant use of the technology would be to identify all possible patterns for retirement planning.

INDIVIDUAL OPPORTUNITY MANAGEMENT

If customer marketing for the chain is about variations on a theme of cross-sell, for shops it is about projecting a capability to solve problems and a methodology designed to inspire confidence in the customer. CRM needs to explain to the customer what problems the shop can solve and how the shop will solve them.

Too often, a shop's website opens with a fanfare about the firm; instead, it should show how the firm understands the problems its customers face, and project its capability to solve them. A shop must broadcast its knowledge of its customers' issues and its capability to resolve them. For example, Wolff-Olins is a leading global branding consultancy that creates unique brands for many leading firms. Cross-selling – 'you bought that, now buy this' – does not apply. The value proposition for the firm is built around the construction of innovative individual solutions. While the existing customer base can be used as references, customer marketing for the firm projects its capabilities to solve unique issues, and its innovative methodology that differentiates its approach from the competition.

Yet most shops build websites more appropriate to chains (or worse, not appropriate to customers at all, only to staff or shareholders). *How* is as important as *what* for the shop. Methodology is irrelevant for chains. Customers do not care how chains build cars or books. For shops it is fundamental. One of the key ways in which shops differentiate themselves from each other, for instance PWC from Accenture from CSC, is in their methodology and how they apply that methodology to solve a unique problem.

For the shop, although cross-sell is a desirable outcome it is not an appropriate objective. Even for the product leader, such as the CRM consultancy or specialist architect firm, cross-sell is not applicable. Rather, the objective is to extend the depth and breadth of the shop's relationship with the customer. This is achieved by focusing the marketing agenda upon projecting capability and methodology.

MANAGE CUSTOMER ACCOUNTS

Customer interaction is a complex problem for any shop. The customer may have an event (the construction of a new brand, or a hospital operation) in which multiple customer representatives have been exposed to multiple staff from the shop to define the eventual solution. Almost all chains can rely upon staff who have no knowledge of the individual customer to manage the customer relationship; technology provides the basic customer knowledge necessary during the conversation to allow the call centre operator to interact successfully. All shops can only succeed if they display deep knowledge of their individual customer needs.

Account management

In a value shop, the role of customer interaction is to maintain an already customer-intimate relationship to drive out new opportunities. Again, this is totally different from the priorities of the chain that focused on customizing products – the shop always customizes its 'product'. A good solution is to manage customers as accounts.

While account management may seem an overly grand term for the management of customer relationships by a two-person decorating firm, the principle still applies. The two-person firm needs, as much as a global consulting firm, to ensure that the customer offers repeat business.

This applies in both the business-to-customer and business-to-business relationships. An account may have periods of high activity and low activity, but there must always be someone within the organization to maintain that customer connection. Perhaps it is nothing more than a letter or telephone call every year. The account structure can be relevant for all shops but is particularly important in the business-to-business sector. It applies regardless of the chosen value discipline.

Self-service shops

A shop differentiates itself by its ability to deploy its corporate knowledge to achieve a particular goal. However, internet-based self-service problem resolution is a radical possibility for a shop, whose value proposition has always been to solve individual problems by bringing a combination of resources to bear. If a shop tells the customer 'Do it yourself on the web,' then the customer may ask 'Why go to a shop in the first place?' For the chain, self-service problem resolution is always likely to be a winner; for the shop, it conflicts with the firm's value proposition and this is a dangerous game to play. However, John Charcol, a UK broker, launched an internet-automated advice service (www.charcolonline.co.uk) authorized by the regulator to provide self-service advice. Given that the value proposition of the broking business has always been product knowledge developed over years, automation of the advice process challenges this value proposition in a more profound way than selling cars over the internet. A radical possibility of CRM for the shop may be to change the business model.

Conversely, the e-shop offers chains and networks the opportunity to create shops to add value to their existing products and services and compete in areas dominated by shops offering

45

bespoke solutions. For example, companies can use the internet to offer automated garden designs at a fraction of the cost of traditional services, bringing them within the reach of a new audience. This mirrors how chains can build networks as community marketing initiatives.

The e-shop needs sophisticated software. The process of finding facts about customer's requirements, integral to any shop's proposition, demands software that can capture and analyze potentially complex data. It certainly demands the recording of data about individual customers, since by definition the solution is unique. Although in their infancy, e-shops open interesting possibilities:

☐ Doctors' surgeries could provide initial patient assessments through the internet or digital TV. The UK government's NHS Direct (part of the UK's state health care system) is an attempt to reduce the pressure on doctors' surgeries by providing a preliminary assessment over the telephone. It is a short step from there to an e-shop.

☐ Architects and building firms could provide customer templates that enable customers to plan their own home extensions at a lower cost than the traditional service. This may allow shops to extend their services to new groups of customers.

☐ Financial services firms can provide advice online. Meridien Research predicts an explosion in such services in the UK over the next five years.

There is a huge risk for any shop in going virtual, since it potentially destroys the value proposition. Where chains and networks provide potential, albeit less customized, replacement or alternative products to the shop, the shop risks destroying its differentiator by automation.

SUMMARY

1 The process of customer information management for the shop is as much about knowledge management as it is customer management. Do not try to shoehorn CRM technologies into your business if knowledge management technologies would play a more valuable role in managing customers effectively.

2 The analytical CRM technologies central to the chain's ability to increase the value of existing customers may be irrelevant to the shop, particularly in the business-to-business market. Even where such technologies could add value, be sure to concentrate on understanding opportunity points rather than product purchasing patterns. This may not imply a change in technology, but it changes and broadens the questions asked of the technology.

3 Consider customer interaction to be as much about account management as anything else. It is only through constructing an account management structure that the shop can ensure that customer 'events' are leveraged effectively. There will, in any case, be an intense relationship between customer and shop during the resolution of the problem – the account management structure needs to maintain the relationship in between 'events'.

4 Virtual shops, or e-shops, offer exciting possibilities for some shops. However, they must be handled with care, because they can destroy a shop's business which is, ultimately, about the provision of knowledge-based services.

CHAPTER 6

DELIVERING SERVICE

INTRODUCTION

Value networks – the third of the four value configurations introduced in Chapter 3 – provide an infrastructure to which customers subscribe in order to connect, either directly or indirectly, with other people. They include banks, utilities and ISPs. Value networks are service companies, yet many are finding that their investment in CRM is not delivering results. *The Economist* succinctly summarizes the anguish not just of many banks but of many service industries:

⟨ For a while, bank chief executives hoped that the answer was CRM . . . But in many cases CRM has turned out to be the opposite of what its name suggests . . . The reason is that [it] is being used to sell products rather than improve service. ⟩ [1]

Service sector firms typically and wrongly pursue a CRM agenda based on pushing products. But customers have higher service expectations than before – particularly, and unsurprisingly, from service industries. CRM is more relevant than ever for value networks, but it requires an agenda founded upon service. This is a different agenda again from that described in Chapters 4 and 5.

NETWORKS HAVE SUBSCRIPTION RELATIONSHIPS

A network's relationships with its customers are different from those of chains or shops. A customer 'subscribes' to a network, contracting to become part of an association of people that the network mediates across its own and other firms' infrastructures, either directly or indirectly. It is a network of customers that may, or may not, also be a network of companies – the other common use of the term value network.

The subscription may be free, especially within e-networks, such as Motley Fool, which provides financial advice and enables financial discussion amongst its members. The infrastructure, at least initially, may be funded by advertising or borrowing. More usually, service must be paid for and the terms and conditions of the subscription represent the 'product'. Thus, a network's relationships are built on the customers' experience of

[1] 'Love Me', *The Economist*, 23 February 2002.

connecting to the service. Customers dip in and out of networks as the need arises (make a call, turn on the oven, pay by credit card), but their subscription, like a marriage, remains even when they are unconnected.

If the subscription is seen only as an opportunity for financial extraction, rather than the basis for service delivery, then CRM will fail. This may sound over-charitable; can someone please think of the shareholders? Nevertheless, as switching suppliers becomes increasingly easy, customers can more readily swap one subscription for another. The only way to retain valued customers is to deliver service, so that in turn those customers reward you with their loyalty. This has significant implications for networks' CRM agenda, as shown in Figure 6.1.

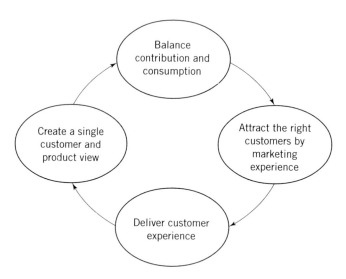

FIGURE 6.1: The network's CRM agenda

CREATE A SINGLE CUSTOMER AND PRODUCT VIEW

Single customer view

Like shops, networks do not have a problem identifying customers – the subscriptions deliver customer data. Yet they do have two information problems:

1 They typically record the same or different data about the same customer in multiple places (e.g. in marketing and administration databases).

2 Where the customer has bought multiple 'products', the customer relationship is often managed as separate product-based relationships.

The network's chief problem is customer data duplication. For example, imagine a retail bank that claims 1,000,000 customers. This may actually represent only 750,000 different people. The difference of 250,000 (33 per cent of the actual total) arises because the bank has a customer database for every product type and therefore double counts every customer with more than one product. These 250,000 customers are bombarded by duplicate marketing and have to write multiple change of address letters – nonetheless they are probably the bank's best customers.

Chains may suffer from the same problem but the implications are not so bad. Product-motivated customers are less likely to be concerned by product-oriented relationships, but service-motivated customers are likely to find multiple relationships within a single brand horribly frustrating. That frustration is compounded when network marketing focuses on service. The brand that promises service will destroy that promise by fragmenting the customers' experience unless it has a single customer view.

Imagine an insurer that, like many networks, thinks like a chain. Its stated CRM objective is to cross-sell more products. When it succeeds, and creates a corps of valuable customers with multiple products, those customers are then exposed to more staff and more departments that manage their expanded policy portfolio. The most valuable customer, with three, four or five products, has to send three, four or five change of address letters and balance enquiries. Marketing letters, driven from the investment product system's customer database, try to cross-sell life insurance – but the customer already has life insurance, with this company. Such firms prove that their customers are numbers and targets. The appalling implication for networks following a chain's product-led agenda is that in addition to finding their CRM efforts unrewarding, they are likely to be unwittingly treating their best customers worse than their worst customers.

Single product view

As Chapter 4 suggested, increasing the product to customer ratio is invariably a good outcome for chains. However, we have also just seen that network customers want access to the network through one relationship, not five different product relationships. The implication is that making it easier for customers to use the network is more effective than traditional cross-selling. This has consequences for product and service design. The network that seeks to become customer-centric attempts to reduce the product to customer ratio to 1:1 through radical product design – with all its technology implications – rather than increase the product to customer ratio through ever more precise customer targeting. A new insurance service launched in 2001, Bluesure, (www.bluesure.com) grasps this concept and offers to mediate a customer's risk through a single policy. The more risk a customer places with the firm, the greater the saving the customer makes. This is good network thinking.

In the UK and Australia, many banks have similarly understood the difference in the thinking. They have developed 'capital mediation' services that include savings accounts, current accounts, credit cards and mortgages managed through a single coherent wrapper. For example, Virgin One is a single account that offers integrated mortgage, current account and credit card. Rather than the customer borrowing on a credit card (at an interest rate of perhaps 15 per cent) and a mortgage managed separately (at say 5 per cent) and then making savings into a deposit account (that accrues interest at 4 per cent), the three products are consolidated.

The corporate mind-set is different: it recognizes that customers subscribe to services that mediate their capital. Traditionally banks have seen selling more products to the same customer as the goal. 'All in one products' recognize that the objective is to mediate more of the customer's capital and reward the customer for this. In another example of network thinking, Powergen was originally an electricity network. It now offers its customers integrated electricity, natural gas and telephone through a single bill. Discounts are offered to customers who buy more services through the network. This creates a 'win win' for customer and utility. The customer receives superior service (assuming Powergen successfully integrates its delivery). Better still, the customer is cheaper to serve – Powergen has to produce one bill not three – and so the utility can reduce its costs and, in turn, its prices. The customer to product ratio is effectively increased, although the important measure is share of wallet; how much of the customer's utility spend is with Powergen?

A network without a single product view provides little incentive for customers to expand their use of it. Why should customers cross-buy when connection to another network is as easy and avoids the frustration of telling the same supplier the same thing multiple times? Operationally excellent networks, with their CRM volume turned low, may get away with the delivery of fragmented experience, price overcoming customer frustration. Nonetheless, for most networks, multiple product-oriented relationships doom any attempts at building the loyalty of their valued customers.

For most networks, the failure to deliver a single relationship, combined with cross-sell initiatives, will result in a growing corps of more valuable but more dissatisfied customers. They will leave. Inertia will always be a more powerful force for customer retention in networks than in chains – changing subscription is more troublesome than buying a different product or visiting a different store. However, inertia is starting to be broken down by self-care systems which enable customers to switch subscriptions more rapidly than before. Building a single customer and product view is increasingly a competitive necessity for networks with broad service portfolios seeking to build wallet share.

BALANCE CONTRIBUTION AND CONSUMPTION

The actions of network customers affect other customers. Take Norwich Union mediating motor insurance risk: every insurance claim will tend to increase premiums for all its customers. Take Powergen: the British love of a cup of tea at half-time in soccer matches causes power surges across the network. Even The Royal and Ancient Golf Club must balance the number of subscriptions against course utilization.

The best customers are those whose contribution exceeds their consumption. The network has to balance the amount customers contribute to the network – through their subscription and otherwise – and the amount they consume. Any network has customers with undesirable behaviour:

- ☐ Insurance customers who have too many car crashes for their size of premium.
- ☐ Telecommunications customers who spend too long using fixed price links.
- ☐ Golf club members who take too long to get round the course.

This is perhaps particularly true of e-networks where the subscription may be more easily obtained, and more readily discarded.

Networks must understand the behaviour of both valued and undesirable customers, and identify mechanisms to grow valued customers by increasing their use of the network, and eliminate undesirable behaviours either by regulating behaviour or expelling undesirable customers. The oldest life insurer in the world, Equitable Life, was effectively destroyed by its inability to balance contribution and consumption. A minority of customers were guaranteed payments from Equitable at a rate far in excess of what Equitable could obtain from investing the other customers' contributions. That minority were consuming more than was being contributed. www.friendsreunited.co.uk is an internet-based network, initiated in 2000, that puts old school friends in touch with each other. However, it became famous for attracting libellous messages about old school teachers. The network now monitors messages and rapidly extracts those that may be libellous. The customers' contribution is different – primarily information rather than subscription – but the same principle applies. Interestingly, like many e-networks, they have found the 'free to customer' model unsustainable and do now charge for contacts.

CRM analytics software helps networks to balance contribution and consumption. The deployment of analytical technologies against a single customer view, to identify desirable and undesirable behaviours is a sensible priority for CRM. For chains the concept of a wrong customer is alien, but for the network it is critical. Product purchase is important, but only as a subset of behaviour. Superficially, successful cross-sell strategies may diminish rather than increase shareholder value. This is an important consideration for firms that have implemented CRM applications piecemeal and that measure their success using simplistic measures such as increases in marketing response rates. A chain typically embeds costs within the initial product price and the customer creates shareholder value at purchase. Network customers create shareholder value over time.

Meridien Research summarizes the problem:

'Extraordinary claims of ROI [Return On Investment] may be misleading. For example, increased response rates on direct marketing campaigns would seem to indicate high ROI for customer databases, but they hide the fact that the programs tend to attract bargain hunters with no potential for retention or profitable growth. The contribution of these customers often fails to recover the acquisition cost, even though the response rates may improve dramatically. Simply put – they are just the wrong customers.' [2]

In the UK, the competitive mortgage industry has enticed customers with low, fixed initial interest rates, but this has simply encouraged the number of 'rate tarts' who grab good deals and then move on.

ATTRACT THE RIGHT CUSTOMERS BY MARKETING EXPERIENCE

You can create brand by creating affiliation to the firm's products, or to the firm itself. BMW, Sony and any chain rightly focus brand creation upon product. In so doing, they create product-led loyalty to the brand. For service industries, it is not product that creates customer value but service, i.e. not AOL's product but their internet environment; not HSBC's accounts but the benefits that subscription offers. This changes customer marketing.

The same four broad categories of marketing that were applicable to the chain (product, affinity, partnership and community) are also applicable to the network, but the marketing message is different. The concept of product marketing is replaced by service marketing. Regardless of the value discipline, customer marketing does not become a tool to push ever more products ever more accurately to ever better defined prospects, but a tool to build desirable prospects' perceptions of their future experience. This is why some insurers focus their marketing upon claims experience. Others who emphasize product features may find customer marketing less successful.

Good network thinking in customer marketing is to identify 'moments of truth' in the customers' use of the network: the defining moments at which the companies' failure to deliver the expected service level will result in customer defection. Customer marketing can address how these moments of truth will be tackled.

---

[2] 'Measuring ROI: Yardsticks for Managing Successful CRM Strategies', *Meridien Research*, 29 March 2001.

Any business can use network thinking to form networks to market product and service more effectively. Film companies (shops) are prominent examples. When it released the first Harry Potter film in 2001, Warner Brothers also created a Harry Potter community (www.harrypotter.warnerbros.com). By facilitating the connection of customers based around the film, Warner Brothers engage in community marketing which creates a virtuous circle where the Harry Potter film becomes a 'must-see'. Such communities nurture the market for related, branded products (soaps, toys, pyjamas and so on).

Chains can also use networks. We have already discussed the Harley Owner's Club in Chapter 4. The formation of these networks is a marketing activity, yet it is far from customer stalking. The network configuration itself becomes an effective customer marketing tool for chains that can create a network around their product. However, such activities are probably restricted to product leaders where shared ownership of common product creates a bond between customers. Support groups for medical conditions work on the same principle: the bond for the community is the shared condition rather than product.

DELIVER CUSTOMER EXPERIENCE

Network customers may pay more to guarantee their ability to use the network's infrastructure when and how they want to. Direct banking over the internet and telephone (significantly cheaper for the customer) has not destroyed traditional branch-based banking, despite customers knowing that they have to pay more to use branches. Sports club members will pay more for exclusivity to ensure use of the machines they want and to ensure that the swimming pool will not be too crowded. ISP customers may pay more to guarantee that they can get onto the internet straight away. Insurance customers pay more to firms who they believe will deliver a superior claims service.

This is not to suggest that network customers abandon price sensitivity; the operationally excellent network will emphasize low price. However, operationally excellent networks typically appeal to a different category of customer. That is why understanding the prioritization of CRM resources is so important. As service firms, networks must focus on delivering value to the customer at the point of interaction through improving service rather than pushing product. This theory has always been hard to prove, except by reference to businesses such as UK retail bank FirstDirect. This organization claims that 94 per cent of its customers recommend it and that 33 per cent of new customers are acquired through referral. FirstDirect focuses upon customer experience – and the results are clear.

The value that network customers obtain is the outcome of making use of the network, not the product defined in the terms and conditions of their subscription. Networks should focus CRM to make it easier for customers to achieve their desired outcome. Yet many networks orient their websites around products.

CRM must be about making it effortless for customers to do what they want to do. This reinforces the motivation that the customer had for joining the network. This may sound obvious, but many networks see CRM as a tool to save money and push products. It is not.

One way to manage customer behaviour is to offer a choice of channels and media. A chain can usefully try to persuade customers to migrate to cheaper channels. However, if customers have selected a particular network because it allows them to interact in the way that they want, then what is important is not customer redirection but cost-effective behaviour management. NatWest Bank, a UK retail bank, markets itself as the bank that keeps its branches open; a competitor, Abbey National, is piloting Costa coffee shops within its branches. This renaissance reflects a realization that significant numbers of bank customers want to interact through expensive channels and are willing to pay for it.

Arguably, for any network, it is more important to understand customer behaviour by channel (and price product and service to reflect these needs) than to understand transaction cost per channel (and enforce use of cheaper channels). If customers want to pay less, they will go to a network with lower overheads.

In networks, customers perceive much of the value to be in the experience they receive during the interaction with the firm or other customers. The more readily customers can connect, the more likely it is that they will perceive value from the network and use the network more. The golf club organizes club competitions; the telecommunications supplier offers cheaper calls to regularly used numbers. Networks need to consider how their CRM program can enhance the experience of its customers interactively while they are using the services of the network.

SUMMARY

1 If you are a value network, create a single customer view. Without it, the more the customer connects with you the more they will realize that your organization has multiple views of them and the worse your service will appear. Consider the construction of a single product view. Multiple product views lead to multiple product relationships which invariably result in your best customers receiving the worst service.

2 Focus analytical technologies upon understanding desirable and undesirable behaviours. Behaviour dictates customer profitability, risk and desirability. Rather than understanding cross-sell potential, understand behaviour and in turn that will identify the customer groups to target.

3 Focus customer marketing not upon cross-sell, but upon expanding the scope which your network mediates for the customer. Emphasize the rewards that customers will receive for cross-buying, and that the more they allow the network to mediate for them, the more benefits they will receive. Good network thinking identifies potential moments of truth in the customer's experience and explains in the customer marketing how these will be smoother for the customer.

4 Change the focus of your operational CRM activities to facilitate the customer's use of the network. Understand how customers want to behave within the network and then construct and charge for the infrastructure appropriately.

C H A P T E R 7

MANAGING CAPACITY

INTRODUCTION

When Fjeldstad and Stabell built on Porter's value chain, they identified shops and networks as the two additional value configurations required to reflect models of value creation in service industries. The previous three chapters have shown that different CRM agendas are needed in chains, shops and networks. However, many organizations do not fall neatly into any of these three configurations. Consider their attributes:

☐ Chains create value by transforming inputs into a product that becomes the mechanism by which value is created for the customer.

☐ Shops create value by undertaking an iterative fact-finding exercise to understand a unique situation and build a customized solution that meets customer needs.

☐ Networks create value by balancing customers' contributions to and consumption from, an infrastructure; they mediate between customers.

Now consider Air France and Lufthansa, Hertz and Alamo, Le Meridien and Holiday Inn, Regal and Odeon Cinemas. They all manage an infrastructure, like networks, but do not mediate between customers. The basis of their value delivery is not customers connecting with each other, whether directly (a telecommunications network) or indirectly (a utility network). They create value by providing a physical product, as chains do, but they rent that product to customers for a defined period. We have called this configuration the value pool, because these companies pool resources for customers to use. Pools include airlines, cinemas, hotels and bus companies. In fact, many are in the travel, tourism and entertainment sectors. Pools create value by buying and operating an infrastructure that customers rent for short periods rather than subscribe to.

RENTAL RELATIONSHIPS

The chain's relationships are transactional, the shop's event-oriented, and the network's subscribed. Pools have customer relationships that have elements of both transaction and subscription. They are transactional because the customer rents a cinema or airline seat one transaction at a time. Therefore, many of the CRM tools used by chains to connect individual transactions are also relevant to pools. Moreover, customers of pools are subscribing to an experience – but it is an experience that is ephemeral.

In the same way as other configurations, pools can pursue any of the three value disciplines and the difference is stark:

1 Operationally excellent pools include the low-cost airlines, for example easyJet, Go and Ryanair and low-cost hotels, such as the UK's Travelodges that offer fixed-price, standard, no-frills rooms. As all pools must, they balance the number of filled units (seats and rooms respectively) against unfilled units and compete on price.

2 Product-leading pools (or rather, service-leading pools) include British Airways, Lufthansa and Air France. Premium airlines compete upon quality of service and not price. While business travel remained buoyant – and business air travellers are one of the least price sensitive customer categories in the world – the strategy worked well to drive profits. During the airline recession in late 2001, the operationally excellent players, as in any sector, began to win share.

3 Pools cannot customize their physical product. They must rent their resources to as many different customers as possible in turn. Allowing customers to change those resources misses the point. Customer intimacy for pools means one or both of two things. Particularly for large pools operating across many markets, understanding individual customers' needs is impractical. Instead, pools recognize loyal customers through loyalty schemes and reward with perks – an upgrade to a larger car, free gifts and personalized messages on the television in the hotel room. Smaller, typically more expensive pools (such as top hotels) may deliver improved and highly personal service. The Imperial Hotel in Vienna offers a customer-intimate experience – but not for the budget traveller. Pools manage product, but can customize service.

These rental relationships mean that customer-intimate and product-leading pools suffer particularly badly when customers' wallets are empty. Many pools offer service that relies upon discretionary spend, and therefore suffer when money is tight. In the travel sector where premium business travel is often a casualty of recession, and the entertainment sector where fun may be sacrificed to getting food on the table, operationally excellent (and cheaper) pools tend to be successful when times are hard.

However, the CRM agenda for pools is much the same, whichever value discipline dictates how they prioritize their assets. It is straightforward, single-minded and distinct from that of other configurations. Pools measure their infrastructure in units for rent – seats (airlines), beds (hotels), cars (car leasing firms) or covers (restaurants). They create shareholder value by managing yield from those units: balancing the price the customer pays per unit against unfilled units. Stelios Haji-Ioannou, the founder of easyJet, was quoted by *The Sunday Times* talking about the creation of an 'easy' cinema:

‘ Our cinema will make money in the same way that easyJet does by selling seats for £45. It is all about volume and utilizing the asset. The cinema industry average – seat occupancy of 20% – is criminal. Going to the movies is price elastic so you can increase usage. ’

The role of CRM is simple. Pools must maximize yield from their assets and balance unused units against charging the highest price achievable.

The value discipline dictates how the pool seeks to optimize yield. It can be the cheapest and most accessible (operationally excellent), have the best products to rent (product-leading), or offer the best service surrounding the rental (customer-intimate).

This CRM agenda dictates a four-stage CRM strategy, as shown in Figure 7.1:

1 Pools may know their individual customers (airlines and hotels do) or they may not (cinemas do not). The first CRM priority is to acquire customer data. The dramatic variations in customer profitability for pools mean that unless staff can recognize important customers, yield may be difficult to optimize. Thus, implementing loyalty schemes is often the first CRM activity, especially in pools focused on customer intimacy or product leadership. For those pursuing operational excellence, the driver is typically market share and acquiring more customers is a higher priority than growing individual customers.

2 Pools need to use CRM to understand which customers use which resources, when, and how, in order to understand and regulate resource usage. This is quite different from chains which must understand purchase behaviour, and networks which must understand contribution and consumption.

3 The customer marketing process for pools revolves around integrating customer and resource usage data to construct campaigns to maximize yield. This marketing is critical even for the operationally excellent. Haji-Ioannou believes he can improve yield in easy cinemas by understanding when the assets are unused (and are leaking money), for example, Tuesday mornings on a sunny English morning – and finding ways to make seats more accessible then.

4 Finally, the management of customer interaction focuses upon differentiating service to loyal customers and making rental as smooth and accessible as possible. The extent of service differentiation increases as the customer intimacy volume is turned up.

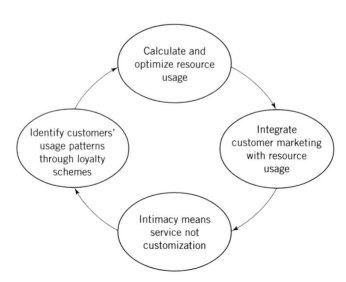

FIGURE 7.1: The pool's CRM agenda

IDENTIFY CUSTOMER USAGE PATTERNS THROUGH LOYALTY SCHEMES

For networks, the single customer view was the foundation of CRM. Without it, attempts to cross-sell are likely to create a corps of ever more valuable, and ever more dissatisfied customers. The single customer view may equally be applicable to pools, although typically only where customer intimacy is important to the value proposition. A single customer view is expensive and, for pools focused on operational excellence, the service benefits of constructing such a view that must be reflected in higher prices may not pay dividends.

Pool customers have no incentive to reconnect with a pool. They do not subscribe as they do to a network. The pool, like the chain, has to connect a series of rentals that can be broken by the customer at any time. The best way to achieve this is to reward the customer through a loyalty scheme. The British Airways 'Executive Club' is often held up as a classic loyalty scheme. The scheme demonstrates a number of best practice features:

☐ The rewards for frequent flyers, business and first class passengers are sufficiently enticing (airport lounges, free flights etc.) that customers have an incentive to record every transaction that they make. This avoids British Airways receiving incomplete information that may misdirect their marketing efforts.

☐ The scheme is sufficiently simple that customers can easily understand it. Customers progress through blue, silver and gold membership categories with the benefits increasing at each stage. If customers do not easily understand what they can obtain from the scheme they will not join.

☐ The scheme rewards loyalty, and penalizes disloyalty. Many business travellers are unwilling to travel with another airline because without that flight to add to their tally, they might lose their gold or silver card privileges. The scheme imposes voluntary handcuffs on its members.

☐ Customers value the status offered by the scheme. Even hard-bitten regular travellers strap their Executive Club card to their bag.

☐ The scheme does not require individual customization of product or service. It did require step changes in customer service for which staff all around the world were trained (but relatively easily). Much of the perceived reward in loyalty schemes comes through such step changes which are noticeable to customers.

CALCULATE AND OPTIMIZE RESOURCE USAGE

Pools create value by renting assets to customers. Any pool has a finite number of such assets to rent at any time. British Airways has fixed numbers of seats on each flight; Holiday Inn has fixed numbers of beds; Hertz has fixed numbers of cars. In an ideal world, the pool would fill all its resources for the maximum period consistent with maintenance needs, at the maximum price that can be extracted consistent with competition.

CRM analytics can answer five questions fundamental to any pool's profitability:

1 Who are the loyal (i.e. repeat) customers, and what are their characteristics? These characteristics, not intuition, should drive the creation of the strategic segmentation model discussed further in Chapter 11.

The difference in profitability between pools' loyal and occasional customers is enormous – much more so than networks whose subscriptions will tend to balance out contribution and consumption between its members. In networks, customers that consume more, pay more. James Varder Patten's quotation from Chapter 2 used examples that are all pools, 'Loyal customers outspend others by ratios of 13 to 1 in the restaurant business, 12 to 1 in airlines and 5 to 1 in the hotel business.'

2   When are the resource peaks, and which customers use services at those peak times? Loyal customers are sufficiently important to be given priority at peak times. Premium airlines and hotels have long understood this – offering preferred standby status to frequent flyers, guaranteeing a room if given sufficient notice.

3   When are the troughs, and what are the characteristics of customers using resources during those periods? Many business-oriented hotels have empty beds at weekends, a period when typical customers are families who seek leisure activities such as sports clubs. Understanding customer behaviour patterns during troughs enables hotels to run schemes to attract their business guests back at the weekend with their families. Pools' facilities that are unused make no money. The empty bed is a bed that makes no money for the pool.

4   What is the relationship between price and resource peaks and troughs? Innovative pricing to fill units during troughs is familiar ground for pools. Theatres may offer reduced price tickets for over 60s during weekdays; airlines offer cheap seats for last minute offers; hotels offer cheap weekend breaks. Customer analytics can take such analyses to a new dimension. By using data mining technologies discussed in Chapter 15, pools can understand the relationship between price and usage and factor in customer behaviours to enable more sophisticated campaigns and even real-time pricing – a concept explored further in Chapter 21. Haji-Ioannou is a master of using flexible pricing to maximize yield.

5   What are popular and unpopular resources with customers? Pools rent units and typically offer different grades of units (such as different classes of seat or car). Understanding popular and unpopular resources and mapping those against customer segments is critical. Hertz has a wide range of cars across the world. It is important that it understands which models are popular with whom, and which are not.

Customer analytics has a critical role to play for any pool. The difference in profitability between loyal and occasional customers is massive. But unlike networks, pools do not necessarily record customer behaviours automatically. Pools have to work harder to do this – but loyalty schemes help. Resource usage is fundamental for pools. If the AOL customer uses his fixed price internet access for only 20 minutes per day then AOL still retains the subscription. However, the full car lot at Hertz is a headache. Every unused asset leaks costs by the hour.

INTEGRATE CUSTOMER MARKETING WITH RESOURCE USAGE

The CRM challenge, and opportunity, for pools is to connect their knowledge of their valuable customers with their knowledge of resource usage patterns. It is the combination of the two that is so powerful. Indeed, keeping them separate may actively harm the firm and destroy shareholder value.

We can demonstrate this with a case study of an imaginary car rental firm, Cars2Rent.

Through his new loyalty scheme, John Doe, Marketing Director, knows that the top 10 per cent of loyal customers – 20,000 customers – generate 50 per cent of the firm's profits. Separately, Jane Smith, Operations Director, knows that the mid-sized car fleet is used to 75 per cent of capacity, but the luxury car fleet only to 60 per cent.

☐ John Doe calculates the characteristics of his loyal customers. They are male, aged over 45, and live within 80 km (50 miles) of a major airport, in detached houses. From a market research firm he obtains names and addresses of potential prospects that meet these criteria and writes to them offering a 20 per cent discount on a car rental with Cars2Rent. This is good CRM thinking.

☐ Jane Smith meanwhile makes what appears to be an obvious decision. Her mid-size Ford fleet delivers consistently better utilization than her Mercedes fleet. She therefore runs downs the fleet of high-end Mercedes and increases the size of the mid-size Ford fleet.

One year on, two things have happened. John has found that the defection rate of his loyal segment has increased from 2 per cent to 20 per cent and profits have decreased. You have probably guessed it is because the loyal over-45 company directors like renting Mercedes.

The failure to hook the customer data to the resource data means that Cars2Rent failed to spot the one crucial statistic that could have resulted in a step-change to their business: 10 per cent of loyal customers always ask for the Mercedes. That superficially compelling 75 per cent of requests for mid-sized Fords are from the 90 per cent of occasional customers who individually generate little profit and are as likely to go to Alamo next door – who are actually cheaper. So what if the mid-sized Fords are popular? It is that 10 per cent of customers that Cars2Rent need to focus on, not the 90 per cent. By doubling the size of that segment to 40,000, the impact on corporate profitability could be profound.

Only by integrating customer data with resource usage data could Cars2Rent identify this pattern. Without it, John was tempting more of his loyal customer group that his operations team could then not serve.

Perhaps the right strategy would have been totally the reverse of what Jane did. If she had halved the size of the mid-size fleet and increased the size of the Mercedes fleet, John could have gone to the board with a proposal to rebrand Cars2Rent as 'Quality Cars', a high end, luxury car rental firm. John's campaign could then have filled the excess capacity at the high end. After all, if John is getting 50 per cent of profits almost without trying from 10 per cent of his customers, what could he do with a solid luxury brand, a focused marketing campaign and a larger fleet of Mercedes at his disposal?

This example is simplistic, but it exemplifies how many pools treat CRM as an isolated marketing initiative. Customer marketing is essential to pools because the difference in profitability of loyal and occasional customers are particularly high – more so than in other configurations because pools are funding an infrastructure that if unused leaks money. Customer marketing for pools is about the relationship between loyal customers and resource usage. Having identified the patterns of data that deliver profit, pools must market hard to the valuable segments with the right resources.

INTIMACY MEANS SERVICE NOT CUSTOMIZATION

Pools cannot change their products to match specific customer needs. Even the Hotel Imperial in Vienna cannot realistically transform its hotel rooms to suit the needs of individual customers. For pools, increasing levels of customer intimacy mean delivering ever more personal service around the product. There are two main priorities:

1   Providing individual service.

2   Making rental more accessible.

Provide individual service

Regardless of their value discipline, all pools rent the same product to many different customers. Customizing each product to each customer's needs is impractical except in exceptional situations (perhaps where a customer takes a hotel suite for years at a stretch). This could imply that pools cannot compete on customer intimacy. They can, but, like networks, they can only do so by competing on the service surrounding their product.

Pools can customize to a particular segment defined by their value to the pool. The very best customers – travel buyers for major corporates, for example – may be recognized individually. For the rest, loyalty schemes are a good way to identify good customers and find mechanisms to reward them by delivering step changes in customer service.

Make rental more accessible

Enabling customers to rent the product rapidly through the medium of their choice is a critical priority for any pool and the direct channel is particularly important. Customers want to know whether the resource they need will be available when they need it – a seat on the airplane, a space in the airport car park and a bed in the hotel are three requirements a business traveller may ask of any international business trip. Pools want to plan their resources efficiently yet allow customers to connect as rapidly as possible.

European low-cost airline easyJet claimed over 90 per cent of its bookings through the internet by the end of 2001 and operated under the tag 'the web's favourite airline'. Bookings have increased in part because of the ease of purchase. Not only does internet booking reduce costs for easyJet, it is more convenient for customers.

SUMMARY

1   The difference between loyal and occasional customers is immense for pools. Do you identify your best customers? If not, how can you do so? Calculate the differential in customer profitability between your most loyal and occasional customers – at least roughly – and consider whether or not the creation of a loyalty scheme would be worthwhile.

2   Consider your use of customer analytics. Only by connecting customer behaviour patterns with resource usage can really valuable data be driven out. Could our Cars2Rent story be yours? If it could, then your analytics efforts may be misdirected.

3   What level of customer intimacy do you want to achieve? Is your service individual enough for your ambition? Can customers rent your resources as easily as possible? Is rental as smooth as possible?

PART 3

LAYING THE FOUNDATIONS

By now, you have considered where you should focus your CRM attentions, and how high to turn the customer intimacy volume control. But where do you begin? If CRM is a component of corporate strategy (rather than a procurement or technology initiative) then you must start at the foundations of your business. Your strategy must explore why customers connect with you and the promise that you make to them. It must be rooted in a business case that the finance department can accept, as well as information systems and marketing. It must learn the lessons of CRM past if it is destined not to repeat its failures. In this section, we ask you to forget CRM as technology and consider how your level of customer-centric ambition must be rooted deep within your corporate strategy.

CHAPTER 8

DEFINING THE VALUE PROPOSITION

INTRODUCTION

Traditional approaches to brand building are too rooted in their product brand origins to support CRM ambition. Product brands are seldom the whole story. The term 'value proposition' means a firm's promise to its customers. Traditionally, marketers called this 'brand' but were largely referring to product brand. As the service sector expanded, the term 'value proposition' grew in popularity and it was recognized that a company's customer promise is more significant than the promise of its individual product brands. The value proposition describes the total customer experience with the firm and its alliance partners over time, rather than that which is communicated at the point of sale.

THE BRAND IS THE BUSINESS?

In 1990, *The Economist* hosted a conference entitled 'The Brand is the Business'. Speaker after speaker declared that in the emerging global, hyper-competitive economy, all product or service innovations could be immediately copied by competitors and executed at lower cost in the developing world. The last bastion of being able to compete on a value-added, high margin basis is brand: the one thing that cannot be easily copied.

Certainly brand owners value strong brands. They provide more cash flow, higher margins, less volatile demand, economies of scale and superior access to distribution networks. Consumer goods firms are sold at multiples of their book value reflecting the assumed value of their brands.

Brands also help organizations to adapt to the changing needs of customers. They construct brands around a core idea or brand essence, expressed in terms of the 4Ps: product, price, promotion and place. For example, a luxury perfume in quality packaging (the product) is expensive (price), promoted with special gifts and not discounts (promotion), and supplied only through selected outlets (place). Businesses align their internal functions to the brand's customers through the 4Ps, adapting them to suit the customers' evolving needs and competitive threats. Staff intuitively know how to act in order to 'be true to the brand'. The 4Ps help the firm define and position its brand consistently.

Customers value their preferred brands as well. Research suggests that brands affect purchasing decisions because they mitigate two types of risk:

1   **Performance risk** – The risk that the offering will not perform as expected. The car may break down; the pension fund go bankrupt; dental cavities increase after changing toothpaste.

2   **Psychological risk** – The risk that the offering will communicate the wrong things about the customer and be inconsistent with the customer's emotional and social goals. Clothes and cars carry high psychological risk.

In business-to-business markets too, brands address both performance and psychological risk. Few would maintain that business purchasing decisions are purely rational and based upon economic considerations alone. Industrial purchasing is a highly complex political and social phenomenon. Brands help organizations decide what to buy by offering reassurance that products will perform to specification and that the decision maker is not taking an undue professional risk (e.g. that colleagues would see your choice of supplier as ill-advised).

Therefore, brands help customers to manage risk and simplify purchasing. For the brand owner, they are a valuable asset and a tool for aligning the firm's operations with customer needs.

ARE BRANDS STILL WORKING?

Four years later, *The Economist* ran an editorial questioning the future of brand marketing[1]. The cause of this angst was the announcement from Philip Morris that it was dramatically cutting the price of Marlboro cigarettes in response to lower priced, unbranded competition. If such an iconic brand could not maintain its added value positioning and pricing, what hope was there for other brands?

The limitations of product branding were reached in the 1990s. Not only Marlboro suffered such indignities. Oil companies found that they could not charge a premium to food retailers for their petrol stations. Grocery brands had to reduce their price premium over retailers' own brands. Financial services customers hopped between current accounts and mortgages in unprecedented numbers.

Nevertheless, people still value some brands. BMW and Harley Davidson still engender a customer commitment and affinity that is the envy of most brand owners. However, in many markets, the leading edge of creating customer value no longer lies with managing risk around the performance of individual product brands.

Customers are finding new means of managing purchasing risk. One is to select suppliers that underwrite risk over a broad category of products and services. UK's Powergen now offers not just electricity, but gas and telecommunications.

It also helps when customers no longer have the same psychological angst in making decisions. A decade ago, you may have hesitated to serve guests a supermarket's own brand wine, but

[1] Death of the Brand Manager, *The Economist*, 1994.

not today. The need for psychological reassurance is reduced in a more transparent market where that transparency drives improvement in quality.

The same is true in business-to-business. Most businesses have created better cross-functional decision-making processes that support more ambitious long-term supplier partnerships. Traditionally, purchasing was in the hands of a 'specifier' who had to understand the complex political currents of the organization when recommending major purchases to executives. If some areas of the business did not agree, the argument could escalate up the hierarchy for resolution and so the specifier took on considerable personal risk. Today, most businesses establish cross-functional teams to recommend major purchases or partnerships. The specifier is now a process leader of a high performing team that can assume more risk and focus purchasing on getting suppliers to provide more added value.

As risk aversion becomes less of a force, customers seek real added value from supplier partnerships. For example, they may want longer-term supplier partners rather than just lowest cost products. Such relationships are founded on trust, built in part on strong brands but also through repeated, positive experiences. These experiences go beyond the immediate products and services consumed. If the UK supermarket Tesco wants to establish what amounts to a 'partnering' relationship with its customers, then those customers will expect a pleasant shopping experience: service across multiple media (shop, internet, phone); high quality, unbiased information about food products; ethical behaviour; consistent pricing across product categories; differential treatment that recognizes the customer's total expenditure; and effective response to complaints. To do all of this, Tesco has developed its business well beyond its origins as a low price stockist of branded products. Its current value proposition is so broadly based that it is hard to describe and capture it through the perspective of 4Ps.

A business-to-business example is outsourcing. When a business outsources a critical business function, its partner's current offer is a necessary but insufficient reassurance for entering into a relationship. Buyers must consider the partner's values, ethics, culture and long-term strategy to assess how they will work together in as yet unforeseen circumstances, and whether this is the sort of firm with which it wishes to connect. In creating their value proposition, outsourcers must communicate trustworthiness, honesty, and commitment to customers' success, as well as flexibility and willingness to invest in new capabilities as customers' needs evolve. Outsourcers do not compete merely on today's brand and capabilities. They must build value propositions that support customer relationships over time.

Relationship-based value propositions, such as those in IT outsourcing, stretch the 4Ps' product brand marketing past its design characteristics.

Therefore, firms moving from a product-focused to a customer-focused brand need to create a new form of value proposition that defines a broader, relationship-based customer value. Trust in the product brand formerly acted as an intermediary between the firm and its customers. When developing a CRM program, the brand must become the window into the company – inviting and transparent.

UNIQUE ORGANIZATION VALUE PROPOSITION®

Instead of trying to stretch 4Ps marketing beyond its sensible limits to accommodate the new relationship-based environment, Knox and Maklan[2] suggest starting afresh with a new value

[2] Knox and Maklan, *Competing on Value*, Financial Planning Institute, 1998.

proposition framework which integrates a company's internal operations with the relationship-based needs of its customers. This customer-centric agenda has two prime features:

1   It integrates the promise and delivery of value.

2   It focuses both on the organization and its offering.

Integrate promise of value with delivery

Creating customer relationships represents a very different challenge to creating a product brand. Traditional marketing created a promise through the brand, and products merely needed to deliver on this. A leading fashion brand did not have to modify its design based upon individual customer feedback; it set the trend and educated the market. It created, made and sold – in that order.

Customers, however, assess CRM every time they experience it. A trusting relationship builds through repeated experiences in which the customer assesses whether the firm delivers on its promise. Managing these 'moments of truth' requires sophisticated business processes, delivered by motivated front-line staff (a subject explored in Chapter 12). Value delivery against a relationship-based promise is more complex and arguably difficult to achieve than against a product-based promise.

For example, a bank's value proposition is delivered by thousands of employees every day. The bank listens and serves – in that order. It needs systems and processes to support mass customization across a huge customer base which accesses it through a wide array of media. The 'product' is the customized experience of each customer at the moment they experience it.

A CRM value proposition requires significant investment to develop new capabilities, new business processes, technology and culture so that staff can deliver it. Brand and process management come together in CRM.

Company and not product is the focus of value

Given that the delivery of the promise is critical to a CRM value proposition, the principal customer risk is not derived from the products or services per se, but from the firm that does not deliver on its total customer promise. Yet the promise can only be delivered by effective cross-functional business processes and committed people. The guarantor of value becomes the organization rather than its individual offerings. Those offerings become events on the relationship continuum, as opposed to the focus of the value proposition. CRM moves 'branding' from product-centric to company-centric because only the company can endorse the values, people and processes that create value.

We use the metaphor of a cable and wires (Figure 8.1) to illustrate this integration of brand and business process. This provides a framework for defining and delivering customer-centric value propositions, such as guaranteed service levels, creativity or convenience. Wires – business processes – conduct these value propositions from deep within the supply chain to the customer. As with electricity, we do not want all the live wires crossing over each, dangling loosely. They must be housed and directed in a cable so that the customer can manipulate the appliance safely. The cable in this framework is the Unique Organization Value Proposition (UOVP)®, which replaces the traditional product brand. The UOVP® directs a firm's processes so that it produces real and differentiated customer value, but retains that element of brand so cherished by firms: the development of a valuable asset that generates superior, stable cash flows.

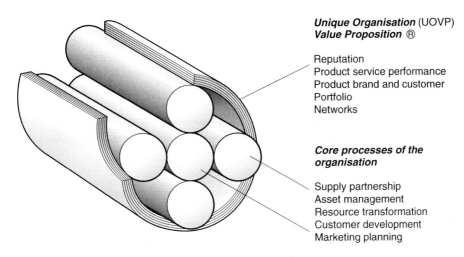

Unique Organisation (UOVP)
Value Proposition ®

Reputation
Product service performance
Product brand and customer
Portfolio
Networks

Core processes of the organisation

Supply partnership
Asset management
Resource transformation
Customer development
Marketing planning

FIGURE 8.1: Cable and wires (S. Knox and S. Maklan 1997)

BUILDING THE PROMISE

The customer value adding processes of the business are 'branded' into a unique and compelling value proposition through four elements that define customer value: the organization's reputation; its portfolio of products and services; its network of alliances; and its performance at the 'moments of truth'. These blend together as a value proposition or promise. The promise is delivered when the UOVP® is aligned to business processes that create real customer value.

Reputation

Reputation defines a firm in a way that cuts across individual lines of business and product portfolios. For example, Toyota is more than just a car brand: it has a reputation for satisfied customers, quality and manufacturing excellence and it leveraged this to create Lexus. Few other mass car brands have managed to enter the premium market except by expensive acquisition. Lands End's reputation extends past clothing to define a customer-centric business. It is renowned for its policy of accepting returns unconditionally, for its helpful call centre staff and for a commitment to quality. This has created a reputation for trust, integrity and service, which the firm has profitably used to extend its business to online media.

Conversely, although many of the innovations that spurred the PC revolution originated at Xerox's Palo Alto Research Centre (PARC), the company did not transfer its dominant position in its existing market to the new PC market.

Reputation is built from the interplay of image and identity. A firm's identity guides the activities of its people, who reproduce that identity in what they make and how they serve customers. The customers' experience forms their image of the firm, in turn reinforcing its identity. Building a reputation requires the simultaneous development of identity and image and integrates the activities of its people in pursuit of both.

Product brand and customer portfolio

Traditional value propositions lead management to focus narrowly on product or business area profitability. Firms that have built up product or business unit structures have trouble creating an integrated customer experience at critical moments for the customer – moments of truth. Managing a product portfolio as a series of discrete brand investments or businesses rarely aligns to the needs of creating integrated solutions for individual customers across business units. One business unit's excellent customer could be another's unprofitable customer; one product brand may invest in leading edge design and product performance while another product in the same company may aim for low-cost, basic products. Sometimes, businesses need to maintain poorly performing products to satisfy good customers, and some customers are unprofitable despite doing a great deal of business with you because of high costs to serve them or excessive discounting. In a product management structure, it is difficult to identify these situations and manage them.

A CRM value proposition helps managers to optimize the product and customer portfolios simultaneously. They need to master both the traditional discipline of good product brand management and the emerging discipline of customer management. Product management will focus on the discounted cash flows of the product portfolio, market entry strategies and market share optimization. Customer management will focus on identifying the high value customers by using more complex measures to address the tangible (cash flow) and intangible (referrals, learning) benefits and strategies to maximize share of wallet.

Networks

Often, in order to meet customer needs effectively, a firm must work within a network of firms. Often, such partnerships are visible to customers and form part of the brand promise. Some hotels place brand name coffee (e.g. Starbucks or Nestlé) in guest rooms; software vendors and systems integrators work together on complex sales; airlines collaborate to cover more routes; global home appliance makers team with local after-sales service brands. Part of being customer-centric is the ability to manage these partnerships on behalf of customers in a manner consistent with your own desired reputation and performance. As global competition intensifies and firms focus on their core competencies, the ability to add network management to brand promise becomes increasingly important. It has been said that in the future, competition will not be between individual firms so much as between entire supply chains.

Product and service performance

Performance delivers the customer experiences at all the 'moments of truth' when the customer evaluates how the firm is carrying out its promise. This is the 'Total Customer Experience'. The capabilities that support this experience include product and service design, manufacturing, logistics, human resources development and customer service. These capabilities are the result of internal processes, but should be guided by customers' expectations which are established by the promise. The British retailer Marks & Spencer, for a long time consistently exceeded customers' expectations of quality, innovation, availability and value. Then it ran into well-publicised troubles. The media suggested that the company's fashion failed to meet increasing customer expectations, while lower priced retailers ate away at its reputation for value. The customer experience may have slipped below Marks & Spencer's desired reputation, to the extent of damaging its reputation. The company has addressed these issues head-on and its performance and reputation is rebounding.

MIXING THE ELEMENTS

These UOVP® elements are not present in equal strength in every value proposition. Management's contribution is to understand the right blend of the four elements to create the right mix for their corporate brand. Virgin's brand (its 'cable') has large elements of reputation and performance. Its product and customer portfolio features less coherence – one is hard pressed to define the Virgin brand by its mix of businesses. Sony's corporate brand also has large elements of reputation and product performance, but it is certainly defined by the product categories in which it competes. Partnerships feature prominently in the branding of systems integrators such as Accenture or CSC: their tight relationships with critical software, hardware and networking firms is a major part of their value proposition.

Conventional marketing focuses managers on creating a single, compelling reason to buy – the Unique Selling Proposition (USP). The UOVP® suggests that CRM branding is more complex and requires the right blend of ingredients.

DELIVERING THE PROMISE

If the UOVP® focuses the organization on a modern definition of customer value, the core business processes deliver on the promise. With the value proposition guiding business processes, CRM is pushed deep into the organization and enables it to create unique and valuable customer experiences.

UOVP® uses a simplified, generic set of processes. Figure 8.2 illustrates the cyclical relationship between promise and delivery of customer value. The process model likens the firm to any living organism: it secures its necessary inputs; transforms them using its assets (intellectual and physical); sells them to customers for profit in order that it might secure further inputs; and has a planning regime to keep the system in balance and growing. The UOVP® model is not meant to replace your existing core processes; it provides illustrative processes that must be tailored to your firm.

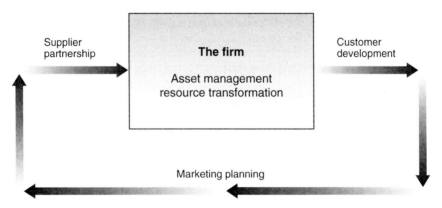

FIGURE 8.2: Business process

Supplier partnership

Traditional supplier strategy is governed by purchasing. It was designed to secure, at lowest cost, what manufacturing required to fulfil marketing's forecasts.

Supply chain management is vital to delivering the UOVP®. Car manufacturers rely on suppliers for an increasing portion of the car's perceived value: new braking systems, in-car communications and on-board guidance are all supplier-led innovations. The trouble is that as global suppliers improve quality, reduce cost and innovate quickly, cars become universally good. Car manufacturers now find that they must expand their value proposition to include, for example, personal car management or financial services in order to differentiate their total offer.

This example demonstrates the interplay between the value proposition and business processes. Supply chain management, originally designed with cost and quality objectives, risks homogenizing the core product proposition and forces firms to customize and extend their value proposition.

Asset management (physical and intellectual)

The customary approach to asset management focuses on utilization, spreading the average cost of a fixed asset. Investment is planned by individual business units or product brands, and many of the firm's core competencies and strategic assets are funded as a by-product of this planning. Early call centres were tasked with maximizing call throughput with little regard for the quality of customer experience or the delivery of the brand promise at moments of truth. Clearly this was wrong. Customer assets must be managed to support the new CRM value proposition.

Customer insight is generally the responsibility of a product or business unit close to operational sales and marketing. Firms that have invested in CRM are finding that this intellectual asset is too critical to be developed in an ad hoc fashion. They are creating separate departments, well-funded, to build that competency for the organization across business units. These firms recognize that what customers teach the firm, for instance the quality of customer data, the firm's ability to develop insight from that data and its ability to create good customer experiences through contact centres, is the most likely source of sustained competitive advantage, differential marketing and superior return on CRM investments. The UOVP® forces firms to align investments in capabilities and assets to strategic ends, and manage such core customer competencies on the basis of cost and utilization.

Resource transformation

Resource transformation is the process by which supplies and other inputs are transformed into products and services. CRM programs often focus on the delivery of customized services to individual customers. This approach of 'listen and serve' potentially requires the greatest investment in new technology and business processes. Failure to integrate process improvements with the development of differentiated brand positioning risks giving away all the improvement. This wastes resources and potentially destroys the business case for CRM.

Many businesses in traditional value chains have focused considerable attention over the past 20 years on the process of transforming supplies and other inputs, i.e. resources, into products and services. A great number found themselves on a process re-engineering treadmill, continually improving their processes to cut costs (and improve quality), only to find that the next organization in the chain had appropriated most of the gains. UOVP® changes the focus from process improvement for its own sake to linking the company's process of transforming resources to its differentiated customer value proposition. This strategic differentiation enables the firm to benefit from its own efforts.

Customer development

Many firms find it difficult to manage an individual customer across the entire business. Traditionally firms built their business around individual product or functional processes, which made it difficult to reconfigure that structure to the needs of individual customers or groups of customers. The ability to have a single customer view, a shared understanding of how to manage the customer and an ability to deliver a consistent experience are essential ingredients of many CRM programs. Differentiated customer management goes beyond providing better service for its own sake and represents a strategic decision about how much of the firm's resources should be invested in each customer segment. This is the definition of customer development and it is explored further in Chapter 11.

Marketing planning

Marketing planning has traditionally been a combination of reconciling top–down demands with a bottom–up collection of individual business unit (or product group) estimates. Popular planning tools such as the Boston Consulting Group Matrix, the Directional Policy Matrix, Ansoff's Matrix and Gap Analysis show that planning's roots lie in product portfolio optimization. UOVP® planning considers customers as well as products, and develops plans for core business processes and strategic marketing assets.

SUMMARY

1   The nature of value is changing away from managing risk towards long-term supplier-customer partnerships that create more value for both customer and company. Brand building is no longer a function of the 4Ps alone; it results from pan-company business processes and an interactive dialogue with customers. The mantra of 'make and sell' is replaced with 'listen and serve'. Consider whether the 4Ps really deliver against your business or whether the UOVP® offers a better model in the relationship-based world.

2   Conventional branding approaches cannot define this new form of customer value or effectively integrate and direct business processes to value adding activities. UOVP® integrates the promise and delivery of value for a customer-centric company. The UOVP® itself is the result of a mix of the key drivers of customer value: reputation, performance, product and customer portfolio and networks. Consider building the UOVP® for your organization to understand the promise you make to customers.

3   It is not sustainable merely to make a compelling promise; that promise needs to be delivered consistently over time. Delivery is accomplished through the firm's core business processes. These are supplier partnership, asset management, resource transformation, customer development and marketing planning. The integration of the value proposition with the means of its delivery creates organizational brands which direct the customer relationship and add value both to customers and companies in equal measure. Consider how well your processes deliver against the promise of your brand.

CHAPTER 9

BUILDING THE BUSINESS CASE

INTRODUCTION

This chapter reviews the financial and business logic behind CRM. Too often, the current practice is to manage a business case as a budgeting and financial planning exercise rather than as a strategic event. We demonstrate that traditional financial analysis, Discounted Cash Flow (DCF) and Net Present Value (NPV) calculations are too limited a basis upon which to make CRM investment decisions. They undervalue returns and focus management attention on short-term cash flow when perhaps the biggest benefits lie in building a strategic asset.

CRM interest has been fuelled by the prospect of the win win scenario for the business and its customers. For customers, CRM promises customized solutions and superior service at reduced cost. For the business, loyal customers improve profitability and shareholder value and release capital.

THE CUSTOMERS' PERSPECTIVE

Economic theory predicts that customers buy from many suppliers to reduce costs and improve service. In reality, customers willingly restrict their choice to a few preferred suppliers or brands. Customer inertia in switching banks and telecoms suppliers is well-documented. Many multinationals have rationalized their supplier base to a core of business partners, abandoning conventional 'sealed envelope' bidding processes to improve collaboration, information sharing and procurement. Customers regularly act contrary to their best economic interests.

Economists explain this through search and transaction costs. In a perfect market, all information is known and there are no transaction costs. In reality, customers faced with purchase decisions generate and evaluate options, choose and negotiate terms and then hope that suppliers deliver their promises. Customers have imperfect information about markets and it costs time and money to learn more. Negotiations cost time and money and when things go wrong, that costs as well. In large-scale purchases, contracts have to be prepared and financing arranged – more costs again. Economists explain that customers restricting their choice of suppliers are acting in a 'rational' manner if we consider the total lifecycle costs of owning an asset or procuring a service. These include search, procurement, installation and after-sales service. The more costly the search and transaction costs, the more value that is created by trusted suppliers.

Some economists extend this and suggest that in some markets changing suppliers incurs 'switching costs'. Switching a software application means that you have to relearn that package. Where telephone numbers are not portable, changing suppliers means that you must contact everyone who knows you. Avoiding switching costs is another 'value' in loyalty.

Marketing people would add a human perspective. When firms remember what they have learnt about you from previous interactions, they can enhance their offer and your experience. Value shops in particular – accountants, lawyers and financial advisors – customize advice, manage complex negotiations and provide a better service based upon their accumulated insight. A tailor that knows your wardrobe and tastes can provide better advice. Marketers know that social and psychological norms create value from relationships: we like doing business with people we like.

All this is also true in business-to-business relationships. Most businesses are complex organizations and effective partnering evolves slowly. Modern just-in-time thinking and alliance management puts a premium on tight process integration between supplier and buyer, because factories grind to a halt if suppliers do not deliver. Increasingly, companies expect their suppliers to participate in product, marketing, sales and manufacturing innovation. Over time, the quality of the suppliers' contribution will improve because they are more likely to invest in process and quality improvements when they have a strong relationship.

Most sophisticated businesses today prefer to deal with a core cadre of supplier-partners rather than procure important supplies in the open market. Relationships add value and buyers demonstrate a strong preference for stable relationships over pure market transactions for all but pure commodities or low involvement brands.

THE BUSINESS'S PERSPECTIVE

Customers have long preferred relationships, but business is just waking up to the profit impact of loyalty. Frederick Reichheld (one of the founding fathers of CRM mentioned in Chapter 1) makes a compelling argument that it is more profitable to focus on building loyal customers than to focus on maximizing market share. Loyal customers generate superior profits because:

☐ It is cheaper to retain existing customers than acquire new ones.

☐ They may trade up to higher margin products and services or buy more.

☐ Their familiarity with a firm's products and services reduces service costs.

☐ Satisfied customers refer other customers.

☐ They are generally less price sensitive.

Reichheld maintains that these effects increase over time, so that the profitability of loyal customers grows exponentially. Small changes in customer retention rates create a disproportionate increase in profitability.

Other researchers have suggested that most firms 'carry' many unprofitable customers who do not generate margins commensurate with the cost to serve them. Firms should discontinue subsidizing unprofitable customers and redirect resources to retaining profitable ones (and attracting potentially profitable ones). This is analogous to product portfolio planning: firms divest unprofitable areas to reinvest in attractive ones. For businesses supporting vast numbers of unprofitable customers, realigning the asset and cost base towards the minority of profitable customers can reduce the total asset base while increasing revenue. The impact upon shareholder value is obvious.

Financial theorists suggest that loyal customers also increase shareholder value by reducing the volatility of the firm's cash flow. Serving large numbers of transient customers makes cash flow volatile and creates fluctuations in short-term assets, such as inventory and receivables. Investors demand greater return on investment to compensate for volatile cash flow.

What's more, loyal customers contribute valuable and unique learning. That which a firm learns from its customers is knowledge unique to the firm, which it should be able to translate into action. Once a customer sees a supplier acting on information it has given, there is a strong disincentive to start again with a competitor. This history creates a 'switching cost' and a sustainable competitive advantage.

Learning from customers is particularly useful in new product development – there will be fewer expensive failures when customers input early into the product development process. The reduced development risk or improved rate of innovation builds cash flow and reduces overall risk. Indeed, many CRM advocates say that customers generate much more than cash flow; they 'teach' firms how to improve their business.

VALUE DRIVERS

CRM creates symbiotic value for both the business and its customers. The more customers 'teach', the more suppliers can support and respond to them. This lies behind certain critical business assumptions in CRM business cases:

☐ **Trust is built** – Research suggests trust is built through repeated experiences that meet or exceed customer expectations. Business cases must address the issue of how trust is to be built and over what time frame. This includes a thorough appreciation of customers' expectations, competitive performance benchmarks and plans to deliver to expectations at each customer contact.

☐ **The CRM program has integrity** – Customers will continue 'teaching' firms about their needs and preferences for as long as they perceive benefit. The business case must address how customer interactions will be managed. The plan must identify how the firm will learn from and respond to customer feedback. It must say how the learning will be integrated with business operations.

☐ **There is mutual commitment** – Business cases must identify how and why customers' commitment will increase over time, and how that commitment will be leveraged commercially through increased sales, referrals and references. Research suggests that as customers buy more, their loyalty increases. However, buying more is not the same as commitment. Commitment comes when the customer recognizes that the supplier is useful for achieving important personal or professional goals.

CURRENT PRACTICE

A major criticism of current practice is that most CRM business cases assume the outcome of the customer learning process at the outset, write those assumptions into sales targets, and design customer relationships around what the firm wanted to sell in the first place. This compromises the win win scenario that underpins CRM.

At the core of most business cases lies a financial investment analysis tool called the Discounted Cash Flow (DCF) analysis and its associated Net Present Value (NPV) calculation. Investment policy ensures that managers create shareholder value by determining whether expected returns on any investment exceed the risk-adjusted cost of capital for that type of investment.

In this financial model, CRM represents an investment in technology, people, new processes and marketing that increases cash flow from customers in future years. The increased cash flow results from customers buying more and incurring smaller sales and marketing costs. This cash flow is discounted by an appropriate charge for capital, to enable managers to compare investment and return on a like basis; that is, the present value of each. If NPV is positive, then risk-adjusted return exceeds cost of investment. Sophisticated users of DCF estimate a residual value for the asset at the end of the planning period.

The NPV is based upon estimated incremental cash flows that are uncertain, and there is no guarantee that the business case is delivered once projects start. However, financial theory assumes that the business is 'an expected value decision maker': it makes a large number of investments, none of which can bankrupt it. If business cases are honestly made, then investments that return less than forecast are balanced by those that exceed their estimates. Across a large number of investments, using DCF tools should lead to decisions that increase shareholder value.

A number of critical assumptions made by this model are not necessarily true for CRM investment. Principally:

1   DCF primarily values measurable cash flow from increased sales and lower costs, but customers are worth more than money. Sophisticated DCF would also estimate the residual value of the investment in the CRM technology; it struggles to measure the non-cash value of enhanced relationships. CRM should encourage customers to recruit new customers, act as test markets for new ideas and teach firms how to continually improve their operations. These impacts can be substantial. As mentioned previously, FirstDirect claims 33 per cent of new customers are generated from referral. A luxury car brand executive once said that the best advert is a clean new car on the neighbour's drive. Software companies have long valued cooperative product development with leading customers. Some firms reduce prices to prestigious customers who will both improve and endorse their offering.

2   The 'expected value decision maker' assumption is equally suspect. If an industry is in flux and there is a clear imperative to move to a more customer-centric business model, the firm may not have the luxury of repeated experiments. You would bet on rolling die repeatedly, giving $100 every time a 6 is rolled but receiving $50 for any other number. With sufficient repetition, you would win, and even if 6s are rolled the first few times, this would not bankrupt you. However, if you were offered even better odds in a game of Russian roulette, you would not take up the offer because the consequence of one failure

is fatal. No one is 'an expected value decision maker' when playing Russian roulette. If customer-centric is a 'bet your business' initiative, DCF fails to value the consequence of getting it wrong.

3 Where there is great uncertainty around the outcome, a business case that looks at the NPV of a best guess scenario is not always helpful. Too many business cases have a wide range of outcomes, which a mid-point estimate with some sensitivity around that estimate fails. This point is made in the hypothetical case of Feeds and Speeds International (FSI), a hardware manufacturer struggling with a CRM business case.

FEEDS AND SPEEDS INTERNATIONAL

Mary First, Marketing Director of FSI, is preparing the CRM business case for a program she believes necessary for the company's survival. FSI provides telecoms network hardware. It has an extensive product and service range, and an established reputation in solving complex, demanding problems. Its high end products form the telecoms backbone of many of its customers and they command high margins. Once installed, FSI can confidently expect the lion's share of upgrades, extensions and ancillary services.

However, FSI is under attack from new competitors who combine solution design with hardware, installation, and network management. These firms are coming between the intermediation of FSI and its customers, and the Board is worried that FSI will become a low margin hardware supplier to these upstarts. Mary was asked to put together a strategic response. How should FSI leverage its undoubted capabilities and extensive offerings to become a broad-based solution provider to its best customers?

Mary divided customers into three segments: profitable; marginally profitable with substantial growth potential; and unprofitable with no prospect of becoming profitable. In the first two segments, FSI was only selling one-third of what it 'should' be achieving. Each business unit was focusing on its own offerings rather than total customer need. FSI was neither maximizing opportunities across business units nor matching sales and marketing expenditure to the opportunity. Each business unit pursued its own targets. To address this, FSI would need to change from being product-centric to customer-centric. Thus, Mary recommended the creation of a key account management function to:

☐ Integrate FSI offerings into bespoke, value added customer solutions.

☐ Coordinate marketing, sales and service expenses, aligning them to priority customers and development programs.

☐ Exploit the potential for referral. Mary knew that her customers networked extensively and that FSI was not actively fostering customer referrals.

This program would require substantial investment in sales and marketing, reorganization and new technology. The Finance Director had advised Mary to use a ten-year cash flow forecast with a discount rate of 15 per cent. Mary felt confident that she could estimate the costs, but assessing increased revenue was more difficult. Mary added her best guesses of incremental sales from key account management, increased referral and reduced marketing and sales costs. However, the NPV analysis demonstrated that the project would only break-even over ten years (Figure 9.1).

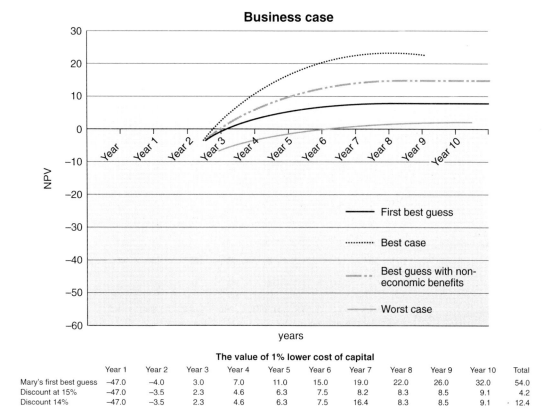

Business case

The value of 1% lower cost of capital

	Year 1	Year 2	Year 3	Year 4	Year 5	Year 6	Year 7	Year 8	Year 9	Year 10	Total
Mary's first best guess	−47.0	−4.0	3.0	7.0	11.0	15.0	19.0	22.0	26.0	32.0	54.0
Discount at 15%	−47.0	−3.5	2.3	4.6	6.3	7.5	8.2	8.3	8.5	9.1	4.2
Discount 14%	−47.0	−3.5	2.3	4.6	6.3	7.5	16.4	8.3	8.5	9.1	· 12.4

FIGURE 9.1

Moreover, the variability was enormous. Nobody could prove how well CRM would work. Mary estimated worst-case and best-case scenarios at plus or minus 50 per cent of her realistic estimate (Table 9.1). But she had no basis for this. The worst case generated NPV of almost −$60 million and the best case +$84 million. She knew that an effective account management program would deliver unquantifiable benefits: new product development ideas and opportunities for reducing non value added activities. Yet nobody could identify these until the program was in place. Nevertheless, she created a second best guess business case, adding in two non-economic (not directly measurable in cash) benefit lines which assumed that key account managers would be able to identify new product opportunities, and identify means of eliminating non-value adding activities.

This took the estimated NPV from break-even to $50 million, and adding non-economic benefits to her best-case estimate resulted in NPV of $114 million.

Mary consulted the Finance Director before going to the Board. He advised her to upgrade the incremental revenue estimate on her best-guess scenario:

‹ If being customer-centric is such a good idea, then it had better do more for our top-line than your initial estimate. We are only selling one-third of our potential in our best account. Triple the revenue line! If we're not confident about CRM, we could get more return increasing investment in our business units without turning our organization inside out. As for

CRM BUSINESS CASE BEST GUESS
Millions of dollars

	Year 1	Year 2	Year 3	Year 4	Year 5	Year 6	Year 7	Year 8	Year 9	Year 10	Total
COSTS											
Technology	40	5	5	5	5	5	5	5	5	5	85
Reorganization	5	0	0	0	0	0	0	0	0	0	5
People	5	5	5	5	5	5	5	5	5	5	50
Marketing	4	4	4	4	4	4	4	4	4	4	40
Total	**54**	**14**	**14**	**14**	**14**	**14**	**14**	**14**	**14**	**14**	**180**
BENEFITS											
Increased cross-sell	2	4	7	9	11	13	14	15	16	18	109
New referrals	1	1	4	5	6	7	9	10	12	14	69
Marketing cost reduction	4	5	6	7	8	9	10	11	12	14	86
Total	**7**	**10**	**17**	**21**	**25**	**29**	**33**	**36**	**40**	**46**	**264**
NET BENEFIT	−47	−4	3	7	11	15	19	22	26	32	84
DISCOUNTED AT 15%	−47	−3.5	2.3	4.6	6.3	7.5	8.2	8.3	8.5	9.1	4.2

CRM BUSINESS CASE BEST GUESS WITH NON-ECONOMIC BENEFITS
Millions of dollars

	Year 1	Year 2	Year 3	Year 4	Year 5	Year 6	Year 7	Year 8	Year 9	Year 10	Total
COSTS											
Technology	40	5	5	5	5	5	5	5	5	5	85
Reorganization	5	0	0	0	0	0	0	0	0	0	5
People	5	5	5	5	5	5	5	5	5	5	50
Marketing	4	4	4	4	4	4	4	4	4	4	40
Total	**54**	**14**	**14**	**14**	**14**	**14**	**14**	**14**	**14**	**14**	**180**
BENEFITS											
Increased cross-sell	2	4	7	9	11	13	14	15	16	18	109
New referrals	1	1	4	5	6	7	9	10	12	14	69
Marketing cost reduction	4	5	6	7	8	9	10	11	12	14	86
Operational effectiveness	0	0	2	3	4	5	6	7	8	9	44
New business ideas	0	0	1	3	5	8	10	12	14	16	69
Total	**7**	**10**	**20**	**27**	**34**	**42**	**49**	**55**	**62**	**71**	**377**
NET BENEFIT	−47	−4	6	13	20	28	35	41	48	57	197
DISCOUNTED AT 15%	−47	−3.5	4.5	8.5	11.4	13.9	15.1	15.4	15.7	16.2	50.4

CRM BUSINESS CASE WORST CASE
Millions of dollars

	Year 1	Year 2	Year 3	Year 4	Year 5	Year 6	Year 7	Year 8	Year 9	Year 10	Total
COSTS											
Technology	40	5	5	5	5	5	5	5	5	5	85
Reorganization	5	0	0	0	0	0	0	0	0	0	5
People	5	5	5	5	5	5	5	5	5	5	50
Marketing	4	4	4	4	4	4	4	4	4	4	40
Total	**54**	**14**	**14**	**14**	**14**	**14**	**14**	**14**	**14**	**14**	**180**
BENEFITS											
Increased cross-sell	1	2	3.5	4.5	5.5	6.5	7	7.5	8	9	54.5
New referrals	0.5	0.5	2	2.5	3	3.5	4.5	5	6	7	34.5
Marketing cost reduction	2	2.5	3	3.5	4	4.5	5	5.5	6	7	43
Total	**3.5**	**5**	**8.5**	**10.5**	**12.5**	**14.5**	**16.5**	**18**	**20**	**23**	**132**
NET BENEFIT	−50.5	−9	−5.5	−3.5	−1.5	0.5	2.5	4	6	9	−48
DISCOUNTED AT 15%	−50.5	−7.8	−4.2	−2.3	−0.9	0.2	1.1	1.5	2.0	2.6	−58.3

CRM BUSINESS CASE OPTIMISTIC WITH NON-ECONOMIC BENEFITS
Millions of dollars

	Year 1	Year 2	Year 3	Year 4	Year 5	Year 6	Year 7	Year 8	Year 9	Year 10	Total
COSTS											
Technology	40	5	5	5	5	5	5	5	5	5	85
Reorganization	5	0	0	0	0	0	0	0	0	0	5
People	5	5	5	5	5	5	5	5	5	5	50
Marketing	4	4	4	4	4	4	4	4	4	4	40
Total	**54**	**14**	**14**	**14**	**14**	**14**	**14**	**14**	**14**	**14**	**180**
BENEFITS											
Increased cross-sell	3	6	10.5	13.5	16.5	19.5	21	22.5	24	27	163.5
New referrals	1.5	1.5	6	7.5	9	10.5	13.5	15	18	21	103.5
Marketing cost reduction	4	5	6	7	8	9	10	11	12	14	86
Operational effectiveness	0	0	3	4.5	6	7.5	9	10.5	12	13.5	66
New business ideas	0	0	1.5	4.5	7.5	12	15	18	21	24	103.5
Total	**8.5**	**12.5**	**27**	**37**	**47**	**58.5**	**68.5**	**77**	**87**	**99.5**	**522.5**
NET BENEFIT	−45.5	−1.5	13	23	33	44.5	54.5	63	73	85.5	342.5
DISCOUNTED AT 15%	−45.5	−1.3	9.8	15.1	18.9	22.1	23.6	23.7	23.9	24.3	114.6

CHARTING

	Year 1	Year 2	Year 3	Year 4	Year 5	Year 6	Year 7	Year 8	Year 9	Year 10	Total
First best guess	−47.0	−3.5	2.3	4.6	6.3	7.5	8.2	8.3	8.5	9.1	4.2
Best guess with non-economic benefits	−47.0	−3.5	4.5	8.5	11.4	13.9	15.1	15.4	15.7	16.2	50.4
Worst case	−50.5	−7.8	−4.2	−2.3	−0.9	0.2	1.1	1.5	2.0	2.6	−58.3
Best case	−45.5	−1.3	9.8	15.1	18.9	22.1	23.6	23.7	23.9	24.3	114.6

TABLE 9.1: The CRM business case

those two revenue lines for future product enhancements and cost savings – how am I to evaluate them? They're so speculative that if you present them to the Board, I'll have to suggest that they are removed. *

Mary pondered what to do. Should she be even more ambitious about the revenue and margin, even though she had no firm basis? Could she scale down CRM investment and still justify her growth assumptions? Should she try to convince the Board with 'soft' unquantifiable benefits? Should she try frightening the Board by painting a vision of doom if FSI allowed competitors to consolidate their hold on FSI's best customers?

Analysis of the FSI problem

FSI needs to become customer-centric. However, the only way to make the numbers work is to make heroic assumptions about increased revenue, reduced cost and the risks of 'do nothing'. Forecasting large increases in revenue (derived from large reductions in cost to serve) based on belief, experts' claims and hard to verify estimates of best practice is risky. Moreover, it assumes that you know the outcome of relationships before entering into them. While FSI might have an idea about how it could 'help' its customers further, it has not validated this in the real world. All businesses think that they can help customers by selling them more. Do customers see it like this?

The Finance Director's advice to invest more in the current business would show immediate return. Smaller initial investments giving short-term returns are favoured in NPV calculations because the discount rate – the time value of money – dramatically reduces benefits that are realized only in the long term. Nevertheless, what will happen to FSI if Mary, and the Board, are right about the shift in their customers' behaviour? How should FSI assess the risk of being cautious? If it fails to implement CRM now, can it come back later or will it have missed the chance forever? DCF is not a good tool for assessing low probability, but potentially fatal, risks. It also favours the short over the long term.

What about the 'soft' benefits? Mary is convinced that once the new organization is in place, FSI will find opportunities to reduce non-value added costs and identify winning new offerings. FSI would also be at the 'top-table' with its customers – gaining inside knowledge both of their evolving needs and leading business practice innovations. Without this access, FSI would lose its edge. The Board would recognize this, but the Finance Director was right. There is no valuation basis. Any assumption must be speculation. DCF, not surprisingly, is best used when the situation can be described in cash flow terms. It fails to value that which FSI will learn from customers – but learning is a major CRM benefit. If Mary's speculation is right, then the DCF undervalues the benefits of CRM investment.

FSI solution

Leading thinking in valuing customer relationships is to adopt an asset valuation rather than cash flow approach. Assets create shareholder value by providing both cash (economic) and non-cash (non-economic) benefits over time.

Mary's analysis identified cash benefits that arise from increased purchase, referral of new customers and lower marketing, sales and service costs. She also identified non-economic benefits in terms of learning and what that could mean for new products and operational efficiencies. Another non-economic benefit that should have formed part of her case is risk. CRM investments that improve loyalty, reduce cash flow volatility. This reduces the firm's risk, and improves share prices. Investors considering two firms generating equal cash flow, all other things being equal, will place a higher value on the firm with less volatile cash flow. This would show up in reduced cost of capital – which Mary accounts for in the 15 per cent discount rate. And, because CRM investments tend to produce longer-term benefits, NPV is very sensitive to that discount rate. This is normally handed down, unchallenged, from Finance. If CRM will reduce FSI's overall risk, then perhaps 15 per cent is too high. In Mary's initial best guess, where CRM investment breaks even after ten years, each point of reduced discount rate is worth $8.2 million.

This still puts no value on the unquantifiable learning aspects of CRM and the risk of stopping intermediation with customers. Even without this, asset valuation thinking suggests that FSI should consider taking a 'real option' on becoming customer-centric.

UNDERSTANDING REAL OPTIONS

Consider a hypothetical European company investigating the potential for its luxury ice cream in the Philippines. There are considerable economic, exchange rate and political risks. It decides that it does not have the management, investment or risk capacity to invest now, but believes that it might do so in two years' time.

The owner of a local firm facing temporary liquidity problems approaches the European company, looking to sell. Our European company could invest some money immediately to keep the business afloat by buying an option to acquire a majority share in two years at a price agreed today. It now has two years to learn about the market and assess the risks. If, two years on, it decides that this is not a good investment, it will not exercise the option. All it would have lost is the option price. However, if after two years the opportunity looks attractive, it can exercise its option.

The option has bought the firm the right to participate in the market in two years' time. The value of this right lies in the firm's ability to assess the opportunity better at that time.

Mary's business case is similar. CRM investment is risky, but failure to invest could be riskier still, reducing FSI to a very low margin business. Most of the benefits cannot be assessed by FSI in advance. It must engage with key accounts for a number of years before it can estimate the potential 'relationship effects'. The shape of Mary's revenue and non-economic benefits curves suggest that real growth will become apparent in years three and four.

FSI should buy an option to become customer-centric in two to three years' time. It will exercise that option only if, over this time frame, it can validate optimistic economic and non-economic benefits. If those benefits prove illusory, then it will not exercise its option.

Mary's agenda is now to create a market test of her program with selected key accounts supported by lower cost, temporary processes and technology. Instead of incurring initial costs of $54 million and complete business reorganization, FSI should look at testing CRM on, for example, 20 per cent of its business for less than 30 per cent of the cost (say, $15 million).

After two years of learning, the firm will then have the option of changing its entire business to a new model based upon validated business benefit assumptions. Or, if the worst-case assumptions look more likely, then the firm will have lost most of its initial investment ($15 million) but saved $39 million and the pain and diversion of reorganization.

The question then becomes how much should FSI pay for this option? In the Finance world, there is an accepted standard for options pricing[1] which looks at the risk of cash flows, the time frames and interest rates in making this determination. The Finance Director would be more helpful if he helped his managers learn how to use real options pricing rather than rigidly sticking with NPV spreadsheets.

SUMMARY

1   The CRM business case is a major strategic document and not merely a financial forecasting exercise. CRM represents a fundamental change and should be evaluated as a strategic, risky and therefore contingent investment in an unknown future. Consider your CRM business case in this context. Do you have one, and is it a strategic, financially rigorous document?

2   The business logic is based upon creating a win win scenario. For customers, relationships reduce the total lifecycle costs of owning an asset or procuring a service inclusive of the search, procurement, installation (where necessary) and after-sales service. Moreover, partners can meet customers' deeper, more profound, needs based upon better mutual knowledge and trust. For firms, committed and loyal customers are more profitable to serve as they tend to buy more, demand less discounts, attract lower sales, marketing and service costs and act as excellent references for the firm. Equally, firms that enter into genuine learning relationships with their customers will find that customers teach them to improve operational efficiencies and develop successful new products and services. Finally, CRM reduces business risk, further increasing the value of the firm to shareholders. Factor this logic into your CRM business case.

3   The foundations of win win are trust, integrity and mutual commitment. Unfortunately, most business cases for CRM emphasize purely the commercial, economic benefits of the seller rather than the mutual learning and the firm responding to that learning. Factor intangibles into your business case.

4   The FSI example demonstrates the limitations of a financial tool that managers typically use when building the business case for CRM: the Capital Asset Pricing Model (CAPM) and its Net Present Value (NPV) calculation. CAPM forces managers into making heroic assumptions about increased revenue (lower cost) per customer before really engaging in the relationship. The value of learning from customers, arguably the key to CRM, is not properly valued in the cash flow analysis. Major risks, such as discontinuous business change, are poorly handled.

5   Write the business case in a manner that views customer relationships as assets, generating both economic and non-economic value. The business case then focuses not only upon revenue, but on learning, trust and commitment to the relationship. If there is extreme uncertainty about CRM benefits, consider using real options pricing as a way around the limitations of the DCF analysis. Use CRM trials to validate the key growth assumptions and quantify the value of that which customers 'teach' you.

[1] T Copeland and P Keenan, 'How Much is Flexibility Worth?', *The McKinsey Quarterly*, No. 2, pp. 38–49, 1998.

CHAPTER 10

WHERE IS THE ONE-TO-ONE FUTURE?

INTRODUCTION

'Relationship Marketing [i.e. CRM] as it is currently practiced [sic.] has not brought us closer to customers. It has sent us farther afield.' So Susan Fournier *et al* wrote in the *Harvard Business Review* in 1998[1]. This chapter highlights the issues that have led many to concur with this bleak analysis. In Chapter 8, the compelling logic for realigning business from its traditional product-centric to a customer-centric focus was outlined. The strong academic and practitioner evidence that CRM creates value for companies and customers alike, in both consumer and business-to-business markets and across most industries, was reviewed. In this chapter, customer management initiatives are assessed on how well they deliver their promise, and why the majority of them fail to achieve their objectives is explored.

THE CRM REPORT CARD

CRM has been on the management agenda for the last decade. Its implementation has spread globally, affecting millions of workers in hundreds of organizations. Business embraced it with enthusiasm. Forrester Research Inc[2], in May 2001, reported that 20 per cent of the Global 3500 leading companies had implemented CRM programs and 61 per cent intended to invest in CRM software. Forrester also estimated that typical investments by the Global 3500 range from $15 million to $30 million. There is now enough history and experience to assess the results, but there has been remarkably little rigorous and objective research.

Most of what is publicly available originates with research firms, consultancies and software vendors. While consultancies and vendors provide well-documented examples of best practice, client references and case histories of successful implementations, these sources must be treated with caution. Software vendors and their allied systems integrators have a commercial stake in CRM and some of the research firms' predictions about new technology have proven optimistic. Yet, despite the potential bias towards optimism in the research,

[1] S Fournier, S Dobscha and D Mick, 'Preventing the Premature Death of Relationship Marketing', *Harvard Business Review*, Vol. 76, No. 1, Jan–Feb, pp. 42–51, 1998.
[2] R Chatham, D Weisman, L Orlov, T Nakashima and E Howard, *CRM: At What Cost?*, Cambridge, Mass: Forrester Research Inc., 2001.

publicly available results still suggest that the majority of CRM implementations fail to achieve their objectives.

The first consideration in assessing CRM effectiveness is that, as we discussed in Chapter 2, there is no accepted definition of CRM. This makes it hard to know what is being measured. A report from consulting firm Hewson Group[3] claimed that only 18 per cent of projects identified as CRM implementations met their strategic definition. A major IT research firm puts the figure at only 3 per cent. Although surveys report that most firms are doing some CRM, in reality many are only implementing tactical applications such as database marketing, call centres, online information sites or sales automation. Research suggests that few firms have fully embraced a strategic, enterprise-wide concept of CRM. Clearly, the first step in assessing CRM effectiveness is defining what it is.

Research firms and consultancies also try to measure the success of CRM programs. The methodologies they use are not always given, but at least some draw on managers' assessments of the extent to which they have achieved their objectives. Academics have long cautioned against relying on an individual's opinion of his or her activities and the success achieved. Even despite this potential bias, most surveys show that only 20–30 per cent of CRM programs are deemed successful. Here are a few examples:

☐ PWC published a report in 2002 on multi-channel marketing, claiming that CRM was failing to meet its objectives in 55–75 per cent of companies surveyed. Furthermore, despite the widespread implementation of CRM, customer satisfaction in the US is declining.

☐ A recent McKinsey study[4] quotes Ernst & Young research that almost two-thirds of US banks do not know if their investments in CRM increased sales, and that despite large CRM investments, customer satisfaction with banks fell during the period 1995–9.

☐ A CSC report published survey data that only 27 per cent of European companies that implemented a data warehouse could quantify its financial benefit; only 16 per cent of UK data warehousing projects delivered tangible ROI; and only 21 per cent of sales automation projects met or exceeded expectations.

There is not enough rigorous research to determine the real impact of CRM programs on customer satisfaction, loyalty and corporate performance. However, from that which is available, CRM appears to be compelling in theory, but in practice is failing to fulfil its potential.

THE MAJOR CAUSES FOR FAILURE

Research and experience leads to some suggestions for senior managers, marketing and information systems to address the core managerial issues in the poor performance of so many CRM programs:

Note to senior managers: CRM is not a panacea

There is a clear need for a more strategic and well-founded business case for CRM, such as that laid out in Chapter 9. Management cannot dismiss CRM as just another fad or set of technologies; boardroom interest in it has already outlasted quality, re-engineering and the dot.com bubble. Few doubt that for many firms the future lies in building productive partnerships with customers. However, senior managers often seem to add CRM to an ever-

---

[3] David Reed, 'Waiting for the Customer Management Revolution', www.eccs.uk.com/suppliers/newsanalysis/april2001_5.asp., April 2001.

[4] G Olazabal, 'Banking: The IT Paradox', *The McKinsey Quarterly*, No. 1, 2002.

expanding list of corporate initiatives without understanding its implications. They expect that new technology and organization structures will 'implement CRM' and deliver against poorly defined and often nebulous objectives.

The start of senior management involvement should be with the business case – planning the economic and non-economic potential of customer relationships. If the 'soft' benefits are not identified at this stage they will probably be ignored during implementation, and the CRM focus will be on cross-selling and exploiting customers. Putting a value on what customers 'teach' the firm is a strategic issue rather than a financial or accounting one. Senior management must engage in the debate so that the organization plans for listening and responding.

The foundation of the customer relationship program is trust, integrity and mutual commitment. This must be the focus of the senior management agenda. These qualities will not automatically result from management initiatives, nor impressive new technology. For companies used to prioritizing operational excellence or product leadership, creating principled partnerships with customers represents a profound change in ethos, working practices and corporate identity. CRM will not happen as a result merely of business process re-engineering assisted by enabling technology.

Note to marketers: CRM is not 'just more marketing'

Marketing may treat CRM as another form of promotion: direct mail on steroids. The hypothetical case of FSI in Chapter 9 illustrates what is often true in practice – that CRM is compromised at its inception. To make the business plan work, marketers too often focus upon how they will sell more of their existing product portfolio, rather than how they will develop their overall service and product portfolio in collaboration with their best customers. To achieve their sales targets, marketers build ever more sophisticated campaign management systems to instruct them when to intervene with each prospect and what to say at the point of intervention. These systems are supposed to learn by trial and error, leading to ever higher yielding marketing campaigns, and thus generate ROI.

As the survey results indicate, in the majority of cases the expected ROI has not materialized. Anecdotal evidence suggests that a growing customer backlash to this interpretation of CRM threatens its future. Customers resent the relentless assault on their free time. Click-through rates on electronic ads are reported to be falling. Internet-savvy customers filter junk e-mail. Direct mail response rates remain low overall – despite some well-publicised examples of highly successful campaigns – and telemarketing often irritates customers.

The overtly managerial approach to building relationships is not working. Trust and respect build idiosyncratically between individuals over repeated 'moments of truth' or experiences. Customers are not amenable to manipulation through repeated direct marketing campaigns. In 2001, Alan Mitchell[5] wrote: 'At worst, this frenzied attempt to gather ever more information about customers becomes a form of customer stalking.' He quotes James Milojkovic, CEO of www.KnowledgePassion.com, who claims that CRM is an oxymoron, because you cannot manage a relationship – it is something that you negotiate.

Marketers need to move beyond direct marketing and campaign management and develop new competencies for a more interactive, relationship-based era. In the age of 'make and sell', marketers were brand engineers, configuring well-known marketing stimuli that could predictably deliver specific customer behaviours. Today, they must become value architects who understand customer needs and know how to configure their organization to deliver

---

[5] A Mitchell, *Right Side Up*, HarperCollins Business, 2001.

against them. Marketers must learn to engage with customers interactively, understanding them through dialogue as much as through conventional market research. Traditional marketers have been schooled in mass communicating predetermined product benefits; tomorrow they must understand their firms' supply chains and their partners' capabilities so that they can create bespoke solutions for customers. Where customers act within communities, marketers must engage with those communities and establish a legitimate presence there. Marketing understands individual customer behaviour and motivation rather than individuals' behaviour in communities or networks, so new marketing competencies will be needed. To develop these competencies, marketers need to experiment with interactive CRM practices in the context of their business, before a full-scale CRM implementation. Best practice cannot be expected to create powerful customer relationships and competitive advantage straight out of the box – some experience is needed first. This is the CRM leadership focus for marketing.

Note to IS: CRM is not an extension of back office re-engineering

Too often, CRM was treated as just the 'next big thing' to be implemented. Teams of skilled software engineers and program managers finished big ERP projects and started on CRM, sometimes without pausing for breath. But CRM is different from back office re-engineering and the enterprise technology that is associated with the back office in many ways:

☐ Failure is more immediately evident to customers and potentially more damaging to the relationship.

☐ Customer-facing business systems affect customers' experiences, which are judged against experience of competitors and not merely against internal benchmarks and past performance.

☐ Operational CRM applications are used by large numbers of customer-facing staff, most of whom are not as highly qualified technically as users of ERP systems.

☐ The ROI is driven more from the quality of the customer experience created, than through improved operational effectiveness.

☐ The business sponsor, often marketing or customer service, is normally less technically sophisticated and understanding of IS thinking than manufacturing. The brief is less likely to be 'right' early in the development process.

☐ CRM systems need to develop flexibly in response to as yet unforeseen customer input. The business sponsor's brief will not be stable through the development process.

☐ The front office solution needs to be connected to the back office. There is little point in a learning relationship with the customer, developing a solution together and agreeing on its value to each party, only to find that the solution is not deliverable or profitable. Customer-facing staff need to be able to see deep into the supply chain in order to conduct their customer conversations intelligently and with integrity, and make promises the firm can keep – at a profit.

☐ Customer-facing staff could cover up failures of ERP or back office systems in interactions with customers. CRM failures leave nowhere to hide.

CRM writers tend to assume the program has worked when the sales are made; the reality of being customer-centric is that the program works when the customers are loyal and committed to you, and tell you what a wonderful experience you provide. Delivery is everything.

For IS, this creates many challenges. Traditional enterprise solution development is sequential and managerial and/or top down. The top team creates a new vision that is then translated into a new structure. New business processes are developed in workshops with operational level staff, and finally the technology is bought to do the job. There are even occasions where, in a rush to implement the new vision, the technology is decided upon almost immediately and the rest of the organization changes its structure and business processes to fit the solution. CRM is more likely to succeed when technology is built iteratively in step with the development of new customer insight. IS must find new ways of implementing enterprise solutions that focus equally upon learning and the development of competencies, as they do on speed, predictability and cost. Tying marketing to a tight specification up front and then slavishly following a Project Plan to deliver it does not add value to the organization. It may even ensure the delivery of a system that is outdated the day it goes live.

LAY THE CRM FOUNDATIONS

CRM is about developing a win win relationship between customers and their suppliers that creates value for both sides, and managing that relationship on the basis of trust, integrity and mutual commitment. This principle is as powerful today as it was when marketing writers first introduced it over a decade ago. However, businesses were distracted from the basic tenets of CRM by the high-tech investment bubble and promises of quick riches and technological solutions to what are fundamentally human problems of building relationships. It is now time to return to basics.

☐ Corporate leaders must first agree on their definition of CRM and the extent of their ambition – the point made in Chapter 2. Those opting to become highly customer-centric must determine the value that both customers and the firm will get from the relationship and answer a series of related questions:

1 Is the value proposition strong enough to justify a relationship?

2 What does the firm need to do to fulfil its end of the bargain?

3 Realistically, how long will it take to make those changes?

4 How will we build trust with our customers?

5 How will we listen and learn from our customers?

6 How will we value that learning and reward those in the organization that acquire the learning?

These issues should be embedded in the business case. Executives need to be aware of whether their financial planning tools help the planning and achievement of CRM.

☐ The toughest challenge for marketing leaders is to change from their traditional orientation, where customers were the object of their marketing planning, to one where they interact with customers to develop value together. More sophisticated, high-tech selling techniques will not enable CRM because they rarely operate in the interest of customers and fail, therefore, to build the trust and mutual commitment. In Chapter 8, it was suggested that the traditional approach to thinking about value is too limited to meet the needs of CRM and an alternate framework was suggested – the Unique Organization Value Proposition (UOVP)®. In this chapter, the need to develop new marketing competencies in advance of the major investments in new technology has been identified.

87

Customer-facing functions need to learn how their customers will interact and extract value from the firm as it develops new CRM business processes and plans for the associated IT support.

☐ IT leaders play a pivotal role in CRM. They understand what technology can make possible and, if they can engage their marketing colleagues, they can help the business to innovate in ways that are relevant to the customer, and are executable. This requires information systems to move beyond being a helpful implementer of well-defined business briefs and to assume a broader leadership role within the firm. IS must accept that the business cannot predetermine the outcome of engaging with customers, and find ways to enable rapid, low-cost experimentation to promote learning about customer relationships.

SUMMARY

1   Senior managers cannot see CRM as a panacea: it is a long-term, pan-company change program. Start with executive involvement in the business case. Trust, integrity and mutual commitment need to underpin the creation of customer partnerships. Consider how your senior management team understands CRM and whether that perception is sufficiently mature.

2   Marketers must treat CRM as more than 'just more marketing' and develop new competencies for building successful customer relationships. This involves understanding how to develop partnerships based on mutual commitment through repeated positive experience. Engage in a dialogue with your marketers to understand the relationship between marketing and delivery.

3   IS leaders must not manage CRM as an extension of back office re-engineering. They must take a broader leadership role throughout the planning and implementation of CRM. Consider the list of reasons why CRM is different for IS than previous initiatives and ask which are relevant in your firm. If any are, then intervene in your CRM strategy now before your customers are handed further evidence of your inability to treat them as anything other than numbers on a marketing dartboard.

CHAPTER 11

SEGMENTATION WITHIN CORPORATE STRATEGY

INTRODUCTION

How many customers does your firm have? Hundreds, thousands or millions? While you can use CRM to acquire, attract, retain and perhaps terminate relationships with individual customers, large customer volumes make it impractical to allow them to drive your corporate strategy.

Customer segmentation is a management tool that enables companies to plan and deliver improved profitability by differentiating the delivery of product and service between different customer groups, based on those customers' needs and their value to the organization. There are two primary uses of segmentation:

1   **Strategic segmentation** – Involves driving corporate strategy based on differences between customer groups. It is primarily focused on high level long-term direction and treatment of customers. Typically, a company is unlikely to define more than a dozen strategic segments. While strategic segments do change over time – indeed they must – changes are relatively infrequent.

2   **Marketing segmentation** – Differentiates the marketing activities directed at customers. Marketing segments may be numerous and may change from campaign to campaign. A company such as Tesco may use thousands of fluid segments to make marketing ever more precise. Marketing segmentation is at a lower level than strategic segmentation, because it is limited to sales and marketing activities.

This chapter describes the role of strategic segmentation within corporate strategy. Marketing segmentation is touched upon in later chapters. While a template for segmentation could be given, this would impose an unnecessary constraint. As with all aspects of CRM, there is no one right answer for strategic segmentation, nor one accepted version of the contents of a segmentation model. Different companies will define their strategy to different levels of scope. The approach in this chapter is to lay out a series of components, any or all of which can be used in the strategy in any combination. Think of them as a palette of tools that you can mix in combination, as you require. Table 11.1 describes these components or tools.

COMPONENT	WHAT QUESTION DOES THIS ANSWER?
Customer segmentation	How will you group customers who have common characteristics (needs) at a level that is manageable but at the same time draws sufficient differentiation between customers?
Competitive context	How (and why) do customers share their purchasing between you and your competition? What is the strength of the affinity between you and your customers, against that for the competition?
Customer base quality	What is your penetration to your valued customer segments? What is your share of these valued customers' wallets? What is the quality of the customer profile?
Intimacy levels	What different levels of service intensity are required for different customers? How should different intimacy levels be delivered?
Relationship management	Who owns the relationship with the customer? Does the customer appreciate the relationship? Do you actively manage the relationship to the standard your brand dictates?
Growth trajectory	What is the growth potential of customers within each segment over time? What strategies can be adopted to grow customers (or discard those that are failing to perform)?

TABLE 11.1: Components of the strategic segmentation model

CUSTOMER SEGMENTATION

Customer segmentation depends on understanding your customer base well enough to group (or segment) customers according to their needs. You need to answer six questions:

1 What do customers need and how do their needs differ?

2 Why do they differ?

3 What different styles do they require?

4 What is their motivation?

5 How much revenue do they bring in?

6 How much do they cost to service?

One approach is to follow the template in Table 11.2 for each of your customer segments.

Building the segmentation model is a repetitive process. Begin with intuition and then refine this by using fact-based analysis (some useful tools are described later in Chapter 15). You need to answer two questions:

1 **How many segments?** This is actually relatively straightforward. We are discussing strategy, and from a strategic perspective you need to restrict the numbers of segments. The Marketing Director may use hundreds or even thousands of segments built specifically for different marketing campaigns. This level of complexity cannot work in a

SEGMENT		PRODUCT NEEDS	SERVICE NEEDS
SEGMENT NAME What differentiates this group of customers from other customers?	Style	What does this segment want to buy from you?	How do they want to be serviced by you?
	Motivation	What are they buying from you and why?	Why do they want to be serviced in this way?
	Profitability	What will you make from them?	How much will it cost you to service them?
SEGMENT NAME What differentiates this group of customers from other customers?	Style		
	Motivation		
	Profitability		

TABLE 11.2: Template for a customer segmentation model

corporate strategy – it becomes unmanageable. If segmentation is to mean anything it must drive the actions of the organization and the organization will only be able to cope with a limited number of segments. As a guideline, with fewer than five segments you may find you cannot differentiate customers sufficiently, while more than 12 will probably be too many.

2   **What criteria should define the segments?** This is the hard question. However, your value discipline may well help drive the criteria. Operationally excellent companies may find it valuable to begin segmenting based on a combination of cost to serve and how customers access product or service. Product leaders may begin using product purchase behaviours and brand affinity. Customer-intimate firms may change the focus to the products or services that customers need. The traditional method of categorization was demographic data – combinations of, for example, age, sex, salary and address. However, modern application software provides considerable behavioural data (e.g. frequency of performing certain transactions). Value networks in particular may find behavioural models more valuable than demographic models.

COMPETITIVE CONTEXT

Unless you operate a monopoly, your segmentation model will be incomplete without an understanding of the competitive environment. It is likely that the competitive context will vary by customer segment. If it does not, then perhaps the initial segments need to be refined. The competitive context model poses and answers three questions:

1   How do customers share their purchasing between you and your competition?

Measuring purchase share is rarely scientific. However, market research, published lifestyle data and your own intuition can provide a solid basis for action. Measuring the reasons why customers share their purchases is necessarily still less scientific – although market research, focus groups, surveys of customer's can all contribute. Within most industries, for each segment, it should be possible to define:

☐ The types of products or services that this segment is likely to purchase.

☐ The approximate proportion of customers within the segment that have the products or services you offer, for example, Segment A typically shops with you for white goods but not for kitchen supplies – why?

Compare these figures to the overall structure of your product or service portfolio to establish whether certain segments are over or underweight in particular offerings.

2   How does your customers' affinity for you compare with the affinity they have for your competitors?

Measuring affinity is also unscientific. However, you can use past purchasing behaviour to identify the degree of loyalty that each segment displays by estimating the likelihood that they would buy from you if they were given the same offering at the same price by your firm and a competitor.

3   What motivates customers to share their purchases between you and your competition, and what are the factors that drive the level of affinity between your customer and your company?

This approach for building a competitive context model is illustrated in Table 11.3.

SEGMENT	PURCHASE SHARE	AFFINITY STRENGTH	WHY?
SEGMENT NAME What differentiates this group of customers from other customers?	How does this segment share its purchases between companies?	What is the strength of the affinity between this segment and the company and other companies?	What are the factors motivating this purchase share? What are the factors motivating this level of affinity?
SEGMENT NAME What differentiates this group of customers from other customers?			

TABLE 11.3: Template for a competitive context model

CUSTOMER BASE QUALITY

It has already become clear that the quality of the information for your segmentation model is imperfect. However, you must judge whether the information remains a valid basis for action despite its imperfections. There are two aspects to this:

1   How good is the quality of the customer data that is being used to make decisions? There will be errors in the data, but have these skewed the results unacceptably?

2   How effective are you at penetrating the market of the market of the customers that matter, and what is their potential for growth?

The segment quality is reflected in two models. In the first (Figure 11.1) each segment is mapped against penetration and value to the business. Value may reflect revenue (current and future), but as we have already seen customer value is more complex than that and includes such things as how likely customers are to refer other customers. Constructing a value/penetration model will begin to highlight the strategies that need to be developed to increase (or decrease) penetration within each segment.

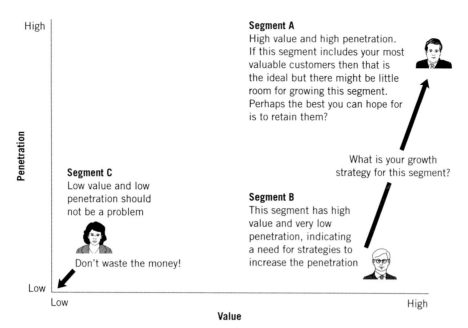

FIGURE 11.1: The value/penetration model

The second element is an assessment of the quality of the customer profiles and segments (Figure 11.2).

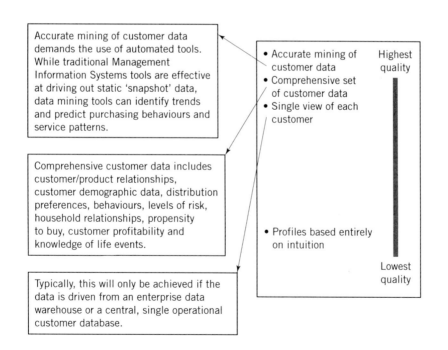

FIGURE 11.2: Assessing segment and profile quality

There is nothing wrong with an intuition-based model. The depth of understanding that you have of your business may well mean that such a model offers real insight which no amount of number crunching could ever provide. The important point is whether or not the business understands the basis for action.

INTIMACY LEVELS

Intimacy levels define how close the organization will get to each segment, and the strategies to adopt in order to deliver the required level of customer intimacy. For each segment, ask three questions:

1 **How will you magnetize, or attract, new customers?** Every business needs to develop strategies to acquire new customers. However, it is likely that acquisition strategies will vary by segment, and linking acquisition strategies to the segmentation model should improve their effectiveness. For example, an airline's segmentation model may define annual holiday travellers and frequent business travellers as separate segments. The tools to acquire new customers in the first segment are different to the second. Business travellers may be attracted by preferential airline lounges and faster check-in procedures; the occasional holiday-maker may be more interested in discounts.

2 **How will you fortify your relationships with this segment?** This is done by establishing mechanisms to increase the level of affinity of existing customers. For example, this may involve a telephone call every month for most valuable segments, sending a personalized magazine, offering discounts against subsequent purchases, running a competition. Again, the strategy may vary by segment. The individual buyer of Dove soap may be encouraged by traditional two-for-the-price-of-three offers, or discount coupons. The corporate buyer (a different segment) may be attracted by bulk discounts or internet ordering tools.

Fortification of relationships is a more useful concept than retention. Many companies 'retain' customers who create no value for the company; in many industries a majority of customers are actually a drain on corporate resources. Customer strategy should not necessarily seek just to retain customers, but to fortify relationships with valued customers.

3 **How will you magnify the customer relationships?** In other words, how will you drive out additional value from each segment? What will you offer customers to get them to buy more from you? Again, consider the differences by customer segment – mechanisms to increase revenue from young single men may be very different from those for middle-aged married women with children. It may be impossible to magnify some relationships. If you produce soap, and the customer is already loyal to your brand then you are unlikely to be able to persuade the customer to buy more.

Differentiating intimacy levels by segment is important for any company that is seeking to move away from a 'one size fits all' approach. Most companies will find that their segmentation model throws out marked differences in the intimacy needs of different customers. Not only does constructing an intimacy level model help to increase the value of relevant customers, but it can also reduce costs by eliminating expenditure on customers that are not valuable to the business.

RELATIONSHIP MANAGEMENT

Relationship management is managing how a customer is treated across different channels and media. Again, it will vary by segment unless you are seeking to deploy a 'one size fits all' model and offer all customers equal treatment. There are three aspects to relationship management:

1 Who manages the relationship? In many companies, the relationship is managed by the call centre operators, or even (in a self-care environment) by website designers. However, if your website designers are the primary influence on how the customer relationship is managed, are they trained in your CRM strategy? In value shops (such as consulting firms) in particular, with complex event-driven relationships, a web of individuals loosely coordinated through an account manager may manage the relationship. Only by understanding this web can the firm truly grasp the impact it is having upon another (probably equally) complex organization.

2 How are relationships with the segment managed through each channel or medium? How often is it used? If 80 per cent of a customer's interaction is through a website, and 20 per cent through a branch, then perhaps focusing more attention on the branch program will miss the point. How effective is the communication through each mechanism? Does one channel or medium stand out as being ineffective? If it does, then is it the favoured medium of your key segment? If it is, then maybe you need to adjust your strategy.

3 Chapter 12 argues that companies need to measure their CRM competence not against a benchmark company, but against the promise of their brand. The third question that the relationship management model needs to answer is how well each channel or medium delivers against the expectations created by the brand. This is illustrated in Table 11.4.

	SEGMENT A	SEGMENT B	MEASURED AGAINST BRAND
CALL CENTRE	What influence does this channel or medium have on this segment? How often is it used? Is communication pro-active or re-active? How confident are you that the right view of your company is being portrayed?		How successfully does this relationship manager deliver on the promise of the brand?
WEBSITE			
COMPANY AGENT			
THIRD PARTY (PARTNER)			

TABLE 11.4: Template for measuring delivery against the promise of the brand

You should create two versions of this table, one reflecting how the relationship is managed now, the other how it will be managed in the future.

GROWTH TRAJECTORY

The potential for growth may itself be the driving factor behind the segmentation model. Different segments will inevitably have different growth potential for the business. For example, many retail banks target university students as a distinct strategic segment – they may be poor now but they have potential.

All the other components of the strategic segmentation model have been essentially static – they examined each segment at one point in time (and perhaps at a point in the future). A growth trajectory model seeks to understand the potential for growth within each segment.

Table 11.5 suggests a possible starting point for a growth trajectory model for a brand that increasingly appeals to men with disposable income. You may need to create such a model for each segment where there is wide variation in potential growth. Where there is less variation in potential growth (probably because growth potential was a significant factor in the initial segmentation criteria) then a single growth trajectory model may work for the entire customer base.

SEGMENT	CHARACTERISTICS	CUSTOMERS	REVENUE IN MILLIONS (DISCOUNTED) 2000	2005	REASONS AND STRATEGY
ROCKETS	Over 3 × revenue growth 2000 to 2005	270,000	0.8	7.2	Graduating male students will enter market – our brand leads in this field.
EAGLES	1.5 to 3 × revenue growth 2000 to 2005	372,000	6.3	10.4	Older middle-aged men – children leaving home, disposable income.
RACEHORSE	Up to 1.5 × revenue growth 2000 to 2005	314,000	14.3	16.2	Late 20s, early 30s men – static expenditure on our brand (cost of children).
TURTLES	Static revenue 2000 to 2005	394,000	23.6	24.4	Our brand increasingly losing appeal to women – see static growth across most age groups.
LEAKY BUCKETS	Declining revenues 2000 to 2005	1,768,000	40.0	30.4	Customers with disposable incomes under $20,000 will cease to buy our brand and replace it with an own-brand cheaper substitute.

TABLE 11.5: Example of a growth trajectory model

The growth trajectory model is one of the most important components of the segmentation model. Yet many firms construct their segmentation model and then treat it as a static, one-time event. Segments will constantly change and it makes sense to include a review of the segmentation model and how well the growth trajectory model is performing against expectations, as part of your strategic planning cycle. You may find that the growth model highlights such profound variations in potential growth that your overall corporate strategy needs to change.

SUMMARY

1 Do you use strategic segmentation within your business? If not, consider the value that it may add. If your firm does not have a 'one size fits all' approach to its customers, then a strategic segmentation model may well reduce cost and enable the provision of more appropriate levels of service.

2 Build a customer segmentation model. Consider what criteria you could use and how many segments would provide the required level of granularity. Understand the different product and service needs of each segment.

3 Try constructing a competitive context model. You may find that you simply do not have the competitive information. How much effort would it take to obtain it?

4 The information that you have about your customers is imperfect. Whether or not you currently use strategic segmentation within your corporate strategy, consider the quality of your customer base in terms of your penetration to the customers that you value most. If you have constructed customer segments, consider how accurate these are. Is the likely error rate acceptable?

5 It is probable that different customer segments will require – or you will wish to provide them with – different levels of intimacy. Build an intimacy model that explores how you will magnetize, fortify and magnify the relationships within each segment.

6 Who manages the relationship with your customers? The answer may not be the obvious one.

7 Your business probably has growth targets in terms of revenue. However, such targets probably hide wide variations in growth. Consider deconstructing your company's growth projections by customer segment. The results may be so profound that they change your corporate strategy.

PART  4

CREATING THE CUSTOMER-CENTRIC ORGANIZATION

An increasing body of evidence suggests that it is the failure to change the organization, rather than an inability to implement new software, that is the primary cause of CRM failure. This makes sense. Intuitively we know that it is how an organization delivers on its promise to the customer that makes the difference. However, perhaps because organizational change is necessarily more nebulous than bits and bytes and boxes, most CRM initiatives fail to treat organizational change as a coherent initiative, or even acknowledge the need to approach it scientifically.

In Chapter 8, the case for developing your Unique Organization Value Proposition (UOVP)® was argued and the importance of aligning the promise and delivery of brand explored. In Chapter 12 on brand-driven relationships, a bridge is built to the UOVP®. Delivering your brand promise makes demands of your organization: different behaviours, different measures, different processes. With brand consultancy Wolff Olins, we consider how to drive brand into the organization. Wolff Olins is the world's most influential brand consultancy. Amongst its clients are many market leaders that have delivered business success by connecting their brand to their organization. Visit Wolff Olins at www.wolff-olins.com.

But how to approach organizational change? Chapter 13 lays out a framework that explains the scope of CRM. An eight-stage organizational change road map is presented that can be applied to any CRM initiative, large or small, to drive change into an organization.

CHAPTER 12

DRIVING BRAND INTO THE ORGANIZATION

INTRODUCTION

An inevitable consequence of increasing competition is that the balance of power in customer relationships tips towards the customer. In this environment, firms must differentiate themselves. As globalization makes product and service offerings more alike, how firms treat their customers becomes an increasingly important differentiator. As businesses differentiate customer experience, industry standards for customer service keep rising: customers want and expect to be treated well, and if they are not, they defect. Good service is not enough to create sustained competitive advantage because it can be copied. As each improvement in customer service is matched by the competition, the playing field is levelled and customer decisions either become once again based upon function, such as price, convenience and product innovation or upon emotion.

Brand encapsulates all that makes a firm different in the eyes of its customers, but before becoming brand-centric, firms must first understand how to be customer-centric.

Consider the behaviour of monopolies or oligopolies, such as telecommunications firms, energy providers and airlines prior to deregulation. With few exceptions, they had no interest in treating customers well and were not very good at it. Few such enterprises did, or do, remunerate staff or management on the competence with which they deliver customer experience. Good service was an individual staff option rather than an institutional competence. The majority of these companies failed to develop this competence, and are only now starting to do so.

CRM can play different roles and be executed in many different ways; in choosing the best options, it is critical to understand what impact they will have on the brand.

DEFINE THE EXPERIENCE YOU DELIVER FROM YOUR BRAND

As customers' expectations from the experience of doing business are raised, how should organizations respond? The two most obvious approaches are both potentially wrong.

Do not try to jump a notional bar of experience excellence

An obvious strategy is just to try and do better: if currently only 80 per cent of calls are answered within three rings, take action to raise the percentage to 95 per cent. However, customer expectations are not delivered just because you have met some arbitrary target of experience excellence. Customers have different expectations, even from different firms within the same sector. A customer may perceive a poor experience at an expensive restaurant, although by any objective measure it is superior to an outstanding experience at a burger bar – more intimate, more attentive, more customized, more personal.

The underlying principle in creating a customer-centric organization is not to direct your firm to jump some notional bar of service excellence, but to meet or exceed the customers' expectations of your firm. These expectations are set through a complex pattern of experiences, rational and irrational beliefs, individual preferences and peculiarities that are more the domain of the psychologist than the CRM program manager. The primary tool available to firms to establish a base level of expectation is the promise made in the brand.

Do not benchmark experience against a best of breed

This approach – seeing who is doing it best and copying them – is also flawed. In attempting to copy, you are delivering another firm's promise. Benchmarking exercises for systems performance may be valuable, but systems performance is rarely a firm's unique differentiator. Organizations have to stand for something that is unique, and what is correct for one is not right for another. British Airways and Lufthansa can receive high marks for customer experience, as can Ryanair and easyJet. Of course premium airlines provide a 'superior' service experience if the customer's expectation is of a free gin and tonic, and a personalized and flexible booking service. However, from an organizational change perspective, Ryanair and easyJet should not and do not seek to match the service levels of those premium airlines. Rather, as with most operationally excellent firms, they make a point of sacrificing 'unnecessary' services and deliver lower prices in return.

Benchmarking against the best of breed may improve your service, but it will not help deliver on the promise of your brand, because that is unique. If your direct mail clothing brand is about youth, low cost and rebellion, then who do you benchmark against? Certainly not the market leader that has built its experience on quality, maturity and deference to its customers.

Few firms, as part of their efforts to improve CRM, initiate a coherent program to drive their brand promise by altering the behaviours of the staff that deliver on that promise. Where firms do initiate an organizational change program, they will often use a benchmark. However, you do not delight your customers by meeting or exceeding the standards of your selected best of breed, but by exceeding the promise of your brand. The fact that brand is unique and differentiated (and if it is not, then it is flawed) means that benchmarking your organizational competence risks delivering to another firm's promise rather than to your own. At best, benchmarking may deliver undifferentiated service; at worst it may result in your taking actions that fail to address the issues underlying the delivery of your own promise. Do not prioritize call waiting times if the bigger issue is whether your staff can solve the problems that the callers are reporting.

THE BRAND PROMISE

Therefore, rather than simply setting your sights high, or benchmarking against a best of breed, you should build an organizational change vision that reflects your brand. The problem is how to do it.

Begin by establishing what your brand says. Most successful brands have a single strong idea that sparks consistent behaviour amongst their customers. For examples, see the six brands in Table 12.1.

BRAND	IDEA
Walt Disney	Magic
Sony	Miniature perfection
Virgin	Challenger
Nike	Victory
Coca-cola	Life
Orange	Optimism

TABLE 12.1: Brand ideas

The brand idea encapsulates a core philosophy which informs the business how to behave. The brand idea is not used overtly. The objective is to invoke a coherent positive emotional response from and to customers and stakeholders. It is akin to a corporate promise. Nevertheless, as argued in Chapter 8, it is no longer sufficient just to promise. That promise must be delivered. This can only happen if the philosophy captured in your brand pervades and informs the service competence within your organization.

BRAND-DRIVEN CRM

The challenge is to understand how to move the whole organization in a direction which appears so nebulous. Figure 12.1, the Wolff Olins brand framework, offers a tool to do this. By using the brand idea to paint a vision of what the brand represents to customers, firms can begin to institutionalize the organizational behaviours that will meet or exceed the brand. In Chapter 13, we will describe how to build these into an organizational change program.

The framework is straightforward to use. Begin by considering the brand idea that sits in the middle. Now consider in turn each of the 12 aspects that are encapsulated within the brand and start to understand the current state. How well does each aspect support the brand? Finally, consider the future state. What has to change in each of those 12 aspects to deliver on the brand?

Below we consider in turn each of the 12 aspects of brand and how these have to be driven into the relationship.

Competence

Competence is tangible, measurable and can be changed by altering how staff are trained, how the firm partners with other firms and how the firm is structured. There are three aspects:

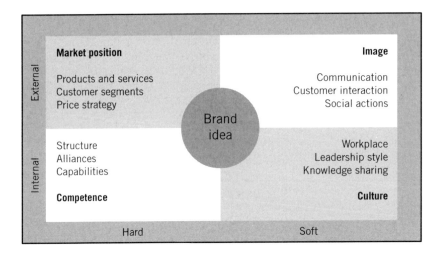

FIGURE 12.1: Wolff Olins brand framework

1 **Capabilities** – Changing the capabilities of an organization is easier than changing its culture. Any CRM program that demands a step change in the service provided by staff will require a change in their capabilities. Such capability changes are often limited to running courses in complaint handling or telephone manner. However, unless the brand promise is already being delivered, the changes required may be more dramatic. They may demand that customer-facing staff are empowered with greater decision-making authority; that supervisors are given authority to make financial decisions previously the domain of management; or that staff responsible for one process have to take responsibility for other processes if that is what the customer wants.

The British Airways customer care program received much attention because it achieved a step change in the capabilities of its staff. It suggests three components of best practice. First, the change in capabilities was sufficiently dramatic to be noticeable to customers – why bother otherwise? Second, the changes were consistent across the organization. Patchy experience is almost as dangerous as poor experience. Third, the changes were relatively straightforward for employees to grasp. The brand promise had been distilled into concrete actions for employees to take, rather than a nebulous framework to be read then forgotten.

2 **Alliances** – Partnerships may have a profound impact on brand perception. Many firms rely on partners, for example to distribute their products. A partner that is visible to the customers will have an impact on their perception of your brand as significant as you do yourself. Yet few CRM programs consider the impact of alliance partners upon their customers' expectation – an omission that in the current climate may be a significant oversight. One of the most traumatic experiences of any air traveller – lost baggage – is outside the control of the airlines, but airlines have to manage the consequences. Incidences of food poisoning in fast food restaurants may be the responsibility of the partner supplying burgers – but it is not the partner that the customer will sue. Customers who are dissatisfied because their furniture is not delivered on time will not blame the delivery company but the furniture store. Customers understand the concept of 'prime contractor' better than most businesspeople; they will deem the firm whom they contract

responsible for any and all aspects of value delivery. Your organizational change program must consider how partners can reinforce or destroy your brand promise.

The need to consider how alliance partners deliver upon customer expectations reinforces the break away from benchmarking, which will always tend to compare like with like (by definition). Partnership structures are always unique and the patterns of influence upon customer perception profoundly complex. Britain's railways have become notorious for delays, overcrowding and overpricing. However, at least some of the damage to the perception was due to the blame culture between the train operating companies that run the trains, and Railtrack that used to run the tracks.

3   **Structure** – In most organizations, customers connect with many representatives of the firm, but the organizational structure should be invisible except when customers choose to access it by speaking to someone in authority. Then, the hierarchy should be clear. The CRM program must identify potential pain points where customers may identify organizational disconnects – focusing particularly upon the interface with partners.

Another sensible option is to construct access mechanisms for customers to use. In the US, over 100 billion letters were sent in 2000, and 4 trillion e-mails. E-mail is the channel of choice for many, and yet many leading firms fail to accept e-mails. A clear access channel, and an escalation process for complaints, are essential in a customer-driven world. The only thing worse than a complaining customer is one unable to complain. How many business units is the customer expected to connect with? Different telephone numbers for claims, service and sales may save you money but can adversely affect customer perception. Customers want one number to call, one address to write to and one URL to bookmark.

Market position

Capabilities are the hard, internal aspects affected by brand; the market position covers the hard, external aspects.

1   **Products and services** – Products and services are clearly fundamental to any brand. But do the offerings support the brand promise? A firm's offerings will either reinforce or destroy the brand and conversely, the brand sets customer expectations about the offering.

2   **Customer segments** – Businesses increasingly divide their customers into segments, as discussed in Chapter 11. Such segmentation is often a foundation of CRM programs. However, what does the brand say to each segment? Is this what it should say? Perhaps most importantly, should the brand say different things to different segments?

The Financial Services sector offers interesting case studies of how distinct brand promises force fundamentally different strategies. Natwest and DirectLine are both owned by the Royal Bank of Scotland, but are fundamentally different brands both from each other and from their parent – and not just because their products are different. NatWest promises geographical convenience through its local branches. DirectLine promises low prices and direct convenience. This difference is reflected through the service experience they deliver. Consider the implications of your brand upon how you treat each customer segment. In some circumstances, meeting customer expectations may demand the creation of a separate brand. Where quite different segments are managed under a single brand, does each segment require the same service?

3   **Price strategy** – The pricing of products and services must also reflect the brand's corporate promise. Price strategy is not necessarily just about balancing the price of the product

against the cost of delivering it. Many firms whose brand promises superior service destroy their credibility by reducing running costs to the level at which service suffers. When the premium airlines were hard hit in late 2001 and lost market share to low-cost airlines, many cut their own costs in response. However, when this cost reduction affected the customer service for which customers were paying a premium, the brand promise was compromised and dissatisfied customers defected. Cost reduction is an extraordinarily hard game to play against operationally excellent competition: you cannot compete on price unless you turn your business upside down and become operationally excellent as well.

Make sure you are true to the promise of your brand. Mobile telecommunications provider Orange has a brand philosophy about optimism and being transparent. When Orange was launched, the established mobile phone firms rounded charges up to the nearest half-minute or even minute. Orange charged by the second. While the charging structure cost Orange considerable time and money to implement, it had a disproportionate impact on the value it earned the company.

Price strategy must also be integrated with the customer service strategy. The customer service strategy must reflect the price the customer expects to pay. Wal-Mart and Gucci both provide outstanding service – but the service levels are clearly different.

Image

Implementing change in the soft, external aspects of the brand is easier to do practically, but much more difficult to achieve the desired results. A TV campaign, for example, is simple to produce, but you need people to believe it. To do this, the products and services, capabilities and culture must all be aligned to deliver on what the TV advert might promise.

1 **Communication** – Communication is what you make known to your customers – the messages you transmit to them. For many firms, what they communicate is not what they want to communicate. Repeated, unsolicited telephone calls made by double-glazing firms in the UK and aluminium siding suppliers in the US have damaged the companies' brands by communicating a message that says their customers are nothing more than impersonal targets. Credit card providers have become equally unpopular with repeated direct mailings that take no account of customer's preferences or circumstances. These are perhaps extreme cases, but many firms have treated CRM not as a tool to improve how they communicate, but as a mechanism to pester customers more frequently at lower cost. Some insurers make it an objective of their CRM program to contact their customers at least three times a year. However, at what point does attentive become intrusive? This depends not upon guesswork but upon the brand promise. What does the brand philosophy have to say about communication? If the promise is 'cheap' then frequent mailings to 'dear householder' may be just the ticket. If it says 'we care' the same mailing is counterproductive. A customer holding three policies with the same insurance company does not expect to receive a 'dear householder' letter. That just proves that the brand is nothing more than marketing. Communication is regularly ignored by CRM programs. More is not necessarily better and may irritate the customer to the point of defection.

2 **Customer interaction** – The dividing line between customer interaction and communication is a fine but important one. Communication is the message you are sending; interaction is the effect of the two-way exchanges with your customers. We all know what customers value in an interaction because it is what we value ourselves as customers. That is the beauty of CRM – we can understand it because we are constantly

affected by it. We all know the critical features of customer interaction from our own experience as customers:

- ☐ Do customers have to wait to be served? Is the wait acceptable?

- ☐ Are customers treated courteously? If not, why not?

- ☐ Are customers' needs satisfied by the interaction? Does the customer have to be transferred around the company?

No organizational change strategy is complete without an assessment of the current and future desired state of customer interaction.

3 **Social actions** – Whether or not it is a universal sign of growing social conscience, many brands are built at least in part upon a promise of social or environmental altruism. Where social action is part of the brand promise then the CRM program must understand the nature of that promise and deliver against it. Consider some firms that have made social action part of their brand promise. Shell has focused brand building in recent years upon its investment in renewable energy sources and commitment to the environment. Indeed, its website homepage, www.shell.com states: 'Shell businesses exist to meet the energy needs of society in ways that are economically, socially and environmentally viable.' Part of the promise of UK supermarket chain Waitrose is 'environmentally friendly' and it delivers by, amongst other things, refusing to stock any eggs laid by battery hens. The intention is that the customers' perception of social action is transferred from the eggs to the broader proposition. Social action is arguably the most important element of The Body Shop's promise.

Social action is a dangerous card to play. Hungry journalists like nothing better than to toy with the carcasses of the holier-than-thou. However, where the brand does promise social action, then that promise must play throughout the organization so that staff understand and can deliver on that message through every interaction.

Culture

Although image is more obvious to the customer, culture is more obvious to staff. Changing image without changing culture is likely to lead to a disconnection in the customer experience.

1 **Workplace** – Workplace culture strongly influences the customer experience. If a customer collapsed in a supermarket, would the manager go with the customer to the hospital in the ambulance, contact relatives and wait until they arrived? Would the shopping be put to one side and delivered to the nearest relative at no charge? Or would the staff just call an ambulance and leave it at that?

How are your staff empowered to deliver in the workplace? Do your staff see customers as 'punters', or partners? While you cannot train staff to be more human, you can foster behaviours and attitudes towards customers. The British Airways customer care program changed the workplace culture by instilling a different vision of the importance of the customers. Such a change takes time. It is much harder to achieve than any technology implementation, but it is potentially more important.

Call centres have become notorious as the twenty-first century sweatshops. Call centre culture is dictated by a range of factors all under the control of the employer. Targets that reward call throughput will never produce customer-intimate results; they will enforce operationally excellent behaviour. The trend towards outsourced call centres highlights a real issue for firms seeking to improve customer intimacy. The culture of the outsourcer is more likely to be reflected to the customer than that of the brand owner.

The workplace has an enormous impact upon how staff connect with each other and with customers. This is why UK retail banks have invested heavily in transforming their branches from grim, barred complexes to open, airy rooms.

2 **Leadership style** – Leadership style dictates the priorities of the business and so organizations that seek to emphasize customer intimacy must nurture leadership behaviours that deliver it. Management bonuses based on delivery against cost targets will deliver a cost-focused customer experience. For the operationally excellent, this is fine. For the customer-intimate, it will inevitably result in customer disillusionment because customers attracted by a promise relevant to their needs find that relevance is compromised by the focus on cost.

Some influential business leaders of the past century – Henry Ford, Jack Welch, Bill Gates, Walt Disney, Tom Siebel, Richard Branson – were so influential that their personalities become an integral element of the brand. Branson is a challenger and Virgin's brand idea reflects him. When customers picture the brand they may even picture the leader rather than whatever logo the brand has adopted.

Leadership, at all levels of the company, dictates how staff deliver on the brand promise. Leaders set the example of their firm's attitude to customers. They create structures that reward behaviour that they deem important. If the UK double-glazing industry has developed a poor reputation for intrusive direct selling, the direction of its leaders is to blame.

3 **Knowledge sharing** – Chapter 5 highlighted how knowledge management was the foundation of the CRM program for value shops. Therefore, particularly for shops, but to a lesser extent for all organizations, how knowledge is shared within the organization can have a significant influence on the brand.

In many organizations, knowledge is power, yet knowledge sharing is poor and poorly rewarded. Even value shops, which depend on knowledge transfer between their staff, tend to reward staff for knowledge obtained rather than knowledge shared. In many organizations staff are effectively discouraged from knowledge sharing because it will reduce the organization's dependence on them and thus their importance.

SUMMARY

1 How you would rate the relative importance of organizational and technological change in your organization? What are the respective priorities that your firm allocates to each?

2 What is your firm's brand idea? What is your corporate promise to your customers and other stakeholders? Could you articulate it? Could all your stakeholders write it down – especially key customer contact points like call centres? Do all your brand vehicles deliver it? To what extent would your version of the brand idea be aligned with those of your colleagues? How well do customer-facing staff understand the brand promise?

3 How well does your organization support your brand? Consider each of the 12 aspects of the Wolff Olins framework from the perspective of the current state and the future state.

CHAPTER 13

CREATING THE CUSTOMER-CENTRIC ENTERPRISE

INTRODUCTION

Followers of fashion are among the few who relish change. For most people in most organizations the status quo is a comfortable place to be. When change is threatened, the feelings of anxiety, loneliness, powerlessness, and putting your personal reputation on the line are perfectly normal. How understandable, then, to deem CRM as being about technology – boxes do not have feelings. How common to find CRM initiatives, large and small, ignoring the people aspects of change. From a new call centre system to a new segmentation model, from a new brand to a new set of business processes, CRM affects not only your customers but also the staff who make relationships happen.

Organizational change addresses a critical component of the enterprise's delivery of CRM: its people. Effective and rapid deployment of business solutions and realization of the desired business results requires active management of the 'people issues'. Organizational change mobilizes individuals and groups at all levels. It implements a disciplined process that enables people to work in new ways, making breakthrough results possible.

If management wants to change how the firm connects with its customers, it has to change the organization. Whatever the strategic context, shifting the organization and addressing the human side of change is the hardest thing to do and getting it wrong is the most frequently quoted reason of why CRM initiatives fail. Unlike technology change, organizational change is intangible. IS departments may have well-understood methodologies to implement new software, but few companies have as clearly understood methodologies to change how their people think, act and do their work with customers.

How many people would make a start on their dream home by ordering 1000 m (3280 feet) of 15 mm (0.60 inches) diameter copper pipe for plumbed central heating without first checking whether the architect had specified warm air central heating? Yet many CRM programs begin this way because they are seen as a technology procurement decision. Most technology, no matter how functionally effective, economically efficient or technically elegant, will fail to realize its potential value until it is integrated into the business along with the organizational changes needed to support it.

This chapter looks at the goals of organizational change, then describes the seven drivers of change – the seven factors that will have to be changed in order to realize your CRM ambition. It then lays out an eight-stage strategy for making organizational change a disciplined process to define future organizational characteristics within your business.

WHY DO ORGANIZATIONAL CHANGE?

Failure to manage the human side of change is the major reason why CRM fails – particularly in value shops and networks that are service industries. Many managers and executives simply do not have the experience necessary to manage the speed and complexity of change because it demands a different set of skills. The organizational change required to implement CRM has the following goals:

☐ **Enable and accelerate CRM** – Without organizational change, CRM remains a technology initiative and will probably only highlight the disconnects between your staff and your systems.

☐ **Support stakeholders** – Stakeholders – affected parties – may experience increased levels of anxiety and stress (e.g. because they have to use new systems). Organizational change must plan initiatives to help those stakeholders deal with the disruptive effects of change.

☐ **Integrate with process and technology changes to provide holistic solutions** – Processes, technologies, applications, data flows – even locations and facilities – may be affected by CRM, and must all be integrated into the change program.

☐ **Build and maintain processes for organizational learning** – Change programs must identify and implement responses to unexpected organizational challenges as well as to the expected ones.

☐ **Build the organization's capacity for sustaining change** – The pace of change is accelerating. Organizational survival is now more dependent on maintaining the agility to respond to an unending series of change requirements. 'We've done change' is no longer an option; creating a process for continuous change is hard but necessary.

The key to realizing the maximum potential benefits from CRM programs is to successfully manage the transition for each of the stakeholders, all of whom may exhibit apprehension and resistance to change. Allowing change to 'just happen' rather than systematically managing it, will delay the implementation of new and more effective processes and systems, cause unwanted attrition and lower productivity. The transition, therefore, needs to be managed carefully.

Experience increasingly suggests that many CRM implementations are accompanied by degradation in customer experience – as customer-facing staff struggle with new technologies that they are ill-equipped to understand.

THE SEVEN DRIVERS OF CHANGE

Experience has shown that seven characteristics are the most significant enablers or drivers of organizational change (see Figure 13.1).

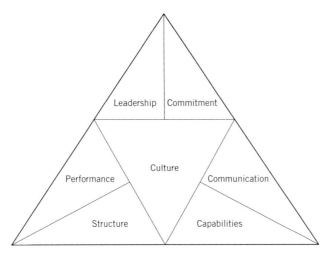

FIGURE 13.1: The seven drivers of change

How should these drivers influence plans to introduce a CRM program?

1 **Leadership** – The leadership team must align with the CRM ambition and engage in driving behaviours and practices to mobilize people and accelerate change. They have to inspire staff to go the extra distance to deliver value for the customer. CRM may, and perhaps should, also change what leaders do, how they think, how they are remunerated, what measures concern them, what departments they manage. The greater the extent of CRM ambition, the greater the leadership challenge.

2 **Commitment** – Employees throughout the organization must be ready and willing to overcome resistance to change, let go of old methods, and rapidly embrace new ways to think, behave, and perform in the service of the customer. An essential stage of the change program is to map staff resistance and readiness.

3 **Culture** – Culture lies at the heart of the framework because all the other elements shape the organizational culture. The organizational work climate and the employee values, norms, and behaviours must continually adapt to new business situations and encourage excellent performance. It is hard to change the culture, but documenting, sharing and encouraging a set of values and behaviours will ensure that at least your staff understand your vision. Culture cannot be transformed by revolution, but it can be nurtured and shaped over time.

4 **Communication** – Employees at all levels must be actively involved in change. They need to share critical information in a timely manner and be engaged in honest, interactive dialogue. You must develop a communication plan to explain to staff what is happening, when, why and how it will affect them. Too many CRM technology initiatives are initiated without staff understanding why.

5 **Capabilities** – Employees at all levels need to develop and share the skills and knowledge to perform in new ways, quickly. If you are changing how you connect with your customers then you probably need to train staff in complaint resolution, adapting their delivery to different customer segments, and detecting customer issues early. Different training may be needed for different levels of empowerment. Will your CRM program help staff to make it work?

6 **Performance** – Performance processes, incentives and management practices must consistently recognize, reward and reinforce the achievement of CRM goals. For example, the program may seek to implement new customer-oriented targets such as successful customer outcomes and customer satisfaction rather than call to win ratios and product profitability measurements. The greater your desire to change, the greater the need to change your targets – and the greater the need to use these to drive different performance from staff.

7 **Structure** – Jobs, work groups and departments, and roles, responsibilities and relationships may all change.

The greater the gap between where you are and where you want to be, and the greater your level of CRM ambition, then the more critical the organizational change program becomes.

THE ORGANIZATIONAL CHANGE PROCESS

All of these seven drivers play through the eight stages of an organizational change program listed in Table 13.1.

1 Define the purpose and scope of change.

2 Develop an organizational transition strategy.

3 Complete a gap analysis.

4 Prepare the organizational transition plan.

5 Develop, test and implement initiatives.

6 Mobilize stakeholders.

7 Perform architectural integration; monitor and adjust.

8 Measure organizational change process outcomes.

TABLE 13.1: The organizational change process

Define the purpose and scope of change

Start with an understanding of customer value. Consider your UOVP®, a concept explored in Chapter 8. Establish when and where the customer wants what, and how the offering is to be delivered. Stand in the future and create a vision of the firm that can deliver on your promises. Establish a compelling reason to change.

Is the nature of the planned change incremental, step, specialized, or far-reaching? Slow, incremental change is often not enough. Setting stretch targets that are far-reaching, complex, and so radical that you may not know exactly how to achieve them, can be a powerful way to alter the mind-set of the organization. The impact on the organization is significant; it requires business re-engineering, which is fast and frightening.

Are you up to the task? Is the management team or leadership group aligned to the change imperative and committed to it? Do they believe that they are ready and capable to take these issues on and provide effective personal leadership?

Gather the leadership team and discuss the following questions to test their alignment and resolve:

- [ ] Why do we have to change? What are the consequences of no action?

- [ ] How urgent is the need? How much time is there for mobilization and how much time is there to carry it out?

- [ ] How great a change is needed? Who is most affected and receives the most value? For customers (of course) there must be a close fit between their needs and the value offered; for shareholders there must be profitability over time with the appropriate return on assets and growth. But for employees, will the organization be a place where people learn to grow and reach their potential? For society, will it provide employment and prosperity in a responsible way, contributing to the economy as well as local needs?

- [ ] What is the outcome you want? Will it strengthen the organization's business value? Will it support delivery of the promise made in your UOVP®?

- [ ] From what direction should you approach change? Do the measures proposed match the targets set?

- [ ] Are you setting your priorities correctly? Is there conflict within your organization – do marketing and engineering want to be product leaders while manufacturing are striving for operational excellence? In that case, should manufacturing be spun off to pursue its own agenda?

- [ ] What should be the scope of the change? What are you willing to take on? Should the changes be piecemeal, or should you tackle information and IS, business processes, management and control systems, job skills and cultures, beliefs and values all at once?

- [ ] What should be the pace of the change? Are redundancies required, or a major recruitment drive?

- [ ] What should be the style of the change? Do you have the skills and capacity to manage it on your own or do you need help?

Develop an organizational transition strategy

With the sponsorship and commitment of the leadership, you can develop a high level organizational transition strategy that defines the content, direction, and scope for the needed organizational change. Some elements of the strategy will be sufficiently clear to define specific early actions, such as initial stakeholder communications and enrolment activities, which need immediate attention. Others (e.g. enabling a culture change, implementing a new performance management system, or changing the organization structure) will probably need to be informed by more assessment and analysis before acting.

Complete a gap analysis

Gap analysis is the key process for converting the organizational transition strategy into an organizational transition plan to enrol stakeholders and prepare them for the impending business change. The gap analysis provides an objective assessment of the distance between the desired organizational future state and the current state of the organization. This clarifies the specific challenges that the transition plan must address.

Prepare the organizational transition plan

The organizational transition plan converts the transition strategy into initiatives that are appropriately sequenced and integrated with other components of the complete business solution.

The plan includes the designs for these organizational initiatives, which address stakeholder transition needs, bridge gaps in stakeholder readiness, and respond to sources of resistance. For example, initiatives might include producing technical education programs and user documentation to develop stakeholders' abilities to perform new processes and use new business applications; developing high-performance team models; and designing and implementing performance management and reward programs.

The organizational transition plan is also used to communicate the organizational change strategy and approach to key stakeholders, and provides the basis for the development of organizational initiative work plans. In addition, it is used to estimate the resources required for developing, testing and implementing organizational initiatives. The transition plan keeps a focus on the higher level transition issues to be managed in parallel with the deployment of specific initiatives.

Develop, test and implement initiatives

Some organizational initiatives will result in physical products (e.g. technical education and user documentation). These will typically be carried out in parallel with the systems development stages of conceptual, logical and physical design. Other types of organizational initiatives (e.g. building high-performance teams) are less tightly integrated with specific technology and process activities. These initiatives will follow development paths that are appropriate to the content and context of the initiative.

Organizational change requires some different models from those used, very successfully, in the service of systems architecture. The 'products' of organizational change initiatives are, at times, emotional or behavioural. Yet outcomes, such as high-performance teams and aligned and committed leadership, are no less important than physical assets, such as technical training programs, in achieving the intended business results.

Organizational initiatives are monitored for effectiveness as they are deployed and progress towards critical organizational outcomes is continuously assessed. This will indicate which initiatives need to be modified or replaced.

Mobilize stakeholders

Some organizational change activities may need to be developed and deployed before the comprehensive organizational transition plan is ready – for example, to strengthen leadership competencies, build awareness and commitment to the business change, or to mobilize stakeholders.

Many of these early stakeholder mobilization activities need to continue throughout the business change program, and so are incorporated into the organizational transition plan as organizational initiatives.

Perform architectural integration; monitor and adjust

Significant organizational change is almost always affected by unexpected events. Changes in business strategy, new technology solutions, and organizational restructuring (including mergers and acquisitions) can quickly render a transition plan obsolete. The structured organizational change process must include continuous assessment and monitoring of changing organizational conditions and requirements, so that these changes can be accommodated in the planning process. It must also measure progress towards targeted organizational change results, and use that information to modify plans to enable the transition to be more effective. For example, results and information received from stakeholders during a roll-out of a specific initiative may suggest changes to the organizational transition plan, or even the previously endorsed overall organizational transition strategy.

It is best to view the organizational change process as a continuum of responses to changing organizational transition requirements rather than strict movement through discrete stages. It is an iterative process that takes account of the changing business needs.

Measure organizational change process outcomes

The effectiveness of an organizational change process is not determined by thoughtful analysis, thorough organizational assessments, comprehensive plans, and well-designed and appropriately deployed initiatives. Rather, it is judged by the achievement of stakeholder transition goals and the intended business results, in coordination with effective technology and process changes.

Structured organizational change places significant emphasis on the measurement of results. It measures overall progress in achieving the transition goals throughout the duration of the change program. These targets provide early confidence in the organization's progress in managing the business change – or early warnings of lack of readiness or continuing resistance that will need planned responses.

SUMMARY

1   If you have ongoing CRM initiatives, or have previously implemented such initiatives, consider how well each initiative managed organizational change. Understand where organizational failures compromised either the success of those initiatives, or, worse, became obvious to customers.

2   Consider each of the seven drivers of change within your organization. Understand where you are and where you want to be, and the implication of that journey for your CRM program.

3   For all subsequent CRM initiatives, frame an organizational change strand in the project and follow the eight-step strategy. Even if the level of ambition is low and the scope of change is limited, this will take little effort but will mitigate one of the largest risks to success.

4   In any and every CRM initiative, make someone responsible for organizational change. Never embark on any CRM project, however insignificant, without putting a structure in place to address the organizational implications.

PART  5

DELIVERING CRM

The scope of the technologies that fall under the CRM banner is as ill-defined as the CRM definition. Some restrict CRM to customer analytics; others perceive it as call centre software. There is no right answer. The scope is so broad that we must break it down. The danger in doing this is that we leave you with the impression that CRM technology is distinct 'silo' initiatives. It is not. A CRM delivery program will typically involve some or all of the initiatives described in this section. Read each chapter with a notional volume control beside you and turn it up, down or off, depending upon its relevance to your business.

The first three chapters of this part look at non-customer facing technologies: the internal technology initiatives normally bracketed under the heading of analytical CRM. Chapter 14 looks at customer consolidation – exploring the single customer view. Chapter 15 on customer intelligence considers what we can and should know about customers. Chapter 16 opens up campaign management and discusses how marketing to individual customers has grown to be a central component of CRM.

In the subsequent three chapters what the customer sees (operational CRM) is examined from three perspectives. Chapter 17, on multi-channel customer care, discusses the challenges of constructing a multi-channel and multimedia strategy. In Chapter 18, sales and service self-care explores the implications of self-service, primarily the internet. Finally, Chapter 19, on sales automation, examines how CRM can improve the sales process.

CHAPTER 14

CUSTOMER CONSOLIDATION

INTRODUCTION

To misquote Jane Austen, it is a truth universally acknowledged that a company in possession of customer data must be in want of a single customer view. The single customer view is a sacred cow of CRM and often regarded as its foundation. Particularly for value networks, the single customer view also becomes a legitimate customer expectation. If a business cannot understand the entirety of its relationship with a customer then it cannot understand that customer's value. For example, call centre staff cannot see that this customer visited an outlet the day before; an internet customer cannot accept a quotation delivered by post; marketing sends the same letter twice to the same customer, and both letters offer the wrong product at the wrong point in the buying cycle; customers must send three address change letters because the customer details associated with their three products are held in three different systems.

The single customer view is often an essential foundation of corporate attempts to improve CRM but many get it wrong. Organizations have invested in customer databases in order to create a single view. Yet OTR Group[1] surveyed 1500 firms in six European Union countries and found that only 27 per cent of those who had implemented a data warehouse were able to identify quantifiable financial benefits. Attempts to create single customer views regularly run over budget, start (and end) without a clear definition of tangible benefits and cost millions. One problem is that two concepts share the same expression. We need to investigate this and clarify the expression.

TWO CONCEPTS, ONE NAME

Single customer view disguises two concepts worth differentiating. A single view of a customer means that a relevant picture of an individual's relationship with a firm is available to staff or systems at the point of connection with the customer. Staff are able to perform transactions across products (change one, update many) and offer service that reflects knowledge of customers' previous interactions. A single view of customers means data

[1] OTR Group, 'Do the Benefits of Datawarehousing justify the Costs?', report published by OTR Group, 1997.

regarding all customers is stored in one place. This delivers specific value: it is easy to make comparisons between customers to enable segmentation; to perform profitability and risk analysis; and to construct marketing campaigns. There are four reasons for making the distinction:

1 **The physical implementation may be different** – The technology emphasis of a single view of a customer is primarily operational and is typically implemented through channel management systems such as call centres and the internet, or data stores within a line of business or operational CRM system. Data stores are often delivered with CRM applications. There may be multiple systems of this kind, so that not all customers will necessarily be stored in a single place. Conversely, a single view of customers has a primarily analytical purpose and the technology emphasis is upon storage and analytical tools. Data marts and data warehouses offer the central storage point.

2 **They are used for different purposes** – A single view of a customer is typically a sales or customer service driven initiative and enables staff and systems to have a relevant view of a customer during an interaction. A single view of customers is typically marketing driven. The emphasis is upon collecting comprehensive data that enables marketing campaigns to be derived, and profitability, risk and propensities to be determined across the customer base.

3 **The data captured, stored and deployed by each concept is different** – The emphasis in a single view of a customer is to display the subset of relevant data necessary to manage the interaction effectively. In a single view of customers, comprehensive data is required to enable patterns to be analyzed. Thus 'click streams' – web page hits – will never be required in a single view of a customer, but are increasingly important within a single view of customers, to help understand internet behaviours.

4 **The applications implemented by the organization are different** – In a single view of a customer, the application emphasis is on connecting customer data to data in line of business systems. In a single view of customers, the emphasis is on storage and analytical and marketing tools to understand customer profitability and risk and to build campaigns.

A single physical customer data store could perhaps drive the organization's CRM efforts, but particularly for large organizations the differentiation between operational and analytical customer databases is important. The sheer volume of data may mean that a single corporate database is impractical. And for technical performance, brand, business unit and feasibility reasons, splitting customer data may be appropriate, to enable different units to own and manage operational data while the data required for analysis is managed centrally.

We will return frequently to the distinction, but where we refer to both concepts we will use the phrase *customer consolidation*.

A SINGLE VIEW OF A CUSTOMER

In most businesses, customer data remains an attribute of product or channel data. Few firms have a single overarching customer data store across all business systems. Fortunately, this does not necessarily matter. The larger the scope and reach of the enterprise, the more likely it is that it can operate through multiple data stores. A single view of a customer is only required for the likely scope of a firm's interaction with that individual customer. There is no need to guarantee that the customer will not find discrepancies. The business must balance the risk of poor customer service caused by disconnected views, with the customers' expectation of service. Use the matrix in Figure 14.1 to determine whether or not a single view of a customer should be a priority.

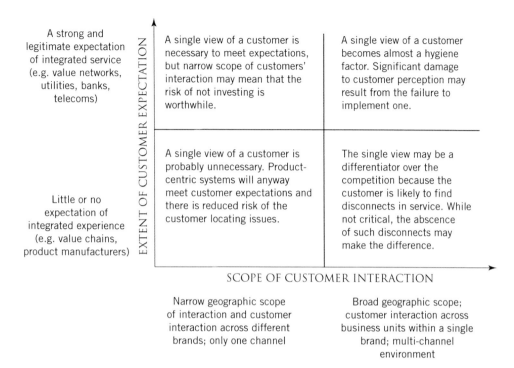

FIGURE 14.1: Single view of a customer

The greater the extent to which customer service is integral to the customer's perception of value, the greater the risk a firm takes by not ensuring the availability of a single view of a customer. That is why for service companies, particularly value networks, customer consolidation becomes an essential CRM foundation.

For example, for a car manufacturer (a value chain) operating in the Netherlands, Italy and the UK, the chances of a customer experiencing the disconnects in service between those three countries is minimal. Each country can have a separate customer data store. However, an airline (a pool) that operates in the same three countries must ensure that customer service is coherent, and so needs a single data store. Here, the scope of the operational customer data store will typically be a single country, but is ultimately bounded by: the scope of individual customer interaction points (across all three countries); the extent to which service is critical to the customer's perception of value (high); and the risk that the firm takes by irritating the customer (defection is likely).

Where a firm operates under different brands, then operational data stores may have to be fragmented. For example, a customer whose home is insured with UK insurer Directline will not expect Directline and its owner Royal Bank of Scotland, which manages their bank account, to share their contact details. Quite the reverse: they may be irritated to discover that the two brands share information. Customers have allegiance to brand not corporation (one of the points of developing brand), so separation of brand legitimately means that different brands can, and possibly should, operate with separate customer views of the same customer.

However, this is not the case for consolidated brands – particularly for value networks, where consistent experience is paramount. When insurers CGU and Norwich Union merged, customers were informed that their relationships would be operated under the Norwich Union brand. At once, this created an expectation of consistent experience, and customers with both CGU and Norwich Union policies had a legitimate expectation that one contact could resolve all queries.

In such mergers, brand consolidation almost always runs ahead of customer consolidation. The customer-centric firm must consider consolidating customers before or alongside brand. If it does not, it risks simultaneously promoting the brand and damaging it by providing fragmented service. Worse, the customers who notice the fragmented service will be the customers with multiple products or services (at least one in each of the merging companies), and these are likely to be the best customers. Brand consolidation without customer consolidation risks your most valuable customer relationships.

A SINGLE VIEW OF CUSTOMERS

A single view of customers has an analytical purpose. It delivers the capability to analyze the customer base for marketing, strategic direction, profitability and risk. The framework shown in Figure 14.2 helps determine whether or not a single view of customers is worth considering.

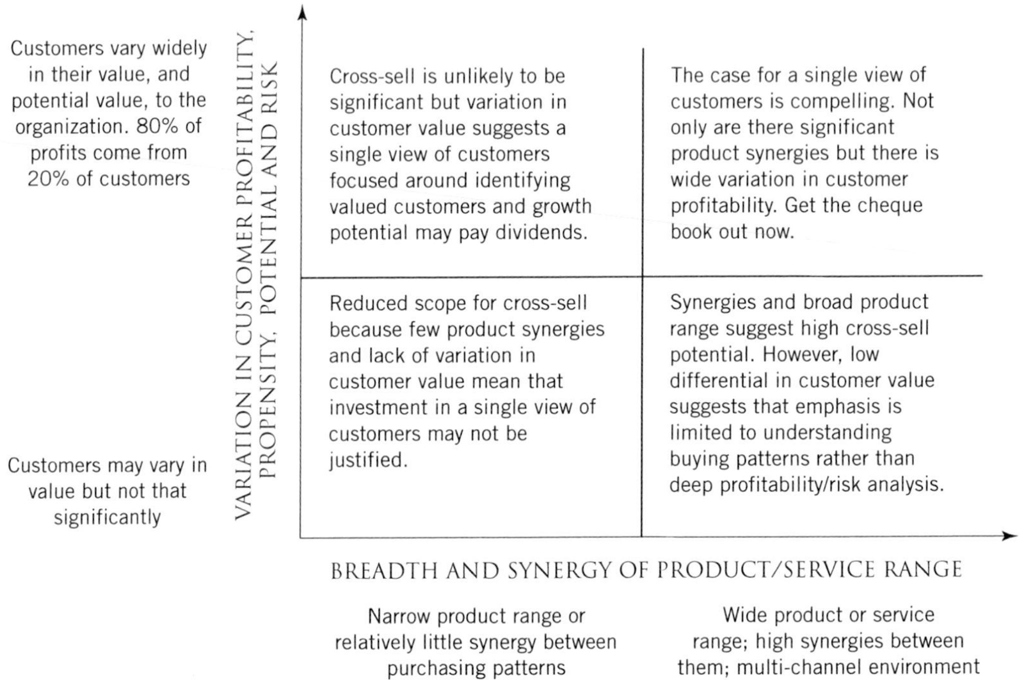

	VARIATION IN CUSTOMER PROFITABILITY, POTENTIAL AND RISK →	
Customers vary widely in their value, and potential value, to the organization. 80% of profits come from 20% of customers	Cross-sell is unlikely to be significant but variation in customer value suggests a single view of customers focused around identifying valued customers and growth potential may pay dividends.	The case for a single view of customers is compelling. Not only are there significant product synergies but there is wide variation in customer profitability. Get the cheque book out now.
Customers may vary in value but not that significantly	Reduced scope for cross-sell because few product synergies and lack of variation in customer value mean that investment in a single view of customers may not be justified.	Synergies and broad product range suggest high cross-sell potential. However, low differential in customer value suggests that emphasis is limited to understanding buying patterns rather than deep profitability/risk analysis.

BREADTH AND SYNERGY OF PRODUCT/SERVICE RANGE

Narrow product range or relatively little synergy between purchasing patterns   Wide product or service range; high synergies between them; multi-channel environment

FIGURE 14.2: Single view of customers

The wider the potential scope of the relationship and the greater the degree of potential synergy between products or services, the more worthwhile a single view of customers is. This does not mean that products or services must be similar – supermarkets have synergy between products because customers purchase shampoo and cat food in a single transaction.

The benefits of a single view of customers are driven by three perspectives:

1   Service behaviour towards customers can be based on customer value – you can treat more valuable customers better. However, this needs customer value to be integrated into operational systems – typically requiring costly and demanding interfaces, application development and staff retraining. Any publicity about such discrimination may damage the brand.

2   Customer marketing can be adapted in line with calculated needs and propensities. Marketing is typically central to the business case for a single view of customers. Success ratios (and customer satisfaction) should increase because the customer is more likely to want the offering, so waste should be reduced. The fly in such ointments is the high implementation cost of the single view. If IT capital construction comes out of the IT budget, and operational management out of the marketing budget, then both IT and marketing may be happy, but the firm may not have a complete picture of the overall value of the investment.

3   Corporate strategy can be directed by customer analysis. For example, if you know that 70 per cent of the most profitable 50 per cent of customers operate by preference through the internet, then additional investment in technology and marketing around self-care makes sense.

Unfortunately, investment in a single view of customers has a poor record of delivering tangible ROI. Certainly the construction challenge is considerable, but more significant is the disconnect between analysis and doing something differently as a result. To address that, a customer consolidation strategy is required.

DEFINING A CUSTOMER CONSOLIDATION STRATEGY

Many organizations view customer consolidation as an IT function because it depends on databases. Technology enables customer consolidation, but other groups besides IT should be involved in the formulation of the strategy. These include:

☐ **Marketing** – A primary use of customer consolidation is in customer marketing – analyzing data, and creating and executing new strategies.

☐ **Sales** – Customer consolidation can provide a wider range of data to the salesperson. The strategy should identify sales data needs.

☐ **Customer service** – A primary driver should be improved customer service. However, without organizational intervention, customer service staff will not make use of the data effectively to drive improvements.

☐ **Legal** – The growing data protection implications of data storage should be considered.

Branding customer consolidation internally as a change program, rather than as a technology project helps establish the right mind-set. The strategy should answer five questions:

1 **What are the processes for owning, maintaining, refreshing, accessing, and using customer data?** How will the consolidated data be used? This may sound obvious. It is not. Many firms invest in customer consolidation without a clear understanding of exactly what is going to be done with it. You must define processes to determine, for example, how and how often, data will be extracted from what sources and consolidated; and how and how often, data be will cleansed and data quality monitored.

2 **Who in the organization is responsible for these processes?** Figure 14.3 shows the four categories of information users. A particular organizational unit will typically fall into two or more categories.

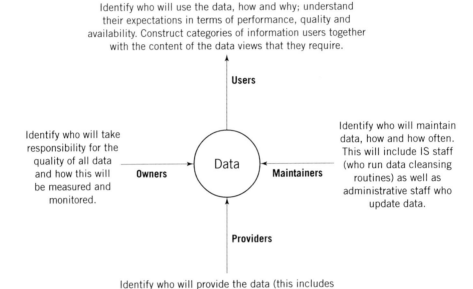

Identify who will use the data, how and why; understand their expectations in terms of performance, quality and availability. Construct categories of information users together with the content of the data views that they require.

Users

Identify who will take responsibility for the quality of all data and how this will be measured and monitored.

Owners

Data

Maintainers

Identify who will maintain data, how and how often. This will include IS staff (who run data cleansing routines) as well as administrative staff who update data.

Providers

Identify who will provide the data (this includes customers), how and in what format. Identify likely quality issues with the provided data and use this analysis to understand where duplicate data can be provided from multiple sources.

FIGURE 14.3: The four categories of information users

Remember that customer consolidation only delivers benefit if people use the information. It may sound obvious but it is worth stating in the strategy before spending millions.

3 **What data will be consolidated, how and where?** Three aspects of data should be considered: scope, structure and quality.

Data scope

An instinctive reaction may be to assume that a consolidated view is a comprehensive view. It is not. Storing click streams in an operational data store will adversely impact performance and provide no value. However, in data warehouses such data may be critical to determine customer behaviour patterns and website effectiveness.

We can characterize data scope at five levels, as laid out in Table 14.1. The strategy should identify what data is available in each category, how it will be used and by whom.

DEMOGRAPHIC	Largely static information, such as name, sex, address, contact numbers and date of birth. Consolidation of this data is integral to all customer consolidation programs.
TRANSACTIONAL	Information about interactions with customers. This includes contact history. The quantity of data is far greater than demographic data. Transactional data required for analytical purposes by marketing will typically be significantly more sophisticated than that required by the operational customer service user.
BEHAVIOURAL	Information about customer behaviour, incremental and accumulated over time. An example is click stream analysis. It is of prime importance in a multi-channel environment because it dictates how, when and where your customers want to connect.
RELATIONSHIP	Information about relationships between customers. Depending upon the industry, knowledge of the relationship between customers (and prospects) is becoming more important. Purchases can be made at individual, family or household level. For example, home insurance will be a household decision: writing to both husband and wife separately, offering the same insurance service is redundant. Typically, relationship data needs to be derived, but it can often be derived quite easily (two people live at the same address, share the same name and have birth dates within ten years of each other).
DERIVED	Data about a customer that the customer does not necessarily know, calculated using analysis tools. Typically, derived data includes customer profitability, customer growth potential, customer propensity (to buy, to die, to leave) and customer risk. Data protection alarm bells ring loudest in this category.

TABLE 14.1: The five levels of data

Database structure

A specific structure is one that embeds specific corporate structure and practice into the database. For example, a company that manages all customers through a network of branches could implement 'branch ID' as an attribute of each customer. This would mean that every customer would belong to a branch. Conversely, it could make the structure generic and implement 'owning unit ID' and 'unit type'. The latter structure will be more flexible if the firm installs a contact centre and acquires direct customers through this channel. However, the former is more understandable to the business as it exists. Owning unit type would be either 'contact centre' or 'branch' and the owning unit ID could be the number of the branch or the contact centre. This is harder for system users to understand, but it is more flexible. Similarly, 'post code' could be structured as XX99 9XX but this format is specific to the United Kingdom; a generic postcode structure could not impose such formatting. There are advantages and disadvantages of each, as shown in Table 14.2.

SPECIFIC	GENERIC
✔ Understandable	✘ Understandable
✔ Accessible	✘ Accessible
✘ Flexible	✔ Flexible
✘ Extendible	✔ Extendible
✘ Stable	✔ Stable

TABLE 14.2: Specific generic data structure

The analysis of structure is time-consuming but critical. The millions spent on customer consolidation could end up being duplicated if two specific customer databases are merged following corporate merger – or even worse, the objectives of the merger defeated because the databases are kept separate.

Data quality

Perfect quality is impossible both to achieve and justify. However, firms must determine acceptable tolerance levels. What is an acceptable delay in updating data? For example, after receiving written notification of an address change how long is acceptable for that change to be disseminated across the organization? What percentage of error in fields is acceptable? The cleansing of significant data volumes requires automated tools, which cannot be perfect. How many and which fields can acceptably go wrong?

Data quality represents one of the biggest challenges for customer consolidation. Quality issues are either pragmatic or inherent, as shown in Table 14.3.

QUALITY ISSUE	DEFINITION	EXAMPLE PROBLEM	PROBLEM CAUSES
PRAGMATIC	Whether the data is fit for purpose	A user has hit enter by mistake on the first answer 'agricultural worker' in the occupation drop-down box – so the firm thinks its customers are all farmers	1 Field defaults 2 Drop-down boxes 3 Careless entry 4 Delay in running update job
INHERENT	Whether all fields are filled with recognizable values	50 per cent of all postcode fields are blank preventing effective geographic analysis	1 Optional fields 2 Previous data conversion exercises

TABLE 14.3: Pragmatic and inherent quality issues

A customer consolidation program should include three data quality projects:

1 **Data cleansing** – To measure data quality and take corrective action.

2 **Quality contamination** – To identify where poor data quality is being introduced. This should identify clerical processes that introduce errors and software application problems that lead to poor quality (such as field defaults).

3 **Quality strategy** – To define future processes including executive responsibility for quality, penalties and reward schemes, quality targets, quality standards, and staff training in data quality.

4 **What applications will feed the data? What applications will be used to run it?**

The major application decision is whether to build or buy the customer database. All operational CRM applications, and many analytical CRM tools, include a customer database in their package. You need to assess whether this is the best solution:

☐ The data structures, which will be generic, may be difficult to adapt to your corporate needs. If your proposed structure is generic this may not matter.

☐ The data sources may be difficult to integrate. There are three options: replication of data from existing product and service applications; conversion of data from an old system onto the new system; and data integration, where the CRM tool accesses data in real time.

Conversely, building your own database also has drawbacks:

☐ The cost may be prohibitive. Building the structures for customer databases from scratch is one of the most complex CRM activities an organization can undertake.

☐ It is likely that the structure will be specific to your business. This may make it more difficult to integrate third-party applications at a later date.

5 **What technologies will be deployed?**

The technology requirements depend on the data volumes and data usage. A single view of a customer may be introduced as part of a wider operational CRM implementation. However, the customer consolidation strategy will help significantly to shape the core of that operational CRM program. Alternatively, the single view of a customer may be pulled into existing operational systems from a single view of customers.

A single view of customers will normally be constructed as a data mart or data warehouse. A data mart represents a smaller investment and is focused upon a specific purpose such as marketing.

SUMMARY

1 Consider how relevant a single view of a customer is to your business. Factor in the importance of the customer's expectation of service and the likely scope of the customer's interaction.

2 Consider the relevance of a single view of customers. Factor in potential product and service synergies and the breadth of your offerings.

3 Define a customer consolidation strategy as part of your overall CRM strategy. Consider all five aspects of the strategy as defined in this chapter.

CHAPTER 15

CUSTOMER INTELLIGENCE

INTRODUCTION

Knowledge about customers, whether inside people's heads or stored in databases, is CRM's fuel. Without it, you are blind to customer needs. You can target only markets, not customers. You can measure satisfaction only by the absence of complaints; retention only by maintaining the customer base; and loyalty not at all.

Use of data analysis for direct marketing grew rapidly during the 1990s and has become standard practice. For example, the technique of 'champion-challenger' models was developed for testing the effectiveness of one approach against another. With this technique, candidates for a marketing campaign are selected from the customer database based upon research or 'gut instinct'. This selection model is then challenged with a more scientific approach – the challenger. If it outperforms the original model, it becomes the champion. In turn it is then challenged using yet more sophisticated models.

Customer intelligence techniques are widely used also to help understand customer behaviour on websites, by analyzing website hits (click stream analysis). Such analysis enables general corporate learning (reshaping of websites to reflect customer behaviour) and individual customer learning (targeting personalized offers).

The technology can provide endless analyses, but advances in analytics have not taught firms to ask the right questions. Successful deployment is driven not by what you *can* know about your customers – which is almost limitless – but what you *need* to know. No technology can tell you that. Customer intelligence technology can never replace customer intelligence strategy.

ONE SIZE DOES NOT FIT ALL

The different value configurations need to gather and deploy customer intelligence in different ways. Value chains (e.g. supermarkets) and some pools (e.g. cinemas) may have detailed transactional data for loyalty card customers, but not for all customers. If the chain analyzes a self-selecting cohort of customers, then it is blind to the rest. It is difficult to determine the characteristics of the customers that join when you do not know the characteristics of those who do not join. These companies typically use customer and transaction data to generate segmentation and targeting models that can be used to cross-sell. They may also develop propensity models to identify the probability that customers will respond to products offered via certain media.

Value shops typically have a wealth of customer data in the heads of their staff, but poor corporate knowledge of those customers. They need a comprehensive knowledge management program that connects data about customers with that about available solutions.

Value networks (e.g. utilities), and some pools (e.g. airlines) store detailed customer information for every customer. They need to relate customer information back to behaviours or resource usage patterns. This enables customer segmentation and targeting, but is not aimed at providing information on the propensity to buy particular products. Rather, it identifies patterns of consumption from and contribution to the network. The technology may be the same, but the questions are different. For example, consider what happens with many insurance providers. Many insurers operate as chains, and see customer intelligence as a tool to identify cross-sell potential. However, calculating the customer behaviours that dictate ratings for pricing policies (e.g. occupation and claims record) is often undertaken separately. The result is that marketing successfully recruits customers who display the right purchasing characteristics but that the actuarial department would pay to avoid. Actuaries should calculate the right price for each customer segment, but a significant number still work at market sector level. For any network, behavioural analyses must be tightly integrated with marketing sales analysis. Indeed, the former should drive, not be driven by, the latter.

For a network, the customers' experience within the network is integral to how they obtain value from it, so obtaining customer feedback is an important component of CRM strategy. The insurer must understand customers' claims experience, the ISP must identify if customers are consistently unable to connect. Customer segmentation becomes crucial in order to group individuals with similar behaviours and experience requirements, rather than with similar purchase propensities.

The way firms create value for customers affects how they deploy customer intelligence, as shown in Table 15.1.

CUSTOMER SEGMENTATION STRATEGIES

There are different approaches to segmentation.

Strategic segmentation

The first approach is strategic – at corporate level, top down and based on market data. Two facets of each segment are particularly significant and must be understood:

1 **Segment potential** – Can the firm address the segment's requirements through its current products and services? Will new players target this segment? What are the barriers and cost of entry? What is the potential market share and value?

2 **Segment profile** – What is the size of the customer group? What are the needs of its customers? Is the segment a growth segment? How many competitors are playing in the market? How mature is the segment? What makes the segment unique?

VALUE CONFIGURATION	KEY DATA SOURCES	TYPICAL CUSTOMER INTELLIGENCE
Chains and pools that do not identify customers (e.g. manufacturers and food retailers)	☐ Loyalty card holders – customer details ☐ External data – based on census data regarding customer types (e.g. Acorn (CACI), Mosaic (Experian)) ☐ Market research on customer buying habits (e.g. shopper surveys) ☐ Transactional information on product/ service take-up	☐ Customer segments based on product sales and demographics ☐ Propensity to upgrade product or service ☐ Propensity to cross-sell product ☐ Propensity to respond to certain media ☐ Price sensitivity ☐ Share of wallet analysis ☐ Cost of product sale by customer group
Shop	☐ Customer demographics ☐ Fact-find on customer needs ☐ Contact history with the company representative(s)/account manager ☐ Transactional data	☐ Customer worth ☐ Degree of match between customer 'needs' and the customized solution ☐ Relationship strength ☐ Understanding complex iterative buying process
Networks and pools that identify customers (e.g. retail banks, insurers and airlines)	☐ Customer demographics ☐ Customer contact data and transactional data ☐ Resource and network usage history against entitlement ☐ Referral patterns (friends, neighbours, work colleagues, family etc.) ☐ Customer satisfaction feedback	☐ Customer behaviour segmentation ☐ Affinity (emotional loyalty) to brand ☐ Customer worth – lifetime value analysis ☐ Understanding of the decision process and the method of interaction preferred by the customer ☐ Resource usage (i.e. behaviour patterns)

TABLE 15.1: Customer intelligence most relevant to the different value configurations

Strategic segmentation is usually undertaken during corporate strategic planning. However it should not be a one-off exercise, but must be updated at regular intervals. See Chapter 11 for more information about strategic segmentation.

Marketing segmentation

The second approach is bottom up, using detailed transactional data that gives an insight into how current and past customers have made purchases and asks: how the customer has been serviced; what the customer purchases, the frequency of purchase, when the customer purchases; and the demographics of the customer. However, even all of this transactional data rarely explains why a customer has purchased from a particular firm, and hence market research data is required to answer questions around purchase motivation. Many geo-demographic (e.g. Acorn, Mosaic), lifestyle (e.g. Peoples UK) and psychographic (e.g. Social Value Groups) segmentation models are available, and many companies factor these into their final marketing segmentation model.

Detailed marketing segmentation can be used for both customer retention and acquisition. Segment profiles should provide insights into the customer experiences, successful communication messages, media used, and response mechanism. A company can draw a profile of its best performing customers and assign more effort to recruiting similar customers.

The segmentation analysis is also key to the development of the business case. Different customer groups are going to exhibit different retention rates, customer product ratios, customer service costs and level of contribution.

For companies not used to working with a customer segmentation strategy, it is important to limit the number of clusters – in practice, probably between eight and 12 groups. Any more may require a complex strategy to manage and to monitor effectiveness, any fewer and the segments may be insufficiently granular.

Customer value measurement

Wherever possible, marketing and sales activities must be measured in terms of the value they add to each customer segment. You need to put targets in place: soft (qualitative) as well as hard (quantitative). Customers always have a benchmark in mind that must be met before they perceive additional value, and that benchmark may rise over time as competitors raise the stakes and customers become more sophisticated. You must also be aware that certain experiences can have a negative impact on the customer. The incremental effects of good and bad experiences, and the interaction between activities need to be considered. Such an analysis will form the basis for constructing a customer retention strategy.

GETTING INTIMATE

All firms need sufficient customer intimacy to meet the accepted standard in their industry. But as the level of customer expectation rises, increasingly firms need to ask how intimate they need to be, and to adjust the complexity of customer intelligence that this requires. These adjustments may be manifested in various ways. For example:

☐ **Address** – This may relate simply to salutation ('Dear John Doe' rather than 'Dear householder'). Some organizations are taking this even further and testing the designs of envelopes on customer perception.

☐ **Timing** – Timing can be irrelevant, for example, direct mail from credit card firms. However, messages may be timed to coincide with a particular customer event, such as policy renewal or birthday.

☐ **Content** – Many firms do not record which offers a customer has received in the past and whether the offer was accepted. Credit cards firms often bombard the same prospects for years with similar offers.

☐ **Relevance** – Finding out whether the customer (or household) has the product already can be a challenge. Trying to sell them the same thing twice proves to customers that they are merely numbers and kills off any attempt at customer intimacy.

☐ **Price sensitivity** – For a customer-intimate firm, price differentiation between different customer segments may be important.

☐ **Customer response** – The operationally excellent firm may direct customers to cheaper media and its call centre targets may be based around the time taken to cover set scripts. The customer-intimate firm should measure successful outcomes from the customer's perspective and monitor satisfaction.

☐ **Conflict** – More than one unit may be communicating with the customer about the same purchase. For example, a car manufacturer interacts with the customer during the buying cycle through a franchise dealer. After purchase, the manufacturer may send the customer a regular magazine highlighting new product innovations or deals established with partners. Simultaneously the franchise dealer will be sending out reminders about service frequency. It is important to ensure that the messages are aligned.

The role of customer intelligence is to take raw data about customer, product holdings, transaction history and value, contact history and media responsiveness, and use this data to support appropriate decision-making processes and operational customer strategies about the level of personalization, customization and relationship that an organization should be undertaking.

Intuitively, storing and analyzing customer data seems like a 'good thing'. This is why so much customer intelligence investment is driven, not by fact-based business cases, but by assumptions that once the business has the answers then the important questions will emerge. Wrong. The business case must be built first – otherwise the firm that has bought a tail will waste millions searching for a dog to wag it.

The customer intelligence strategy should identify the questions to which the business needs answers. These questions can be grouped into eight categories reflecting different possible CRM objectives, as shown in Table 15.2.

CUSTOMER INTELLIGENCE TECHNOLOGIES

There are broadly two categories of technology that underpin customer intelligence.

OLAP (Online Application Processing)

This enables data to be 'sliced and diced' in different ways and to examine underlying historical trends. It answers questions such as 'How many customers that have cancelled orders are female, aged 25–30 and live in the south-east?' However, it does not help you to determine whether this is a relevant question to ask in the first place.

Data mining

Data mining techniques can be split into three categories.

1 Predictive analysis is used to predict a target variable (e.g. response/no response to a campaign; uptake of a product; or claim value). A propensity model can then be generated which determines how likely a customer is to do something (buy a particular product, fall ill, get married etc.) based on the behaviour of other customers sharing similar characteristics.

2 Descriptive analysis looks for data patterns within the customer data. The analyst is not constrained by a target variable but looks for clusters of customers that exhibit homogeneity in some way. Segmentation models are typically built through descriptive analyses initially.

3 Simulation analysis runs through different scenarios and sees the impact on a predefined end objective – such as 'How many customers would be lost if all outlets in towns with a population under 10,000 were closed?'

TECHNOLOGY ENABLES, NOT REPLACES, JUDGEMENT

The thousands of firms that have invested in data mining technologies have the potential to obtain highly sophisticated customer intelligence. They may think that their customer intelligence problems are solved. Far from it. Advances in analytics can result in the fundamentals being forgotten. As techniques become more specialized, the distance between the businessperson with the questions and the analyst with the answers may extend to the point where invalid results are drawn, incorrect targets measured and marketing campaigns fail.

CUSTOMER MANAGEMENT

OBJECTIVE	TYPICAL PROBLEM
Contact analysis:	☐ Who to target with what message
☐ Customer acquisition	☐ How to increase customer numbers profitably
☐ Customer retention and loyalty	☐ Which products to push to which customers
☐ Cross-selling	☐ Which marketing and sales activities are most effective
☐ Campaign analysis	☐ Which distribution channel is most effective for the customer
☐ Media and channel analysis	
Customer profitability (lifetime value)	☐ What the cost drivers are, whether they differ by customer type, and if so, how
	☐ What the customers' value to the organization is
	☐ Which customers you should spend more on attracting
Branding	☐ Whether the brand means the same to everyone – or whether different customer groups have different brand values
	☐ How branding activity links with emotional bonding, and how this adds customer value (especially for a value network)
Location analysis	☐ Which outlets are performing well, and whether this is due to access, competitor activity, size of store, products stocked, location (probably most relevant for value chains)
Basket analysis	☐ What the most common purchases are
	☐ Which purchases are made together
	☐ Whether customers are grouped by transaction type
Customer satisfaction analysis	☐ Whether the customer is satisfied with the products
	☐ Whether the customer is satisfied with the service
	☐ How complaints are handled
	☐ What the satisfaction is with each channel
Pricing	☐ Price elasticity and sensitivity analysis (what happens if prices increase?)
	☐ Optimization of the pricing strategy by customer type
Business planning and control – forecasting volumes/value	☐ Business planning
	☐ Ongoing management targets

TABLE 15.2: Different CRM objectives ask different CRM questions

Consider five areas where analysis cannot replace human judgement:

1 Understanding the quality of and relationship between data and the associated business rules. Vasectomies can only be performed on males, British children under 17 cannot drive on public roads. Analytical tools do not know this unless they are told. So, what is it relevant to tell them? If you are researching unknown patterns, then you risk giving the technology irrelevant rules and ignoring the critical ones.

2 Missing and extreme data values. If only 5 per cent of the occupation fields are filled but those 5 per cent are filled with 'architect', it does not necessarily mean that all customers are architects. It is more likely that 'architect' was first in the drop-down list of occupations. Again, only human minds can assess this.

3   Understanding the robustness and fit of the model, and interpreting its meaning. If DIY enthusiasts are less likely to buy holiday insurance, it may be that they do not tend to travel abroad – although it may be that they are less risk averse and so less likely to take out insurance. No machine can make that judgement.

4   Laying a sensible trail of analyses. The most effective analyses use a basket of different techniques, applying them incrementally to achieve results: the result of one analysis influences the direction, and the appropriate techniques, for the next analysis.

5   Looking at data in isolation. Customer data from websites must be analyzed with data generated through other 'touch points', because customers use different media for different phases in the buying cycle. Closing down the outlet because all the business comes through the web may be the right answer, but what if all research is done in the outlet, and then purchase occurs later through the web?

Customer intelligence technology demands, not replaces, the application of human intelligence. The risk of taking decisions based on false information increases with the complexity of the technology. Thus, before thinking that analytical investments have failed, address the human intelligence issues.

SUMMARY

1   Consider your segmentation strategy. How sophisticated is it? Would your firm find it valuable to construct different strategies to drive, for example, corporate decision making, marketing and customer service?

2   Ask yourself how intimate your customer intelligence needs to be. Consider how granular your analysis must be in the context of your value discipline.

3   Draw up a list of the top ten questions you would like to know about your customer base. Then ask five of your colleagues whether you have that information to hand in your business and whether it informs your decision making. If not, initiate a customer intelligence strategy now!

4   Think through the analyses you would like to have. Would predictive analysis help your firm? What about simulation analysis? Think of a few 'What if?' customer scenarios for your firm and speak to your information systems department about how much it would cost to get the answers.

5   Deploy customer intelligence technology to help the customer intelligence strategy, not to create it.

CHAPTER 16

CAMPAIGN MANAGEMENT

INTRODUCTION

The primary value of customer intelligence for most organizations is when it increases the capability to sell their products and service more effectively and efficiently. Consider a direct mail or telephone campaign that is completely blind – it makes no attempt to determine whether or not prospect A is any more likely to purchase than prospect B. What are the chances of success for such a campaign? The primary value of customer intelligence for most organizations is the capability to sell their products and service more effectively and efficiently than would otherwise be possible. Consider a direct mail, or telephone, campaign that is completely blind – it makes no attempt to determine whether or not prospect A is any more likely to purchase than prospect B. What are the chances of success for such a campaign? The answer is probably limited. But consider the business case if you target the customers that you deem most likely to buy:

☐ Focusing upon customers who are likely to buy reduces the cost of a marketing campaign because each target group to generate a given level of business is smaller (e.g. to gain 100 customers you need only target 1000 prospects instead of 5000).

☐ If the new customer is more likely to want or need the product or service, and less likely to have just succumbed to the marketing, the chances of a long-term relationship (i.e. creating brand loyalty) are increased. In many industries, particularly for networks, customer profitability is created over time rather than on initial product purchase. In saturated markets it is the long-term relationship that becomes important. If campaign management only captures the short-term customers that have succumbed to marketing, they are less likely to be retained in the longer term.

☐ Prospect or customer dissatisfaction is reduced. Prospects that do not have children may be irritated by marketing for children's savings plans; those that have double glazing in their homes may not appreciate calls asking whether they want it. Increasingly, customers provide slight variations in their name and address in order to identify which company is using their data for marketing, and to punish that company by withdrawing their business.

☐ A virtuous circle is created in which the marketing precision becomes ever better. For example, you target a group whose probability to purchase Service X you calculate to be greater than 35 per cent. Based on the actual responses, you find that of this group, men have a greater probability to respond than women. The next campaign you run for Service X is to men only and this increases the probability to 50 per cent. And so on.

This chapter introduces the art (or science) of campaign management. The simplest view of a marketing campaign is as a series of marketing communications to a defined audience. Most are 'push' communications – the organization initiates the marketing contact and pushes the message to the potential customer. However, recent research shows that 70 per cent of marketers are struggling to capture customer attention because of the explosive growth in the volume of marketing messages. Even coordinating their own messages is increasingly taxing for many organizations as mass marketing techniques fail to make themselves heard in a crowded multimedia environment.

FROM 'JUST IN CASE' TO CONTEXT

A primary function of marketing is to communicate the value of the brand or offer. Marketers spend more than $1.3 trillion globally annually on marketing projects. It is estimated that expenditure on integrated marketing campaigns incorporating online advertising, e-mail and direct mail will exceed $63 billion by 2005. Inevitably, a significant proportion of marketing investment is wasted – ignored or thrown away. In the past it was difficult to measure where this wastage occurred. The emergence of marketing communications systems integrated with customer information repositories now enables marketing effectiveness to be measured at an individual level. The communication feedback loop – 'closed-loop CRM' – theoretically creates a virtuous circle in which more precise campaigns are targeted at a more precisely identified audience.

This supplier-centric view of marketing involves finding customers for the company's products. However, CRM thinking demands that marketing leverages the customer relationship by understanding which customers have the highest propensity to be influenced, and targeting communications at the customer events that will generate the greatest return.

Campaign management should be about finding products and offerings for customers, presenting relevant information and offers at appropriate customer events, and seamlessly interweaving these communications with the customer activity cycle. Firms increasingly seek to focus their event-driven communications at an individual level and coordinate these communications with the customer's activities. Marketing communication becomes an ongoing process as customers progress through their buying and consumption experiences. The objective is to deliver the right message, at the right time, to the right person through the most appropriate media. Event-driven marketing has evolved from the historical 'just in case' communications, to communications focused around the customer's activities and delivered in an appropriate context.

KNOW YOUR CUSTOMER

As discussed in Chapter 4, a key challenge that faces value chains, such as retailers, is to identify customers uniquely. Although warranty schemes or loyalty cards deliver basic data, knowing who your customers are remains crucial. Increasingly sophisticated marketing communications require increasingly sophisticated data, which is often not captured by chains. Nevertheless, chains can use point of sale technology to capture customer data at the point of transaction. This can yield a richer understanding and insight into customer behaviour than proxy research methods, such as focus groups and home surveys.

Such insight enables chains to identify prospects. Other sources, such as website visits, previous communications and external lists, enable chains to communicate with these prospects. The minimal marginal cost of delivering high volumes of e-mail and internet communications, compared to traditional media such as direct mail, has led to an explosive growth in the use of new media for marketing. It is estimated that in 2001, over 50 billion e-mail offers were made and 82 per cent of web purchases were prompted in part by an e-mail offer. E-mail marketing communications are expected to double in 2002. E-chains, such as Europe's www.lastminute.com, use e-mail offers extensively. This is an extraordinarily cost-effective way to acquire customers. Note, though, that www.lastminute.com's customers are by definition internet-savvy and receptive to e-mail offers.

CUSTOMER INTIMACY DEMANDS RELEVANCE

The greater the extent to which you pursue customer intimacy, the more strenuous your efforts must be to make your campaigns specifically relevant to customers and to their context. Inappropriate marketing (e.g. sending student loan flyers to pensioners or badly-timed telephone calls) can damage a brand that is trying to say 'You're important to us'.

The irony is that firms pursuing customer intimacy regularly spend millions on mass marketing and advertising to tell the customers that they are more than a number; and then millions more on disproving that with irrelevant customer-specific marketing.

Companies can now deliver offers based on customer profitability and tailor communications to include unique offers that will also benefit the customer. However, a firm can only realize these benefits by integrating its communications approach with its customer insight. UK insurer Standard Life claimed response rates that were 35 per cent ahead of target across the range after it integrated its customer database and marketing communication systems.

While customer-intimate companies know they must coordinate their marketing messages with the customer's lifecycle, it has been difficult to join these two activities together. Unfortunately, in many organizations customer marketing uses separate data marts which are only rarely updated from operational customer data or worse, populated from external sources. The connection then becomes impossible. Campaign management technologies can now effectively monitor which customers have and have not responded, and also how long the response took, when and where the offer was redeemed, how much the communication cost and how the customer's behaviour and subsequent value was influenced by that communication. This detailed communication and transactional history over a customer's entire relationship enables firms to fully understand the customer's lifetime value and their own ability to influence and enhance this.

With a customer information repository, the organization can tailor customer communications based upon unique customer events, which can be identified through their transaction history. Alternatively, marketing communications can be sent on the basis of predicted behaviours drawn from past operational experience and extrapolated using data mining techniques. Thus, a website visitor can receive a targeted e-mail follow up that lists the issues a product addresses, and invites them to explore further, to request further information and to nominate the most appropriate communication channel or to decline further contact.

137

Depending on the response, the customer could be directed to other information on the website, offered suitable alternatives or asked for further information. Furthermore, if the user is identified as a known customer, the organization can reflect this in its communications and perhaps persuade them into an immediate impulse purchase.

OPERATIONAL EXCELLENCE DEMANDS UNIFORMITY

Combining marketing communications with customer interactions enables operationally excellent firms to succeed.

For example, the McDonalds brand is known almost universally and the marketing communications can stress a consistent, common product message: the UOVP® for McDonald's in France is the same as that in the US and Japan. Of course, the products being pushed will vary by country. However, the message associated with the products will be broadly the same.

ORGANIZATIONAL DIFFERENCES

Firms pursuing customer intimacy will naturally have a different communications process from those that pursue other disciplines: the combination of planned communications and the customer interaction process enables the customer-intimate organization to engage in a dialogue with its customers. Such dialogues will vary depending on how the customer interacts with the supplier, and how often. For chains, the customer relationship is based around transactions, and communicating these in context will be an important consideration for developing the communication plan. When you buy a car, Ford is unlikely to cross-sell you another vehicle at the same time, but regular communications about service enhancements may make it more likely that you will buy Ford again. Toyota's customer care scheme has raised customer satisfaction levels and repeat purchases.

As customers re-engage with a supplier via a series of transactions, the supplier has an opportunity to enhance those transactions. For example, rather than sending a generic cross-sell offer to a repeat purchaser, it may be more appropriate to offer reduced shipping charges on all purchases. This is good for both sides: it is worth more to the repeat customer than a 20 per cent product discount, while for the supplier repeat orders have a lower cost to serve and promotional costs are reduced.

The customers of a value network have subscription relationships with the network. For retail banks, that subscription – the account – enables or even mandates customer communications. However, networks often have multiple engagements with the same customer via different business units and need to bring marketing communication approaches together in order to manage the entire customer relationship. When a customer is a potential target for multiple messages, it is necessary to determine which messages should take priority. A network must avoid overloading its customers with communications, and draw up business rules that determine customer contact frequency.

The key to resolving this communication challenge is to identify who owns the customer relationship. Some firms have addressed this by developing 'segment managers' who own all customers in a particular segment and are responsible for all sales, marketing and service activities in that segment. Segment managers become responsible for prioritizing campaigns and maximizing customer lifetime value. Segment migration communication strategies migrate customers to higher value segments in a controlled and predictable manner.

A single customer view enables value networks to evaluate how customers are using the network and influence that behaviour via a series of planned communications. For example, a utility may identify that take up of a particular offer has been relatively low. Customer data analysis could predict customers most likely to respond and the utility could then communicate this offer only to likely responders. Indeed, as the firm builds a rich information picture of its customers, it can ensure that only those customers who have or are likely to become high net worth customers receive enhanced service offers. By combining marketing and service elements for high value customers, a company can reduce its marketing investment through more effective targeting, without damaging return on investment.

It is essential to recognize the correct audience. Once they have developed a customer database, marketers can correlate marketing investment with the changing customer behaviours picked up by customer intelligence systems. There has been considerable focus on managing customer 'churn', but a challenge still facing marketing is to understand how marketing communications encourage customers to move between segments – referred to as segment migration.

MORE THAN JUST TARGETING

Campaign management is not just about targeting customers more effectively. There are at least three strategies that firms can adopt using campaign management concepts and technologies to improve the effectiveness of their marketing, other than developing increasingly precise campaigns.

Customer redirection

All value networks have unwanted customers: perhaps those that overuse the network, or incur significantly higher costs to serve. By identifying these customers, organizations can be proactive. For example, a communication to a high cost to serve customer may illustrate the benefits of using the website rather than the call centre. Combining this communication with an incentive – an online discount perhaps – enables a firm to manage customer behaviours. This is campaign management – but not of the 'customer stalking' variety.

Load balancing

By automating communications approaches, companies can 'load balance' the message delivery media to manage costs. If an airline wishes to launch a new inflight service, it could communicate the offer initially to high value business travellers regardless of their location, then roll it out in stages across geographies to minimize operational impact. A staged roll-out means that marketers can assess their most effective marketing communications processes and refine them over time.

As suppliers learn to enhance the value of their dialogues with customers, customers can also enrich the dialogue by bringing service matters or product issues to the supplier's attention during interactions. For example, customers that have called the service centre could be sent follow-up communications and further suggestions.

Community-based marketing

Internet communities of customers frequently discuss product or service issues, and manufacturers of these products can add value for customers by directing them to the appropriate community. This can build customer loyalty, especially if experts or product advocates become recognized and frequent visitors to the community. Through product communications to these advocates and communities, firms can disseminate marketing messages in a non-intrusive fashion. www.ivillage.com has a number of community sites with affiliated marketing programs, such as www.parentsplace.com. However, the downside is that dissatisfied customers can use the community to address their own grievances.

CUSTOMER INITIATED CAMPAIGNS

Traditionally, suppliers always initiated marketing communications. The campaigns were often planned and prepared over a long time period. However, unplanned customer communications – where interactions are initiated by customers, either via the internet or other real-time media – have transformed this landscape. Customer initiated communication is starting to transform campaign dynamics. Customers can now 'pull' information from firms that meet their specific needs at a specific time. Customers enter marketing communication interactions on their own terms.

The complexity of meeting this new communication challenge is immense. The underlying issues of delivering a consistent experience across channels and media and implementing a centralized customer control mechanism remains. Understanding the relevant factors and customer behaviour which a firm can affect, and using this knowledge to modify and influence that behaviour, remains a critical challenge for marketers, regardless of the campaign.

As firms can now monitor interactions with individual customers, it becomes necessary to understand how these individual interactions are processed. If customers buy after three separate contacts, it is difficult to determine the individual factors that influence purchase behaviour. However, by developing a history of these encounters at an individual level across the customer base, firms can develop an understanding of the value to the customer of discrete components of their marketing communications (such as specific offers or personalized features). This requires more advanced analytical technology.

Marketers have yet to fully leverage all the capabilities of the 'touch points' that a customer uses. Truly personalized communications at every touch point will enable marketers to deliver messages in a more targeted manner, thereby reducing the number of messages that it distributes to its customer base.

It has become increasingly difficult to measure marketing response and attribute it to a particular marketing investment because of the escalating number of campaign interactions. By monitoring the interaction between marketing investment and response attribution, an organization can enhance its investments by improving its understanding of their effectiveness.

The success of a marketing campaign cannot be measured solely by a simple response mechanism, despite vendor claims to the contrary. Nielsen NetRatings finds that banner advertisements on the internet are clicked on by between only 0.5 and 0.25 per cent of viewers. However, almost one-third of all advertisement-driven 'conversion events' (a purchase, registration or other marketing objective) happened after surfers had viewed, but not clicked on, an ad banner. Indeed, research suggests that banner ad campaigns created a 19 per cent lift in sales of items bought on impulse. This level of impulse purchasing parallels activity in real world shopping, where it is known that analyzing marketing spend effectiveness is already problematical.

Regardless of how customers are identified, every enterprise needs to be able to track marketing expenditure against customer behaviour before it can develop more sophisticated future campaign approaches using multi-step, multi-stage, multi-channel and context-based communications. Then it can use the most cost-effective medium for the message at the time of delivery, rather than always using the cheapest method of marketing communication.

An organization that has developed its customer interaction management capabilities can individualize customer communications for a sequence of marketing actions based on its business rules and observed customer behaviour. With real-time campaign capabilities, organizations can reduce the cost of these communications by developing an automatic sequence of marketing events. A customer who abandons a shopping trolley on a website may receive a sequence of three e-mails offering special dynamically priced discounts based on the availability of these products in the inventory. Customers who respond to the first of these messages may be more loyal than those responding to the final offer. The loyalty of the first responder can be strengthened with further communications and an appropriate illustration of service benefits, whereas the last respondent's loyalty can be bought for as long as it is cost-effective to do so.

Electronic business has broadened the type of campaigns that marketers can use, and expanded the avenues that a customer can use to respond or initiate contact. While these developments have made the life of the customer easier, they have also introduced unparalleled complexity for firms that try to provide consistent communication and service across multiple channels and multiple touch points.

The growth of unplanned communications processes has increased the risk for suppliers because customer interactions can be lost in an unconnected or uncontrolled channel.

A multi-channel campaign management capability can enable the organization to take advantage of the many customer touch points available, and by enabling the monitoring and refinement of these interactions over time, increase the return on marketing investment.

SUMMARY

1 Consider the level of integration between marketing customer data and operational customer data. Consider the disconnections that exist and the impact of these upon the customer's likely acceptance of the marketing message.

2 Consider campaign management in the context of your value discipline: customer intimacy demands relevance; product leadership has to create need; and operational excellence requires uniformity. How well does your campaign strategy achieve these goals?

3 Develop a customer ownership strategy. Who is responsible for coordinating and approving all messages that are put in front of a particular customer segment?

4 Assess the relevance of three marketing tools: channel and media redirection, load balancing and community marketing. Could your firm benefit from introducing these tools?

5 Understand how well your firm operates across multiple channels and multiple media from both the customer's perspective (right offer, right time, right place) and firm's perspective (right medium, right price, right outcome).

CHAPTER 17

MULTI-CHANNEL CUSTOMER CARE

INTRODUCTION

Here is something that would revolutionize business: customers browse through products at home, purchase them remotely and have them delivered direct to their door. Eliminating expensive outlets means that prices can be lower, destroying traditional competition. It would mean the death of distance and a new form of business. The revolution was catalogue shopping and it happened in nineteenth-century USA. The catalogue did indeed become the primary sales medium for some companies, but for most it became an adjunct to their existing media. The greater change was that catalogue shopping reintroduced, on a large scale, the most common business model prior to industrialization: a direct relationship between supplier and customer.

Fast forward to the late 1990s. The failure of the internet to destroy traditional business indicates that going digital is not too hard or too expensive, but that many products, services and customers are unsuited to digital delivery. It is a multi-channel, and multimedia world, and any firm operating across multiple channels and media needs to consider the interplay between them. The importance of a multi-channel strategy increases with customer expectation that service will be delivered coherently. It is a brave (and probably foolish) organization that ignores this expectation.

DIFFERENTIATING BETWEEN CHANNELS AND MEDIA

The four channels

The terms 'channels' and 'media' are often used interchangeably, but they are not the same. Organizations connect with their customers through different interaction models (channels) using different tools (media). The distinction is important now and is becoming more so because the same medium is increasingly deployed across different channels.

There are four main channels to the customer:

1 Firms can connect **directly** with their customers. The direct channel (which for some firms in the nineteenth century meant only catalogues) has seen an explosion in the number of media that can be applied to it: internet, WAP (Wireless Application Protocol), telephone, digital television, fax, e-mail, white mail. Increasingly, direct channels use a complex mix of media to support a range of different customer interactions.

2 Firms can operate through a network of human **agents**: representatives or intermediaries that act as interfaces. Almost all value shops operate in this way. In 1990, technology support was typically provided through basic mobile computer applications connected to head office servers. In this channel, too, different media are increasingly used. Laptops predominate, but palmtop applications are growing more popular and even mobile phones can be used for giving directions for customer visits. Firms are integrating their contact centre operations in support of their agents.

3 **Outlets**, branches or stores are used to distribute products or services. They are either owned by firms (e.g. bank branches) or are franchises (e.g. fast food outlets). Historically, outlet systems were unconnected with other channels and had no knowledge of other customer interactions. Increasingly, outlets form part of an integrated multi-channel strategy because customers use different channels at different stages of sales and servicing and have an expectation of integrated service across those media.

4 Firms can rely on **partners** to distribute products and services through the partner's own direct, agent or outlet channels. Partnership constitutes a different connection model again, but partner strategy must also be integrated with other channels. If partners represent your brand to your customer – which they do – then their every contact reflects your customer promise.

Therefore the internet is not a new channel – it was a new medium. This is not to play it down, but rather to play it up. The internet, like most media, increasingly has a role to play across different channels.

Many media work across different channels

The number of media is increasing, and now customers often own the device through which they connect – mobile phone, PC or television. Thus, customers dictate how and when they receive information, and suppliers must configure their delivery across a bewildering range of different devices over which they have no control. They have to decide which media to support, and which to ignore. This is increasingly hard. Take something as prosaic as screen display size: what works on a fixed PC fails on a PDA (Personal Digital Assistant); what works on a PDA fails on a mobile phone.

For example, the internet is clearly a significant medium in the direct channel, but it is equally an appropriate medium for connecting to agents, for connecting outlets to head office, and for connecting partners. However, having four internet strategies within one firm to reflect four different uses makes no sense strategically, technologically or financially. Worse, this delivers incoherently on your customer promise. On the other hand, a contact centre may support direct customer connection, but it can support agents equally well. Indeed, restricting contact centres to supporting a single channel, or developing separate contact centres to support direct and agent channels – as many firms do – fails to take advantage of an expensive investment.

The separation of device and function

The type of device we connected with once dictated what we used it for. We used a telephone to make telephone calls, a PDA to record diary and contact details and a television to watch programs. That relationship has broken down. Increasingly, one device is used for multiple functions: PDAs include phones and digital cameras; digital televisions enable e-mail and TV sites. As a result, we need a media strategy that reflects how the same process may be delivered across different devices, each with its own constraints. How can we achieve this? Should we design differently for every device? Yet how can we, when we do not even know what devices will look like?

THE MYTHS OF MULTI-CHANNEL WORKING

Before considering a framework to construct the answers, it is worth getting rid of some of the myths of multi-channel customer interfaces that have become entrenched clichés of the CRM community.

Myth 1: ʻYou need to let the customer choose the channel.ʼ

Wrong. Most successful firms deliberately restrict channel access and only recruit customers who are willing to connect through a specified channel. Therefore, www.amazon.com operates only directly to its customers, and McKinsey's only through its own agents. It is more pertinent to recruit customers that want to work within your defined channel strategy.

The same is true of media. Use only the media that are relevant to your offering. In the UK, Domino's Pizza (a home delivery pizza franchise) has been successful through two media. Its traditional medium was the telephone, but it was an early adopter of digital TV. Domino's experience demonstrates how media strategy must be based on context – where the customer connects – and on need – what the customer wants to do – not upon a misguided intention to be everywhere.

Myth 2: ʻYou need to allow access any time, any place, anywhere.ʼ

Nonsense. Instead, reflect where and when your customer wants to connect with you. Access 24 hours a day, seven days a week has become a bravado statement of intent. If operating within a single time zone, a bespoke furniture supplier will certainly survive without the tiny corps of customers who will abandon them if they cannot order at 3.00 a.m. Customers have different expectations of access depending upon your industry, their urgency and their required outcome.

Myth 3: ʻMulti-channel is about reducing the cost of managing channels.ʼ

Not true. Although firms focused upon operational excellence may perceive operating the channel as a cost, for many – particularly value networks – the channel is an integral component of creating customer value. Channel strategy is about value to the customer, not price. Particularly for networks, and as some have found to their cost, forcing unwilling customers to move to lower cost channels means that customers leave.

Myth 4: ʻSelf-care is the goal and will destroy other channels and media.ʼ

False. Product and service complexity vary enormously. Self-care is one of a number of models that may or may not be relevant, depending upon the complexity of the product. Value shops in particular may avoid self-care altogether because they offer bespoke services. The more product-oriented the offering, the more relevant self-care becomes. For most shops, self-care will never be significant except at the margins because the complexity of the service offered, and the extent to which that service is customized, militates against customers serving themselves.

Myth 5: ❮ Multi-channel is about integration. ❯

Not necessarily. A common CRM mantra is that multi-channel demands integration. It may do, but it may demand the reverse. For example, Mundial Confiança, a large Portuguese insurer, operates primarily through traditional channels. When the firm wanted to enter the direct market, it created a new brand and new company, Via Directa. Not only did this avoid overt cannibalization of existing traditional channels, it also enabled the new operation to reach customers that would not have been attracted to the existing brand.

There are numerous examples where a new brand has been created to extend the customer offer into other channels, rather than integrating new channels within an existing brand. Egg is a UK credit card brand set up by Prudential. Prudential could easily have launched the service under its own brand. It did not because its existing brand was inappropriate for the customer offer, and the new service fell outside the remit that customers expected of the parent company.

CHANNEL STRATEGY

Defining a channel strategy means understanding the interplay of channels and how customers connect across those channels.

Direct

The direct channel has become common across chains, networks and, particularly, pools but not shops, where bespoke solutions demand repeat human interaction. There are usually three main arguments in the investment case:

1 For new entrants, direct distribution demands less infrastructure investment.

2 Operational transaction costs are lower than agent and outlet channels.

3 Many customers will prefer to deal direct than through other channels.

These are compelling reasons, but there are also clouds on the direct channel horizon:

☐ A direct channel will cannibalize other channels because some customers will switch to it. Since agent and outlet channels are based on fixed, relatively inflexible infrastructures, their profitability may be compromised.

☐ Investment in the direct channel is often predicated on substitution: a legitimate expectation that customers will swap from a more expensive channel to the cheaper channel, thus reducing the cost per transaction. However, evidence suggests that customers actually increase their transaction rate (e.g. checking balances more often). While increasing the time customers spend with you is desirable because it offers marketing opportunities, the business case based on substitution may disappoint.

☐ Higher value customers will also move to the direct channel. You may have opened that channel to service lower value customers at lower cost, but a defining feature of the direct channel is that the customers own the media with which they connect (telephone,

PC, television). Not only are higher net worth customers – usually the most desirable customers – more likely to have access to self-care media, but they are likely to be better educated about products and services and to need less advice.

☐ Focusing on cost may lead to poorer service. Direct initiatives which focus exclusively on cost are often guilty of automation at the expense of customer value. Call centres can be the least popular manifestation of the direct channel strategy – customers do not like holding for extended periods listening to repetitive music interrupted by lies about 'We value your custom'. The danger is real: in 2001, more people in the UK were employed in call centres than in the entire manufacturing sector.

A good direct strategy begins by answering the five questions listed in Table 17.1.

1 What value discipline drives service prioritization?
Companies focused on operational excellence can legitimately offer lower service levels to reflect their lower prices. For others and particularly those in service industries, who seek to emphasize customer intimacy and inflate customer expectations accordingly, holding for 15 minutes will be unacceptable.

2 What impact will there be on other channels?
Any firm operating through multiple channels will see the effects when they add a direct channel. This impact must be anticipated by addressing the structural implications, or avoided by developing a new direct brand.

3 Which customers will go direct?
The dream of channel redirection – lower value customers to lower cost channels, higher value customers to higher cost channels – is false. Most firms will find that their most valuable customers are more techno-savvy and are open to using the direct channel. Estimate likely channel behaviour by customer segment.

4 How will substitution balance against increased transaction rates?
Particularly for networks, which provide an infrastructure into which customers 'dip', the direct channel is likely to increase transaction rates.

5 How will you leverage the increased time your customers spend with you?
If the direct channel increases transaction numbers then your strategy should consider how to grasp that opportunity.

TABLE 17.1: Considerations for direct channel strategy

Agent

The primary channel for value shops is agents (e.g. advisors, account managers etc.) who represent the firm's capabilities and customize the offer to the customers' needs. Agents are mobile, expensive, and may be averse both to technology and processes imposed by head office. Where a direct strategy must consider service prioritization, channel impacts, customer segmentation, substitution and marketing, an agent strategy must consider mobile technologies and integrated head office support.

Most agents could benefit from mobile technologies. Where agents represent complex solutions, particularly in shops, mobile support is critical. Mobile is no longer solely about laptops, but equally it is about mobile phones and palmtops.

The agent channel is most efficient if the agents spend most of their time on activities that create value. Chapter 18 shows in more detail how much time is often wasted on administrative activities, such as booking appointments, completing paperwork and chasing customer enquiries. By understanding that the value of agents is manifested in their sales activities, administration can be devolved to a contact centre or direct channels.

Outlet

Outlets remain the core channel for many firms, including most chains. While commodity products, which require minimal customization – books, pet food, office supplies – can be distributed direct, the need for outlets increases with the customer's need to see, smell, touch and talk about products and services. The greater a customers' purchase risk, the greater the need for outlets.

A legacy of the dot.com boom was that outlets were seen as a high-cost channel. So they are, but outlets must be judged from a value and not a cost perspective. Manufacturers of high value items have always judged outlets on value and not cost. For Gucci, the outlet is essential to customer value, while chains with commoditized products see outlets more as a necessary evil.

Outlets can be a useful ally to a direct channel: customers can research online and buy in the store. However, the direct and outlet strategies must be aligned. Few customers use one channel exclusively where more than one is available. If goods are offered through the direct channel which are not available in outlets, processes must be in place for outlet customers to order them. The car firm that sells direct must allow the customer to test drive at the outlet.

Many firms allow partners space in their outlets – department stores may have partners' branded in-store outlets, and this is particularly beneficial where the partner's value discipline is different from that of the host outlet. For operationally excellent firms especially, product leading or customer-intimate partners can enable the expansion of the overall customer offer. For example, the UK DIY chain, Homebase, prioritizing operational excellence has branded in-store Laura Ashley outlets, which offer a customer-intimate fabrics service. If the DIY outlet offered the bespoke service itself, customers might not trust its capability to provide a customized service. Similarly, Barnes & Noble bookstores house Starbuck's coffee outlets. Coffee brewed by the bookstore staff may not be as good as Starbuck's, and would therefore command lower margins.

The considerations which drive an outlet strategy are summarized below:

☐ Judge the outlet from a value and not a cost perspective. Is the outlet an essential part of your value proposition or a necessary evil to sell your products?

☐ If the outlet is part of a multi-channel strategy, how will you integrate it with other channels? If direct and outlet strategies are not aligned, customers which operate across both will be confused.

☐ Can your outlets support your partners and vice versa? You may be able to expand your offer to customers by offering partners space in your outlets.

Partners

Partnerships are increasingly important. Understanding the relationship with partners is key to multi-channel strategy because your partners will be delivering part of your customer promise. Partners can play three roles in the delivery of value to customers.

1 Transactional partners may take responsibility for aspects of customer care at an agreed price and to an agreed specification (e.g. parcel delivery services). While cost-effective and relatively easy to manage, such partnerships are risky. The customer-intimate firm that employs an operationally excellent distribution firm may find their value proposition compromised when the partner insists on tight delivery windows which sit poorly with the customer's expectation. The greater your emphasis upon customer intimacy, the more dangerous cost-based partnerships may be to the customer promise.

2   At the next level, partners may work with your firm to make customer care more efficient. This may involve storing stock within their own warehouses to reduce turnaround time for delivery or shared contact centres to enable scheduling of visits. Your multi-channel strategy should consider how pooling resources (such as internet collaboration or contact centre connections) could enhance customer relationships.

3   A value partner takes responsibility for some part of the delivery of value to the customer. This is a higher risk but potentially a higher reward. This places part of your brand value squarely in the hands of the partner.

Integrating the partner strategy is important because it demands that your organization answers some critical questions:

☐ If your emphasis is on customer intimacy, will a transactional partnership with an operationally excellent supplier damage your value to customers?

☐ Can you pool resources with partners to make customer care more efficient?

☐ Are you willing to allow a partner to take responsibility for part of your brand value?

BUILDING THE STRATEGY

With multiple channels and a multiplicity of media playing across those channels, it is difficult to know where to start. We suggest two simple approaches that, in combination, will rapidly clarify the multi-channel and multimedia challenge within your organization.

Design from a process perspective

One challenge for multi-channel customer care is that many processes involve different channels and different media at different stages. Consider channel strategy from the perspective of the key processes that your customers execute. Customers may use a direct channel to complete initial product research, visit an outlet to view the product, go away, think, and finally telephone an order.

Consider the major processes that involve customers (shown in the example in Figure 17.1 in the bottom row of the swim lane diagram). Each process is something that the customer does, or is done to the customer by the company. Each process may involve different channels (the second row from the bottom) and different media (the third row from the bottom). Not only will this identify the channels and media that must be supported, it will also show the required integration. Using the process map, you can tell what data must be available at each stage of the process and what organizational units will be involved. Most importantly, this approach considers channel and media strategy from your customers' perspective.

Figure 17.1 shows a simplistic example from a notional innovative kitchen supplier. Even at this simplistic level, the sophistication of the information flow between the different media and across the different channels is enormous. In reality, the integration requirements to provide a seamless transition would be much more complex.

Channel and media matrix

The second approach, which should be used in conjunction with the first, is to construct a channel and media matrix. You need to consider how the same media will be deployed across different channels. This matrix will then make it clear which media are required across which

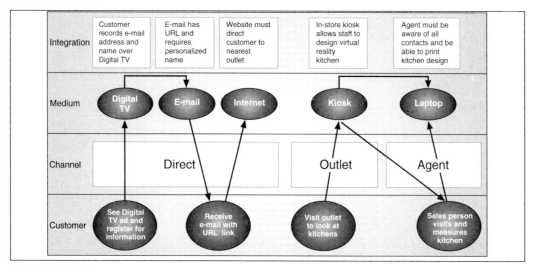

FIGURE 17.1: Multi-channel swim lane diagram

channels. Table 17.2 shows a simple example for a notional organization. At each intersection, you can use the matrix to identify:

- ☐ The current state.
- ☐ The future state.
- ☐ The targets required.
- ☐ The strategy and individual projects within the overall change program.

	E-MAIL	LETTER	TELEPHONE	INTERNET
DIRECT	Metric 50% of customer correspondence by e-mail by 2005			
AGENT		Current state Agents complain about lost mail and response	Strategy Call centre could provide agent support – pilot in region X	Metric 90% of agent interaction through our portal by end 2003
OUTLET		Future state No mail will be received at outlets	Strategy Outlets need head office support – open call centre to outlets and offer priority number	
PARTNER	Future state All correspondence via e-mail			Current state Currently website has no link to Partner A

TABLE 17.2: Channel and media matrix

Some of the cells within the matrix have been completed to show how the matrix can be built up to construct an overall channel and media road map.

SUMMARY

1   Consider which channels and media you use, and understand how well they are integrated. Could customers experience inconsistency across channels?

2   Prepare channel and media strategy from a process perspective. What matters is how customers experience their various interactions. Take a sample number of high volume, high customer impact processes and construct swim lane diagrams to understand the interplay of channels and media.

3   Define the channel and media strategy within a channel and media matrix. Use this tool to understand the current state and to paint a vision of the future state. Draw out the strategies you will adopt to move to the future state and document the targets. Such an approach will at least ensure that you consider where the problems and opportunities lie.

CHAPTER 18

SALES AND
SERVICE SELF-CARE

INTRODUCTION

Self-care means enabling customers to initiate and complete business processes without the need for human intervention on the part of the supplier. Self-care has been important for years – think of vending machines and ATMs – but the internet has become the cornerstone of self-care. Exponential savings in customer transaction costs and the possibility of personalized marketing have caused firms to invest millions. However, self-care involves more than the internet, and self-care strategy is about more than web design. Successful self-care encourages customers to look after themselves. This chapter summarizes the primary considerations for constructing a customer-oriented self-care strategy, based upon the self-care framework shown in Figure 18.1.

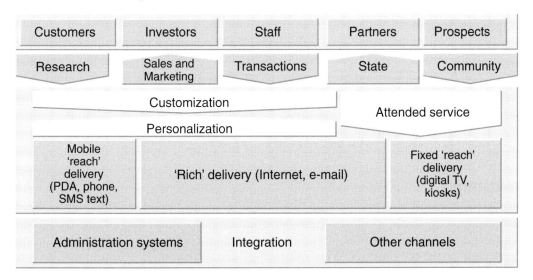

FIGURE 18.1: Self-care framework

WHY SELF-CARE?

There are at least six possible reasons for investing in self-care. A sensible starting point is to understand the balance between them.

1 Sector pressure

The acceptance of self-care varies unpredictably by industry sector. www.amazon.com's success drove Barnes & Noble online, yet Dell's online triumphs have not forced all PC manufacturers to follow. Customized clothing offered on the web (e.g. by Levi-Strauss), although superficially attractive – how many people are off-the-peg sizes? – has failed to revolutionize the clothing sector.

2 Brand reinforcement

A strong self-care presence can enhance brand value. An increasing number of customers use the internet for research. According to Egg, a UK financial services firm, 5.5 million UK citizens had used some form of online banking by the end of 2001 – that is 10 per cent of the population. As more customers surf the internet and are encouraged to do so by their governments, a lack of presence may harm brand recognition.

3 Reduced transaction costs

Significantly reduced transaction costs drove many early business cases for self-care. The analyst Datamonitor has estimated that the operational cost of straight through internet transactions is less than 1 per cent of transactions processed in outlets. However, business cases built on comparative transaction costs can be misleading. They may fail to factor in high capital infrastructure costs. It is not the internet, but straight through integration to back office systems that drives such significant savings. That integration comes at a high cost which must be set against operational savings. Estimates of interaction numbers must also be treated with caution. When self-care is available, interaction levels increase: customers check their account balances every second day online instead of fortnightly at the ATM. If customers continue to spend the same amount of money as always, but add new online interactions, then, as Chapter 17 suggested, the business case looks less convincing.

4 Customer demand

The most internet-savvy customers will not be attracted unless you offer them a self-care environment. The size of this constituency varies by culture (12 per cent of Swedes but only 1 per cent of Spaniards arranged insurance online in a 12-month period, according to Datamonitor), the demographic characteristics of your customer base, and the industry sector. The business case should attempt to identify the numbers of new customers that are likely to be acquired. Such research is relatively easy to conduct. Check the websites of some of the top self-care firms in your sector and you will find press releases or online history proclaiming their successes.

5 Partnerships

The internet enables partnership models that are not possible in other environments. These partnerships extend the breadth of your proposition and may improve customer acquisition and retention. A primary factor in the creation of partnerships is the construction of the interface between the partners. Where that interface can be virtual, partnerships can form more rapidly. Egg built a range of partnerships in its online store, offering discounts for purchases made with an Egg credit card.

6 Customer communities

The creation of a community of customers as a marketing tool is not new. The Harley-Davidson owners' group, mentioned in Chapter 4, has become the cliché of such strategies, in the same way that www.amazon.com has become the touchstone of personalization. Self-care allows communities to be created and managed more cheaply.

The interplay of the above factors can be seen in any business that has integrated the internet into its operations. European low-cost airline, easyJet, exemplifies how self-care can become integral. We mentioned earlier that easyJet sells over 90 per cent of its seats online, offering web customers discounts. As the low-cost airline market grows from its existing 4 per cent share of the European market to an estimated 10–12 per cent, easyJet's low-cost internet customer acquisition model looks sensible. Indeed, for any value pool, the direct channel is a sensible sales strategy. easyJet's model mapped against our six self-care drivers shows a high degree of focus upon cost reduction, brand projection and customer acquisition.

SELF-CARE USER CONSTITUENCIES

There are five different user constituencies and all require different types of interaction:

1 **Existing customers** may be the most important category. Typically, they want to complete transactions (book tickets, notify a change of address, check balances) as efficiently as possible. www.amazon.com's introduction of one-click ordering exemplifies rapid, efficient transactional capability for existing customers.

2 **Prospects** need to research available products or services offered, and to be able to purchase them. If your environment is designed to appeal to prospects as well as customers, good design demands that users are routed through different paths depending upon whether they want to research before they buy. The first is sequential (the prospect needs leading through research and purchase processes); the second is menu driven (the customer wants to select from the different options available). Paths designed for one group may be inappropriate for the other – particularly where the product or service offering is more complex.

3 It may make sense to use the same self-care environment to deliver **staff** services, such as maintaining holiday or sickness records. There are cost advantages in managing a single infrastructure, and integrating a knowledge management intranet with the internet site may be cost-efficient and increase staff awareness of customer-facing information.

4 **Investors** and **research organizations** that comment on your company require different information again. They will be interested in data that is irrelevant to customers, prospects or staff. They require a discrete area where their questions are answered.

5 **Partners** may be either suppliers or distributors. You should ask partners what they want. For example, you might provide advertising for the partner, which can be reciprocated, if the partner is part of your value delivery to the customer. Possibly the partner can process transactions (e.g. invoices) if the partnership involves regular transactional exchanges.

In order to build a successful self-care environment, first identify the constituencies for which the self-care environment is designed. Describe the information that each constituency will seek, and the transactions that each constituency expects to complete. Build a structure that makes it clear to each constituency where to go and what they can do. Self-care environments that do not begin the interaction by asking 'Who are you and what do you want?' fall at the first hurdle. It is the user who defines the success of your self-care environment, not your staff or your web design company.

INTERACTION

Customers may want to do any one of five things through self-care media. The self-care strategy needs to consider whether and how each of these activities will be facilitated.

1 Researching products and services

In January 2002, UK research from BT Finance Industry Solutions and The Henley Centre revealed that the number of people in the UK who used the internet to research financial services information, such as share prices, pensions and mortgages, increased by 80 per cent during 2001. Furthermore, over one-third of the UK population gained some form of financial information over the web. How easy is it for prospects and customers to research the products and services you offer? Many self-care media are poor at quickly and easily explaining what the customer can do. Research does not need to be reactive. Companies (e.g. Netrep) offer software to enable real-time conversations between firms and their customers. This merges the self-care environment with the attended environment.

2 Sales and marketing

The second type of interaction for the customer is to understand the benefits and to purchase or, in the case of complex products and services, to register an interest in purchasing. Any self-care environment has a sales and marketing role. Self-care marketing can be either 'push' or 'pull'. It can work at different levels, from projection (where there is no customer registration and the customer is not identified) to personalization (where specific propositions are targeted at identified individuals).

3 Completing service transactions

The toughest decisions for organizations revolve around the transactions that are self-care enabled. By mapping transactions against the self-care transaction matrix (Figure 18.2), you can consider which transactions are worth enabling in a self-care model. Impact, cost and frequency drive the equation.

4 Ascertaining the status of processes or accounts

A cost-effective deployment is to allow customers to understand the state of processes or account balances. Many insurers find that a high proportion of telephone calls to call centres are chasing claims status. This has three disadvantages. Responding to basic enquiries by phone or letter is more expensive, and places a greater strain on infrastructure than allowing the customer to 'pull' status information from a self-care environment such as a website, or 'pushing' it via e-mail or text message. The customer who wants to determine status by telephone or in writing may be worried about that status, and their perception of your organization could be damaged by your failure to put these facilities in place. Moreover, all call centres have peaks and troughs and high volumes of status enquiries exacerbate the peaks. This could be addressed by a relatively easy to implement self-care status enquiry system.

Your self-care strategy should determine how different status enquiries will be handled. The business case is built around three factors: the number of enquiries received; the cost of

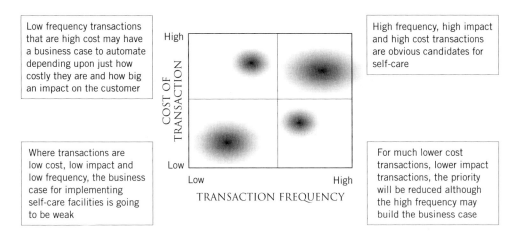

The size of the circle indicates the impact of the transaction on the customer as a reflection of his/her overall relationship with the company (e.g., in insurance, a motor claim has huge impact)

Low frequency transactions that are high cost may have a business case to automate depending upon just how costly they are and how big an impact on the customer

High frequency, high impact and high cost transactions are obvious candidates for self-care

Where transactions are low cost, low impact and low frequency, the business case for implementing self-care facilities is going to be weak

For much lower cost transactions, lower impact transactions, the priority will be reduced although the high frequency may build the business case

FIGURE 18.2: Self-care transaction matrix

answering them through attended channels; and the extent to which the company differentiates itself on quality of service provision.

5 Communicating with other customers

For some companies, self-care may be the tool to enable communication between customers. Indeed, a critical element of the value proposition of an e-network, for instance, The Motley Fool (which provides impartial financial knowledge to its subscribers) is the community of members managed by the company. Such companies must become brokers and enable customers to communicate with each other, but police the interaction to prevent problems (e.g. libellous allegations).

GETTING INTIMATE

Personalization and customization are different: they deliver different benefits, require different investments and are appropriate for different firms. Personalization describes the capability for the firm to adapt delivery media based on expressed or calculated customer needs. A good example is www.amazon.com. Personalization is 'push' technology. Customization describes customers' ability to adapt environments to their own requirements. For example, My Yahoo! (www.my.yahoo.com) allows customers to build their own pages with information drawn from a basket of possibilities (e.g. sports news and television listings). Customization is 'pull' technology.

Another 'pull' technology is attended service. At the end of 2001, this technology was relatively new, but some innovative applications have been developed that enable customers to have a conversation with either a 'robot' (see www.artificial-life.com) or a human through internet chat, voice or video (see www.netrep.com). Only widespread use of broadband technology will secure the place of offerings of this kind.

Personalization

Jeff Bezos of www.amazon.com is quoted as saying: 'Our goal is to provide our 20 million users with 20 million different stores.' The book, *The One to One Future*, by Peppers and Rogers was the sacred text on which personalization was built. Personalization was touted as the internet's killer application. By enabling companies to connect with individual customers, the internet was the e-delivery arm of one-to-one marketing and customer intimacy.

In deciding whether to personalize there are three important considerations.

1   How important is self-care within your overall customer proposition? The less dominant the role self-care plays, the less convincing the business case for personalization.

2   How high is purchase frequency? Unless customers typically make – or can be induced to make – relatively frequent purchases, companies are unlikely to gain sufficient benefits to absorb the high set-up costs. For many value networks, for chains with low purchase frequency (such as car manufacturers), and for shops (where cross-sell may be irrelevant), purchase frequency may be insufficient to warrant investment in personalization.

3   To what extent do you differentiate on customer intimacy? If you pursue customer intimacy, the investment may be worthwhile. Otherwise, unless the industry standard within your sector demands personalization, your resources may be better used elsewhere.

The benefits of personalization are difficult to assess. It is a tool of customer retention rather than customer acquisition. Personalization builds on expressed or calculated customer needs and so customers in effect 'teach' companies what they are interested in. Retention comes because customers are better satisfied, and are therefore unwilling to 'teach' other companies about how they want their world to look.

Personalization is not for every organization. However, it will assume greater importance as self-care itself grows. Nevertheless, handle personalization with care. It is neither the nirvana promised by its disciples, nor the bottomless pit claimed by its detractors.

Customization

The most obvious application of mass customization is to products. However, at least in delivery terms, customization technologies also enable mass customization of information. For financial 'infomediaries' (i.e. an independent web-based purveyor of knowledge and advice about a market), such as The Motley Fool, customization is essential to the proposition. There is a wealth of financial information available and much of the value created comes from enabling the customers to shape the information they see.

The case for customization revolves around two factors:

1   **Complexity of information delivered** – Customers have to find their own way around the world that you present to them. You can offer them a site map but few customers are willing to learn how to use your environment. The more information complexity you deliver, the greater the case for customization. For companies whose business is information enabling, customization is probably essential. These companies succeed by expanding the range of information that they deliver. As information complexity increases, the need to provide customers with the tools to sift through it becomes paramount. Conversely, if the information provided is relatively straightforward, there is little incentive to customize it. Customers will simply navigate through what is available.

2 **Interaction frequency** – If customers only access the self-care environment once every three months, customization may be irrelevant. If the customer accesses the environment every day, it becomes important. If you want customers to establish your environment as their home page or as a favoured bookmark checked regularly, customization may pay dividends – depending upon the information complexity.

The benefit that customization brings is that customers must invest time to customize your environment. Such an investment is likely to deliver loyalty. Customization should be seen as a tool to avoid confusion and to enable navigation through complexity.

RICH VERSUS REACH

In the distant days of the 1990s, self-care came to mean the internet. The internet was never specific to PCs, but even in 2002 most customers perceive it to be. WAP impinged too little on most customers' consciousness. Nevertheless, as devices merge (phones include Personal Digital Assistants, PDAs include digital cameras, laptops become smaller, palmtops become larger, watches become mini-computers, televisions deliver e-mail) the perception that different devices deliver different services is beginning to break down. A more useful framework is to consider richness against reach. Richness is about the provision of higher data volumes, larger files, complex functions and so on – the content that the customer needs. Reach is about immediacy: lower data volumes, mobility and messages.

Mobile reach delivery has capabilities that reflect the customer's urgency to receive information, wherever the customer is.

Some media (e.g. televisions, self-service airport check-in kiosks and ATMs) are fixed but are still 'reach' as opposed to 'rich' media because either they deliver information where the customer is unable to spend significant time reviewing it (e.g. a kiosk or ATM), or because the medium is not suited to the provision of rich information (e.g. television). Digital TV has more in common with the kiosk than the PC as a medium of customer connection. Static TV is unsuited to providing complex information and firms rightly reject it as a primary medium for complex customer servicing. Static reach is about enabling customers to execute straightforward transactions that demand little or no complex information gathering by the customer.

INTEGRATION

In most transactional environments, experience shows that 80 per cent of the cost, and 80 per cent of the risk, lies not in building the self-care environment but in integrating it with the systems that process the transactions.

Beware of all self-care estimates. Many vendors and consultancies reasonably quote for the work that they know they will have to do – the customization and parameterization of the package. However, not only is this the smallest part of the work, it is also the lowest risk. Integrating that environment with a 30-year old business system written and maintained by a programmer now nearing retirement, to enable secure transactions, is far more difficult. This situation worsens as packaged self-care software becomes increasingly easy to customize and parameterize.

Beware, too, of package flexibility and functional richness. It may seem a perverse warning, but all self-care packages require data. That data can either be populated from scratch or (more likely) from existing systems. If the functional richness of the package is greater, more data is required and the integration problem will grow.

There are no short cuts to integration. Data mapping will be difficult. Technical integration may be problematic regardless of the sophistication of the software used to integrate. The older the systems you integrate with and the more complex the data, the worse the integration issue is likely to be.

SUMMARY

1 Build the self-care strategy from the foundation of the user constituencies that the self-care environment is designed for. Consider the various needs of each constituency and how these needs can be delivered most effectively.

2 Broadly, users will want to do five things within your environment: research what you have to offer; consider the sales and marketing pitches and potentially buy product; perform servicing transactions; understand the status of processes, accounts or of any variable aspects of their relationship with you; connect with other customers. Consider which of these are relevant to your firm and how well you deliver them.

3 Approach personalization from the perspective of the importance of self-care media to your proposition, the actual or potential purchase frequency, and the extent to which you wish to pursue customer intimacy. Look at customization from the perspective of the complexity of the information you are offering your customers, and the frequency with which you can reasonably expect them to visit the environment.

4 Understand the rich versus reach debate and how it applies to your organization. Consider the interplay of different self-care media. How integrated are they? How integrated do they need to be?

CHAPTER 19

SALES
AUTOMATION

INTRODUCTION

Corporate sales forces are still, overwhelmingly, the dominant sales model in business-to-business relationships. They remain, despite the growth of direct channels, dominant in business-to-customer relationships, either as mobile agents (typically in value shops and networks) or in outlets (normally in chains and pools). The Siebel software package was launched as sales automation software for mobile agents, and its dominant position in the CRM market created a widespread perception that CRM was a sales automation initiative. As Siebel grew, thousands of firms invested in sales automation. Then two things became clear.

Stories began to emerge of failing sales automation initiatives and of millions spent on initiatives that ended up unused. It became apparent that although software could drive huge improvements in sales effectiveness, success or failure was dependent not upon the software (which by and large was, and is, effective) but on the integration of that software into the business and its acceptance by the sales force. Traditionally, salespeople are independent, competitive individuals who see their value in their knowledge and experience – not in their keyboard skills.

Meanwhile, some claimed that the internet was going to destroy the sales force. Business-to-business relationships would be managed through net-markets, which would enable firms to connect directly with each other, rather than relying upon competitive legions of salespeople. Self-care systems would enable customers to serve themselves, and the old sales force models would founder. CRM was becoming personalization and not sales automation; e-CRM and not CRM. For a short time, sales automation became a ghost town and tumbleweeds rolled down its empty streets. However, slowly people realized that although the internet was a powerful new medium, it did not make existing models redundant.

These twin revelations served to drive a more mature attitude to sales automation and a realization of what works, and what does not. Sales automation remains an important component of CRM strategy for firms that rely on the agent channel to explain the benefits of complex products and services. It will continue to do so.

PLAYING THE GAME WITH DIFFERENT RULES

Although sales automation remains as important as ever, the role of the sales force is changing and the rules are different. This affects how software must be deployed. Agents will remain an important, probably dominant, channel for non-commoditized products and services for the large proportion of the customer base that requires face-to-face, advice-based sales. It is difficult to envisage a situation where most value shops, being knowledge based, and chains that sell high value products, will not be primarily dependent upon their salespeople. The more customized the solution, or the higher the value of the offering, the more the company depends upon someone to sell it. It is hard for a website to explain complexity.

The size of that face-to-face customer constituency varies dramatically by country and industry, and it depends upon a range of cultural and historical factors. A recent Datamonitor report showed that in 2001, 19 per cent of British and Swedish customers arranged insurance face to face, while the equivalent figure was 85 per cent in Germany, and 67 per cent in France. Nevertheless, we can expect to see a continuing shrinkage in, and transformation of the role of sales forces overall. This is due to a number of reasons:

☐ There is a move away from large numbers of less skilled representatives employed on the Darwinian principle of 'survival of the fittest', towards a smaller body of more focused and knowledgeable representatives: 'employment of the fittest'. Commoditized products and services will be sold increasingly through the direct channel in most industries and particularly in the business-to-customer sector.

☐ The impact of direct channels has been to shrink sales forces, forcing firms to consider whether to retain this channel. Fewer competitors each take a (potentially) larger slice of a smaller, and shrinking, cake. Those that remain in the game have to play it better. The management of the integration of different channels (discussed in Chapter 17) becomes one of the greatest challenges for companies still playing the agent game.

☐ The disparity in cost of distribution through sales force and self-care – and the transparency of this disparity – forces companies to focus the sales force's attention more precisely. Inevitably, higher distribution costs can only be recouped through higher prices. Yet prices are increasingly transparent and salespeople need to raise win rates to justify their high cost to their employers. The traditional focus of salespeople is upon large numbers of low value customers – those without the knowledge to serve themselves. This is being replaced by an emphasis upon lower numbers of higher value customers. Using an expensive channel to service lowest value customers does not make sense.

SUCCEEDING WITH SALES AUTOMATION

There are four critical success factors for firms wanting to make a success of sales automation.

1 **An educated sales force** – Salespeople increasingly require better knowledge of products and services than previously. This superior knowledge is required to avoid mis-selling, and to meet stringent qualification hurdles, particularly in industries such as financial services. Most of all, it is an essential differentiator where more educated customers seek not a clarification of complex products, but the provision of relevant, customized solutions to specific needs. More frequently, customers now undertake their research on the internet and the salesperson becomes a customizer of the offering, rather than a proxy researcher for the customer. In this environment, salespeople need to be empowered with corporate knowledge and not trained in cross-sell techniques.

2 **Closely targeted leads** – Salespeople must improve their win rate to sustain their incomes. Sales forces have historically spent significant efforts prospecting, but increasingly it is better to do this at head office, where the more sophisticated data analysis technologies discussed in Chapter 15 combine with a growing wealth of data. Firms must deliver prospects to sales forces, rather than use an expensive channel in less productive research.

3 **Better diary management** – Diary management must be improved so that salespeople visit the right customers at the right point in their buying cycle. Salespeople need to sell more to each contact. Again, the role of technology is critical in understanding the buying cycle. CRM analytics can reveal which customers buy what and when. Delivering this information to salespeople becomes ever more important. Diary management also requires tight integration between salespeople and the contact centre that manages their visits.

4 **Head office support** – Companies must make more effective use of the rich customer data locked into their head office administration systems, to enable more professional sales force support. Campaign management and customer segmentation can all be improved if salespeople have access to embedded corporate knowledge.

MORE THAN LAPTOPS

To most IS staff, sales automation means mobile laptop applications replicating head office systems every night. This picture is too narrow. A successful model focuses staff upon their core competence by making smart use of integrated, collaborative customer management technologies. First, you must discover what sales force time is spent on activities that could be better managed at head office. If you split sales force time into four categories – administration, servicing, sales, learning – then only the third and fourth of these should be primary sales force activities. Many salespeople also spent considerable effort on the first two. Administration can consume enormous amounts of time if salespeople are struggling with complex processes designed for the convenience of head office. Moreover, processing servicing transactions is rarely a sound use of an expensive channel – except where it hides a sales lead. Instead, wherever possible persuade customers to serve themselves or to use remote channels, such as contact centres.

A successful sales automation strategy integrates three technologies:

1 Salespeople require a relevant **knowledge management tool** to enable the collection and distribution of customer data, needs analysis, and calculations. Most of these applications are designed for laptops. Particularly in the Far East, there is an increasing interest in palmtop tools. However, these cannot deliver the same function as laptops, if only because of the physical restriction of the display size.

2 **A contact centre** is needed to contact suspects, identify prospects, plan appointments and conduct initial needs analysis. Integrating the contact centre with the sales force both cuts costs and significantly enhances sales force performance. If tightly integrated with the sales force, the contact centre can answer sales force queries, process servicing transactions, and absorb more of the burden of administration and servicing activities.

3 A **data mining or analysis capability** is required. Many firms' business administration systems have rich customer data that can be used to identify prospects. Combining this with data about buying patterns, supplies contact centres with high quality contact lists to schedule sales force visits and to provide better customer information. You also need a quality control

function to manage basic, but critical, targets (such as the percentage of arranged visits kept and percentage of successful visits). Feeding these results back into the analysis function creates a virtuous circle in which salespeople receive ever-higher quality leads.

TECHNOLOGY INITIATIVES OFTEN GO WRONG

Firms have found three problems with sales automation initiatives:

1. Often generic software has too great a redundancy of function and data for technology-averse salespeople. Conversely, if that software is adapted to the needs of particular sectors, it may become too costly.

2. The cultural integration can be mishandled. The culture of the sales force is very different from that of IS, and an IS-led project will rarely win over salespeople. Salespeople value their interpersonal rather than their technological capabilities. It is a brave manager who disciplines the star salesperson for not using a computer, yet the hearts and minds of the sales force must be won.

3. Replication of data between mobile devices and central servers remains a primary technology challenge. Furthermore, the larger the firm, the more customer data is scattered across different company systems. All of this data needs to be collated into a single storage point to enable salespeople to access it by dialling in from their homes or client sites. The more complex the product and service offering, the harder the challenge becomes – and yet the more important it is for the salespeople to have that data.

Industry has burnt its fingers often enough to suggest that sales automation initiatives which do not integrate relevant applications, prioritize cultural integration and plan a robust replication strategy are doomed.

Best practice suggests that successful sales automation is dependent upon adopting relevant software designed or configured specifically for the sector, and then customizing it to the specific needs of the firm. The data and function redundancy of generic tools will create resistance. Such a relevant application has a six-point checklist, shown in Table 19.1.

INTEGRATE THE CONTACT CENTRE

The contact centre's main focus is to support direct sales and customer servicing. However, the contact centre should also play a role in sales automation strategy. In many firms, salespeople do not know when the contact centre has contacted the customer or vice versa. The contact centre can fulfil a number of roles in an integrated sales automation model:

☐ The contact centre can telephone existing customers, working through pre-defined, context sensitive dialogues to establish channel preferences, basic product and service needs, and propensity to buy. This establishes prospect lists for salespeople. In both the business-to-business and business-to-consumer sectors, some customers want to be serviced by salespeople and some want to serve themselves. Use the contact centre to establish this preference more cheaply than the sales force can. Analytical technologies enable head offices to understand customer needs sufficiently well to construct prospect lists.

☐ The contact centre can take on administrative tasks currently carried out by the salespeople, freeing them to do their core task – selling. These administrative tasks include

1 Can it be readily integrated to the firm's back office systems?
Force vendors to demonstrate this by constructing a prototype that integrates with your most complex back office system. Most sales automation procurement projects focus upon the function within the software, yet integrating sales automation tools with business systems soaks up 80 per cent of the cost, and carries 80 per cent of the risk. If this is not factored into your plans it will be 80 per cent of the overrun.

2 Does it offer relevant capabilities?
The tool must offer integrated capabilities for needs analysis and product and service calculations appropriate to your industry sector. Salespeople will only use tools that do something that they cannot.

3 Does it pass the usability test?
Choose a focus group of salespeople drawn from across the company and see if they can work with it successfully. Most sales automation initiatives fail because sales forces do not use them. Head office executives may see value, but if the sales force does not, the initiative will fail.

4 Will it integrate with your contact centre software?
A smart combination of contact centre and sales force is the most effective method for focusing sales force time effectively.

5 Does it include an event-driven system to understand the buying cycle?
Salespeople increasingly sell complex products and services because the simple products are sold and will be sold direct, more and more. These complex offerings are likely to have a complex buying cycle. Understanding where the customer is in that buying cycle is critical.

6 Can you run a pilot?
A pilot among the more technically literate salespeople prior to full roll-out should be regarded as essential to engage the sales force. An ongoing program of support and education is then required. As discussed in Chapter 9, running a pilot allows you to take an option on whether to proceed to a full roll-out.

TABLE 19.1: Identifying the right sales automation technology

scheduling appointments with named representatives using centrally managed diary capabilities, issuing customer details (such as directions to the customer's location), and calculating purchasing propensities.

☐ The contact centre can answer sales force queries regarding customers, products or services. Salespeople should spend as little time as possible researching questions from customers – they are too expensive a resource. Particularly where the firm operates through both direct and agent channels, it does not make sense to manage two contact centre infrastructures to support the two channels.

☐ Other tasks that the contact centre can take on include supporting administrative work, for example, changing customer addresses and order status chasing. The time that salespeople have to spend on administration can be minimized by initiating a business re-engineering project which discovers where administrative effort is being undertaken by salespeople and diverting it to the contact centre.

A failure to integrate contact centre and sales force misses one of the big sales automation opportunities that is open to many firms. The difficulty of this integration is cultural first and technological second.

THE BUSINESS CASE IS COMPELLING

Evidence suggests that sales revenues from salespeople can be increased by over 25 per cent by using a well-implemented sales automation strategy. More time is allocated to selling rather than administration, leads are better qualified resulting in an improved time to sell ratio, and fewer unproductive visits are made. Telephone qualification ensures more focused visits which allow salespeople to address specific customer needs.

Annual staff turnover amongst the sales force may be 5 per cent and even experienced salespeople may take six months to become fully productive in a new territory. Diary filling and customer knowledge acquisition are primary problems facing new salespeople. A sound sales automation model can help fill the diaries of new salespeople, and help experienced salespeople become more productive more rapidly by providing improved information.

Many firms have a discrepancy between data captured by salespeople (e.g. needs analysis and fact finding data) and that stored within the organization (e.g. derived data and service history). This can be resolved by integrating sales force and contact centre technology and deploying a single customer database to underpin both media is likely to pay dividends.

Salespeople often focus attention upon repeat business and incentive payments often reward such behaviour at the expense of more difficult new sales. Centralized diary management addresses this and ensures that salespeople are given a balance of new and existing contacts.

Although channel redirection has not had the radical impact that internet gurus first promised, it does mean that customers who want telephone or self-service can be serviced appropriately. This ensures that expensive sales force time is not spent on customers who would prefer telephone support.

A close integration of sales force technology and contact centre means that the contact centre is better able to support the customer directly for straightforward requests (e.g. enquiries). Encouraging customers and the sales force to use contact centres for simple enquiries saves money and frees the sales force for selling.

Properly implemented, such a program is popular with the sales force. While an element of control is removed (e.g. over diaries), increases in sales and therefore in commission compensate. If sold as a secretarial service rather than 'big brother', the cultural battle with the sales force can be won.

SUMMARY

1 Design your sales automation strategy as an integral component of CRM strategy – the emphasis of many sales automation strategies is wrong. The strategy should not be to automate salespeople, but to deploy automation to reduce the burden of unproductive activities.

2 Make sales automation an organizational and cultural change initiative, not a technology initiative. Involve salespeople in the selection process, and run a pilot.

3 Consider the integration between contact centre and salespeople. Contact centre technology now offers the tools to enable head office to prospect, fill diaries, answer enquiries and so on. Consider merging contact centres which support direct and agent channels.

4 From a technology perspective, consider three technologies: contact centre, data mining (or analytics) and mobile applications. A strategy that integrates the three technologies will dramatically outperform the sum of its individual parts.

PART  6

TO INFINITY AND BEYOND

We end by focusing on trends that we believe will transform customer relationships over the next few years.

A new breed of customers who have never known life without URLs is coming your way soon, and they are going to place different demands on you. These are people who understand how to programme video recorders and what SMS (Short Message Service) stands for. Are you ready for it? Meet the internet generation.

'The customer is in control' is a mantra of the CRM community and beyond and we believe that it is true. However, the impact is not a nebulous need to invest in 'being nice to customers'. Customer Managed Relationships will force you to change how you connect with customers and move you towards mass customization, but not just of your products and services. Customer Managed Relationships will force you to mass customize everything.

CHAPTER 20

THE INTERNET GENERATION

INTRODUCTION

Today's young people are growing up immersed in technology. They play video games, download music from the web and burn it to CD, program the VCR for their parents and are the only ones who seem to really understand SMS. They are mobile, techno-savvy and entertainment hungry. This is the internet generation. They are different in how they shop, work and think. They are the customers of tomorrow, and you need to start planning how to connect with them.

HYPE OR HIP?

Part 1

The dot.comedy of the internet stockmarket bubble which burst in 2001 was about credulity not technology.

Brand was a creation of industrialization and the need to overcome the new disparities between customer and manufacturer. In the digital world, that disconnection is extreme. The creation of brand from scratch in a global marketplace is expensive. For start ups, the finance can come only from shareholders or borrowing. Internet technology cannot be blamed for expenditure on brand.

Given brand, why did customers not come? When the business model was good, they did – but not in sufficient numbers or buying sufficient goods to cover the cost of the capital investment in brand and infrastructure. Businesses have never constructed customer bases overnight. McDonald's began with one restaurant; Hewlett-Packard began in a garage. The internet accelerates the process of customer acquisition, but not to the point that customer bases are acquired within months rather than years. An incredible statistic was that by the summer of 2000, just five years after its launch, www.amazon.com had acquired over 20 million customers, from a standing start – an unparalleled run rate. Nevertheless, still www.amazon.com only achieved profitability in January 2002. The customer run rate required to deliver profit builds over time, but brand and infrastructure costs run ahead of that curve. The greater the upfront brand and infrastructure spend, the greater the bet on the customer run rate. Firms like www.amazon.com can weather the storm with a strong business model. Even so, on 23 June 2000, Lehman Brothers issued a report suggesting that the company could run out of money within a year, crushed by debt and chronic unprofitability. Fortunately www.amazon.com has flourished. If there are flaws in the business model in terms of speed of access, offerings and so on, then that critical bet on the customer run rate is risky.

Historically, new customer acquisition is organic, typically growing from the locality or niche in which the start up operated at a slow and manageable pace – with investment in marketing keeping step. The challenge for internet start ups is that in a virtual world, the only way to acquire new customers is by getting your URL in front of as many prospects as possible. However, the more virtual the business, the more difficult that is.

With this in mind, consider tomorrow's customers. They do not mistake technology for a potent mix of shareholder credulity, lack of economic sense and poor business models with technology – issues about which they, unlike their share owning parents, care little. To blame the internet for the dot.comedy is to blame flowers for Dutch tulip mania in the seventeenth century, or sailing ships for the South Sea Bubble in 1720.

Part 2

Sibonisiwe Nkomo's introduction to the internet was fascinating to watch. Exposed to the web in one 30-minute school class a week, this Johannesburg teenager revelled in the unlimited access to the internet in the house where she earned a small income as a babysitter. With no additional coaching, she opened her own Hotmail account and spent hours chatting to new-found friends across the world, later corresponding through e-mail. A year later, she spends less time chatting and more time researching. The internet has become important to her life.

Sibonisiwe's generation is the natural target for tomorrow's highly competitive commercial technology-enabled offerings. Yet how much do we know about this market? What are their needs, desires and preferences? What do they consider 'cool'? How do we connect with them? How should we attract them? How can they create value for your company?

THE INTERNET IS THE MOST SIGNIFICANT TECHNOLOGICAL EVENT YET

Forget the bursting of the dot.com bubble. The internet is about connection and convenience. And the internet generation is reaching maturity (and customerhood) with an expectation of convenient connection to anything and anybody. If they are not part of your plans, then they will be soon because they are an increasing proportion of your customer base.

In 1969, it would have been nearly impossible to imagine that a fledgling experiment in computer networking at UCLA and other institutions could emerge as the defining technology of a generation. Yet this technology has become the most ubiquitous, and is still the fastest growing, electronic communication tool. The internet has the potential to provide more communication power, purchasing capability and knowledge gathering reach than print and other electronic media combined.

Even more astonishing is that most of the internet's growth has occurred in less than seven years. In January 1994, when the UCLA Center for Communication Policy, the Academy of Television Arts and Sciences, and US Vice President Al Gore hosted the first 'Information

Superhighway' conference, the internet had little immediate relevance to most customers' lives. By 1997, some 19 million Americans were using the internet. That number tripled in one year and passed the 100 million mark in 1999. Even after five years (1996–2000) of explosive growth, new enrolment remained high. In the month of November 2000, more than 4 million Americans joined the online world – roughly 140,000 new users each day, up from about 55,000 in the first quarter of 2000.

The technology that supports the internet is similarly expanding with unprecedented speed. The internet's capacity to carry information doubles every 100 days. In 2001, the number of online, indexable documents topped 1 billion. Every 24 hours, the content of the worldwide web increases by more than 3.2 million pages and more than 715,000 images. Late in 2000, the total number of hits on US web pages passed the 1 billion per day mark. E-mail, perhaps the most basic of online services, continues to grow beyond all expectations. The number of electronic mail boxes worldwide jumped 84 per cent to almost 570 million in 1999. In 1998, the US Postal Service delivered 101 billion pieces of paper mail; estimates of the number of e-mail messages transmitted that year range as high as 4 trillion. Such expansion raises intriguing questions about how interpersonal communication and commerce are changing.

In the United States, for example, when electricity became publicly available, 46 years passed before 30 per cent of American homes were wired; 38 years passed before the telephone reached 30 per cent of US household. It took 17 years for television to reach the same percentage. The internet required only seven years to reach 30 per cent of American households.

As with the introduction of television, the internet has had a profound impact on society. This has been particularly significant for the generation that has grown up with the internet.

THE INTERNET GENERATION – HUGE AND DIFFERENT

They are the internet generation. Sometimes referred to as generation Y, the millennial generation, or the Nintendo generation, this generation was weaned online. In the US, the older members of the internet generation, born in the early 1980s, are just coming to the end of their formal education.

Generation Y is estimated to number more than 1.5 billion, almost as many as the post-war baby boomers, and dwarfing generation X, who are sandwiched in between. Generation Y are marked by a distinctly practical world view, say marketing experts.

Raised in dual-income or single-parent families, generation Y have already been given considerable financial responsibility. Surveys show that they are deeply involved in family purchases, from groceries to cars. One in nine US high school students has a credit card co-signed by a parent, and many will take on debt to finance college. Most expect to have careers and are thinking about home ownership. Early observations of the internet generation in the US indicate that this generation is different from earlier teenagers in significant ways:

☐ They are more ethnically diverse than previous generations.

☐ They are more tolerant of cultural and behavioural differences.

☐ Members of the internet generation are not interested in devoting their lives to work but cannot wait to start spending.

☐ Health and fitness is a concern, but they are still tempted by fast food, clubbing and drugs.

169

☐ They are interested in spirituality and experiment with religion, but will not necessarily commit to one religion.

☐ They change fashion and style based on times of the day: Grunge by day; exotic by night.

☐ They have grown up in prosperous times and are more optimistic than their older brothers and sisters.

Having grown up in an even more media-saturated, brand-conscious world than their parents, generation Y respond differently to advertising, and prefer to encounter advertisements in different places. Marketers that capture the internet generation's attention do so by bringing messages to places they congregate: the internet, a snowboarding tournament, or cable TV. Ads may be funny or disarmingly direct. Some previously successful marketing strategies may fall flat with this audience.

Soon almost every business is going to have to learn the nuances of marketing to the internet generation. In just a few years, today's teenagers will be out of college and shopping for their first cars, homes, and mutual funds. The distinctive buying habits displayed today will follow them as they enter the high spending years of young adulthood. Firms unable to click with them will miss a vast new market – and could find the doors thrown open to new competitors.

Fortunately, we can gather further clues about the internet generation's future behaviour and preferences by examining their forerunners: today's consumer users of e-business. This is a small (if growing) group, but an important predictor of things to come.

SERVICING STATISTICAL OUTLIERS IN A NEW MARKET

The size and growth of the internet have made it many firms' nightmare. The diversity of technologies, the short attention span of visitors, and above all, the multitudes of new marketing opportunities (e.g. search engines, portals, catalogues, net-markets and more) conspire to create an environment where we build the site – and customers do not come. Even well-established internet businesses, such as stock brokerages, have to accept that only a small percentage of their customers will use the e-business medium exclusively.

With the proliferation of new media, institutions seem more focused on expanding their online and wireless offerings than improving their existing websites. A 2001 survey by Jupiter Communications found that for every CEO (chief executive officer) who says that making the company website customer-friendly is important, there are four who say they are more interested in increasing their mobile and other online offerings.

There is a disparity between what online institutions are building and the services their customers are seeking. Institutions will lose major market share if they fail to offer integrated, customized and simplified online offerings that better suit customer needs. US research over the last ten years indicates that customers' demands largely fall into two categories: convenience and trust. The top qualities that people look for when choosing a financial services provider, for example, are customer service (52 per cent) and accounts guaranteed by the US Federal Government (59 per cent). However, most financial institutions are focusing on innovative features. Fifty-seven per cent of financial services executives believe that expanding online capabilities is their chief priority. The volume and complexity of online financial options spirals, producing new complexity – fundamentally at odds with the customers' top priority of convenience.

SERVICING KNOWLEDGEABLE CUSTOMERS

Products and services that rely on esoteric terminology and consumer ignorance to conceal inherent weaknesses will suffer. Processes that are unnecessarily cumbersome and delay the gratification of customer demands will not be accepted. The internet generation knows what is possible and achievable. You and your systems will be benchmarked against the best in the world. So, publicise your specifications and pare down your processes. New customers want to 'pull' product, not have it 'pushed'.

The internet generation is fickle, not because they do not know what they want, but because they change their minds almost immediately upon experiencing new technology. Websites are already the most important and frequently used banking information source for retail banking customers, second only to newspapers as the most frequently used general financial information source. The internet generation will place even greater demands on this resource.

Organizations should carefully examine the online behaviour of their customers with a view to tailoring and customizing their web-based information offerings.

OFFER LOW PRICE TODAY, CONVENIENCE TOMORROW

What motivates today's customers to buy online? Initially, price. They perceive or hope that they will get good deals. Nevertheless, that influence will decline as today's online customers realize the benefits of convenience – something the internet generation knows already.

In a recent study, 45 per cent of online banking users cited rates and fees as the initial reason to bank online, but only 6 per cent cite them as a reason for continuing to use these services. Price sensitivity is the critical factor in convincing today's consumers to buy online, but over time, convenience and not price becomes the key driver for continued use. The internet generation already has convenience (and speed) as its critical motivator. Firms should implement a two-pronged customer service model:

1 Promote low costs and fees during the customer acquisition phase. With online services, free trial periods should work well – provided they are long enough to experience the service fully.

2 Switch to focusing on service features for post-purchase reassurance – better access, customer service, fully integrated channels, heightened convenience.

Most surveys show that online banking customers are, on average, very satisfied. However, two sub-groups have an even higher level of satisfaction: those who use the internet as their primary banking medium, and the elderly. These findings make sense – the most satisfied users of any service are the ones who actually use it, and the convenience and safety of internet banking are ideal for those who have difficulty travelling to branches. Online banking customers who perform the majority of their banking online are recognizing the time savings and ready availability of information that the internet delivers.

Other noteworthy findings of surveys of online banking customers include:

☐ There is a significant lack of awareness about the specifics of online services. For example, half of online customers do not know whether they can stop payments online. A better understanding of available features and benefits would help to drive usage.

☐ Customers who stop using online banking give reasons including, insufficient benefit, convenience or interest; concerns about security; and unreliable site performance. The first two reasons are communication issues. The third rests squarely on the shoulders of the manager of the site.

☐ Almost one-third of dissatisfied online customers have considered switching banks because of their web experience.

What does this have to do with the internet generation? The basic motivations for the behaviour of today's online customers will be amplified and accelerated for the internet generation.

CAPITALIZING ON THE INTERNET GENERATION

Don't mothball those business-to-customer sites – yet

Business-to-customer (B2C) e-commerce has not been a roaring success. A recent study indicates that concerns about security are the major inhibiting factor. The same study, however, indicates that the internet generation have less concern about security and prefer to shop online. These consumers are about to enter the economic mainstream. It stands to reason that they will turn to the internet for everything from groceries to financial advice.

Many companies will lose market share because they have let e-business initiatives die. Seven per cent of North American consumers already want to do everything online – from researching and buying insurance to buying groceries. Companies that fail to maintain momentum of their business-to-consumer e-commerce initiatives will emerge with smaller pieces of the pie and it will take time to claw their way back.

However, business-to-consumer sites will have to improve considerably to satisfy the internet generation. Take a hard look at your future customers. If you think that your business will depend on generation Y in three to five years, you need an online brand now. Online advertising (which is currently cheap) could help; Pepsi's Pepsi Stuff blitz on Yahoo! netted the company 3.5 million responses and a 5 per cent increase in single-serve sales.

It is not all about money

For generation Y time matters and, specifically, an instant response. If you want to learn about a firm's offering, you can telephone and risk being put on hold or passed around for several minutes, or you can go online and find the information right now – whatever the hour. If you want to communicate with a friend, send an e-mail or SMS and your friend can respond immediately.

It used to be said that the internet was about money – that it let you compare prices and find the cheapest product or service. This causes sellers to focus more on costs and pricing, driving overall prices down and promoting mass commodities. What really makes shopping on the web different is that you can do it instantly, not just cheaply.

It is not all about information

Some search engine and portal strategists believe that the web is about information. The more information you can give the customer they reason, the better. The concept of making every word on the web clickable is destined to fail. We, and especially the internet generation, need more relevance and context, not more information or more links to review.

It is all about convenience and time

Some organizations are reluctant to provide online information. They should reconsider. What they should be providing is not just information, but information that customers want right now, packaged to save them time. The internet is concise. It uses common technology. If you tell customers by e-mail when and where the information is available, they do not have to search – they do not even have to go and look for it. And if customers want to buy, let them buy immediately – 'Press this link and it will be sent to your address'.

So, take a close look at your online content program. Does it revolve around being instantly convenient?

Promote the media of choice

Today's competitive environment is spawning multiple media, and yet only small numbers of users utilize any individual medium. There are 200 million SMS-enabled cellular telephones in use in Europe alone. Do you plan to deliver through this medium? The internet generation will expect excellent service in all supported media. This brings a classic dilemma: which media to service? The appropriate strategy is to prioritize, because you cannot deliver across all media, and promote aggressively to prevent media proliferating.

DON'T MISS THE WAVE

For Sibonisiwe Nkomo, the future is optimistic. She has a thorough understanding of a vital technology, friends around the globe and she has improved her skills in her third language, English. She represents a future inhabited by people who have different loyalties, hopes and dreams.

To your organization, the internet generation seems a giant wave, bearing down fast. Will you have the thrill of surfing down the face of the wave? Will you be smashed against the rocks? Or will you simply be momentarily lifted, then left behind?

SUMMARY

1   Consider personalization and customization capabilities that present each customer with unique offerings, based on the services they request and the usage data you gather. Generation Y will offer you loyalty if you reward them incrementally.

2   Ensure that e-business offerings provide fast and frequent feedback, in order to keep the customer's attention focused and to maintain confidence. If generation Y do not know what is going on when they are on your site, they will go elsewhere.

3   Position online products based on customer needs, rather than on the latest technology: let common sense and not the internet design team, drive.

4   Integrate systems and capabilities to minimize complexity. Aim to elevate and maintain the quality of customer experience over the quantity of new products, channels and features. The breadth of your capabilities may be of interest to shareholders and to your staff, but relevant information conveniently presented is of interest to customers.

5   Construct your connection strategy from the perspective of the customer asking 'What can I do?' rather than from your corporate perspective of 'What do we do?'

CHAPTER 21

CUSTOMER MANAGED RELATIONSHIPS

INTRODUCTION

In 1993, as Peppers and Rogers published their *The One to One Future* manifesto, Hammer and Champy published their manifesto for business revolution[1]. Three Cs besieged all companies: customers, competitors and change. It was time to stop tinkering with existing ways of doing business and rethink how work was done. The goal was to focus on customers and to harness change – particularly the change brought about by 'disruptive' technologies – in order to deliver value to customers faster and cheaper than the competition. Innovation meant new offerings delivered in new ways by employees freed from the drudgery of routine, although specialized, tasks. The routine tasks needed to support value delivery would be automated. There would be no 'standard process'.

Straightforward problems would be forwarded to generalist case workers, empowered to resolve them using their best judgement and the information at hand. When they needed help, the workers would consult the few remaining specialists. By eliminating the time that transactions spent waiting in intrays, these changes could remove 90 per cent of processing time. The walls surrounding departments and business units would fall.

Early re-engineering projects found that customer value was produced by less than 10 per cent of work processes. In most firms, the overwhelming majority of the work was checking, coordinating, and handing off within and between departments – activities that delivered no value to customers. Each step took time and introduced errors that needed correction and revalidation. Re-engineering was the call to focus on process not functional organization, and to use information technology to restructure what was done and how. The goal was to create a new world of work where workers were problem solvers or innovators. Truly routine activities should be automated, replacing humans with machines. Everything else should be obliterated – not done at all.

174

---

[1] Michael Hammer and James Champy, *Reengineering the Corporation*, Harper Business, 1993.

By the end of 1995, 69 per cent of North American and 75 per cent of European firms had at least one re-engineering project underway[2]. Nevertheless, soon after, possibly killed by its own universality, re-engineering was dead and had been replaced by ERP. Best practice – standard processes copied from industry leaders – replaced process innovation.

Then the re-engineering horror stories started to emerge. Tales circulated of massive lay offs, demoralized work forces, and failed technology projects orchestrated by hordes of arrogant young consultants. Looming Year 2000 (Y2K) issues triggered a rush to replace ageing systems, leaving no time for process redesign. ERP projects set firms' processes in concrete, which later required teams to continually break and reset it as the business changed.

Meanwhile, what of the customers? They were infuriated at listening to 20 minutes of tinny Vivaldi on the phone because 'improvement' meant understaffed call centres had replaced local outlets. Trusted contacts were out of jobs because of downsizing. Branch managers had become powerless to take decisions because head office referral was the norm. And head office used automated tools, not relationships to determine who was worthy. Customers of 40 years' standing received letters addressed to 'Dear The End House, Bramley' because marketing had become an extension of the database and analytical tools were blind to data quality.

By making a flawed assumption that creating customer value was necessarily a consequence of eliminating cost, re-engineering as it was implemented was arguably responsible for some of the most rapid and dramatic reductions in the quality of customers' experience. This was never the intention.

In Chapter 1, we implied that mass customization was the approach for the customer intimate. Companies could choose whether or not to model their business around customizing their products and services ever more precisely for the needs of the individual customer. This chapter will argue that that model is changing. The bar of customer intimacy is being raised higher and higher. Mass customization will soon no longer only be the preserve of the customer intimate. Or perhaps it will. Perhaps we are all customer intimate now.

NOT PERFECT, BUT LESS IMPERFECT

What has changed? We are now in a customer managed world where business value means customer value. We remain a long way from a 'perfect market' – the concept that four trends, described below, would destroy the boundaries between customers and suppliers. Nevertheless, consider how all four are to some extent in place, or have become more relevant.

1 **Availability of information** – Most customers in developed markets will soon have internet access that enables an unparalleled research depth on any topic from purchasing an aquarium to obtaining pension advice.

2 **No barriers to entry and exit** – Barriers to market entry and exit remain but increasingly companies can enter new markets, and more easily exit them, by building partnerships with other companies already in the field.

3 **Equilibrium price** – Equilibrium price applies to products and services that can be directly compared. In a truly transparent world, how can you survive if you are not cheap? More than ever the answer is to understand your value discipline. Transparency forces firms to consider differentiating themselves on something other than price, and to choose between product leadership (competing on quality and superiority), customer intimacy (competing

[2] 'Business Process Reengineering: Its Past, Present and Possible Future', Harvard Business School, 13 November 1995.

on relevance), or operational excellence (competing on price and accessibility). Only when the offerings are differentiated, can you break out from being forced to drive down price.

4 **Perfect matching** – In the ultimately connected world, the gap between supplier and customer is non-existent: customers can find exactly what they want, from exactly the right supplier, when they want it. We are rapidly approaching this situation. A new breed of 'infomediaries' sit between suppliers and customers and offer at least superficially impartial advice about who to buy from, why, when and how much to pay.

Only by re-engineering how you create value, can you deliver value in such an environment. Re-engineering is back, but it is different. This round of re-engineering must deliver customer value. And that is going to involve a mass customization of everything.

MASS CUSTOMIZE . . . EVERYTHING

Where the 1990s was the decade of re-engineering to obliterate and automate process, the 2000s will be the decade of re-engineering to deliver customized product and service in real time. If 1990s' re-engineering looked deep into the firm's internal operations and automated how the corporation worked, 2000s' re-engineering looks out to customers and partners and changes how firms connect across a complex web of customers, partners, channels, media. The way to deliver customer value is to accept that the customer is in control and to adapt how you do your business to customer needs. This is the age of the customer managed relationship.

In customer managed relationships, what you offer, how you offer it, how you price it and how you use partnerships to construct it, are all adapted to how you attract, acquire and retain individual customers. This demands that you mass customize:

☐ Your products (or services).

☐ Your processes.

☐ Your prices.

☐ Your partnerships.

Customer managed relationships are not some ethereal vision in which you continue doing the same things, while talking about customers being in control. You have to re-engineer how you create value.

MASS CUSTOMIZE YOUR PRODUCTS

Mass customization was about product, about being able to create differentiated products at mass production prices through re-engineering the business around the smart use of technology. However, mass customization has not changed business. For every Michael Dell there are a myriad of wannabee Henry Fords mass producing, driving down on costs, standardizing across their product or service lines.

The reason for this comparative failure is that the technology has not been up to the job. Where it currently exists – for example, enabling Levi Strauss to have custom jeans built to order – cost and complexity and their effect on the price and accessibility of the product, have failed to transform markets. Levi Strauss's customization efforts counterpoint Dell's success. Mass customization of products has so far failed to change the world because it has been impossible to reconcile customer intimacy with operational excellence.

Nonetheless, the technology is getting better through an iterative process of competitive innovation across different industries. We are starting to see mass customization, if not at the level of the individual customer then for increasingly granular customer segments, across many sectors:

☐ In insurance, more and more customers expect to be able to include or exclude different policy features, and insurers are able to deliver this flexibility without charging excessive premiums by using innovative policy management technologies.

☐ In car manufacturing, customers are given a larger range of options and transparent pricing models at ever lower prices. Simultaneously, lead times are falling as new technologies allow cars to be built to order.

☐ Furniture manufacturers can offer a range of customized options delivered in the same time frame as their standard offers at only marginal premiums.

☐ Publishers can organize ever smaller print runs because computerized technologies reduce the cost and risk of introducing new titles, allowing many more titles to be created for more precise markets.

Computerization increasingly makes customization only a marginal additional cost. Thus, when customers compare your customized offering with standard product or service from an operationally excellent competitor, they can access it as easily, it is delivered as punctually, and the price is much the same. How can an outstandingly successful operationally excellent firm that focuses upon standardization, such as McDonald's, grasp mass customization? The Cadbury's Creme Egg is a British icon. It is sold primarily at Easter. McDonald's partnered with Cadbury's to create a Creme Egg McFlurry; the new product became McDonald's advertising lead over Easter. This was perhaps a small step towards customization – it was geographically limited (the UK) and event-oriented (Easter). However, from this small start, what may be possible in ten years' time using new technologies? Nationally customized products become regionally customized. The number of events expands to regional events. An English town runs a French farmers' market; when the cost of customization becomes marginal, what is to stop the local restaurant creating a French-oriented offering? Consider mass customization not as a switch, but a sliding scale in which products can be customized to ever more granular customer segments until ultimately reaching the individual customer.

MASS CUSTOMIZE YOUR PROCESSES

The mass customization of products is relatively well understood – if hard to find. Now there is a new form of mass customization, which involves process. From a CRM perspective, mass customization of process will enable customers to dictate their touch points with a business process at no, or very little, additional cost to the firm. Companies that have complex processes where process status changes frequently (insurance claims, bespoke furniture orders) used to tell customers when the status changed at their convenience, if at all. Soon – and we can already see this in new mobile services that alert customers when their shares fall below a certain price – customers will dictate when and through what medium they want to be told of status changes. John Doe may want notification of payment being taken for his order, and of product dispatch. Jane Doe may want only to be told of the dispatch. John may want e-mail notification. Jane may want a text message to her mobile phone.

The difference is that technology, which posed so many barriers to change in the earlier days of business re-engineering, now promises to serve radical solutions. New Business Process Management (BPM) systems define and manage business processes. They orchestrate the many software application components needed to carry out routine but complex tasks, such as selecting products or services, placing orders, checking the availability of products, choosing a dispatch method, assessing the credit worthiness of the buyer, and managing payments and credits. These BPM technologies are increasingly integrated with CRM technologies. Existing technology requires the business to design complex processes (e.g. build to order) and then expects IT staff to integrate the packages and proprietary software needed to support the process. Often the business objectives of the new process design are lost between business and IT. With BPM technologies, business and IT work together to design, deploy and revise end-to-end business processes. These technologies provide agility, making it easier for the business to access and use the information flowing through a complex web of customers, suppliers and other partners. BPM technologies work to:

- ☐ Improve the quality of process design – analysis tools validate, simulate and enhance processes before deployment.

- ☐ Reduce the time and cost of building a networked enterprise because they build on, rather than replace, legacy systems, both home grown and best of breed solutions.

- ☐ Integrate from the top down, reflecting the process model, not the myriad point-to-point technical interfaces that cost too much to implement today.

- ☐ Improve your ability to make sense of and react to market dynamics, by providing real-time measurements on process operations.

With these new technologies you can mass customize your processes, change the way you work and who you work with to meet the needs of each customer and market you serve. Your competitive edge will be your flexibility to manage many very different processes and your agility to change processes as fast as your customers and markets demand new services.

Proactivity in the past meant pushing more product and service at customers, however personalized and well directed. It was a sales tool. Process was a corporate black box and unlocking it was almost impossible. Those days are changing. Business Process Management and re-engineering in the 2000s changes the game to one where you must respond rapidly to individual customer needs through the adroit use of technology.

MASS CUSTOMIZE YOUR PRICES

Many firms, particularly value pools, are increasingly able to consider the mass customization of price. In today's relatively transparent market, customers understand supply and demand pricing better than ever before. A powerful combination is now on offer:

- ☐ Price sensitive customers understand what is cheap and what is expensive, and accept and expect supply and demand to drive pricing.

- ☐ Technology allows real-time pricing at a more granular level than ever before.

Prices have always been sensitive to fluctuations in customer demand. What changes now is the rapidity with which firms can respond to demand, and the sophistication of the information available to them.

Hotels, like most pools, are used to adjusting their prices to reflect peaks and troughs in demand. Chapter 7 suggested that managing this sensitivity is a primary CRM role for pools. Consider the potential for mass customization of pricing. Stelios Haji-Ioannou, founder of easyJet, quoted in *The Sunday Times* (May 2002), said: 'As demand increases so does the price. That's why the last Easyjet seat costs more.' easyJet already has sophisticated models to mass customize price.

MASS CUSTOMIZE YOUR PARTNERSHIPS

Increasingly, competition is about partnerships competing with partnerships, rather than individual firms competing with each other:

☐ In the airline industry, Oneworld competes with the Star Alliance. British Airways and American Airlines compete, but at the margins; Lufthansa and Delta are their real competition.

☐ In the fast food industry, of course McDonald's competes with Burger King. However, these firms line up powerful partnerships with Coca-Cola and Pepsi. It is the combination that competes, albeit through different brands.

Historically such partnerships were pre-defined, structured relationships in which taut definitions of products or services to be supplied were entrenched within complex contracts pored over by lawyers. Yet partnerships must be more and more flexible to customer needs. The hotel that partners with the car rental firm will no longer have a rigid price tariff. The receptionist needs real-time access to real-time pricing and availability information, to offer a discount on those hard to shift compact cars that are the only ones left in the rental car park. The insurance firm's distressed customer with an exploding boiler needs to know *now* which plumber, decorator and electrician is closest and available to undertake the job. The firm needs estimates back in real-time, and to authorize the work in real time. This requires re-engineering across corporate boundaries for customer value to be created by seamless connection. The customer's experience in dealing with a firm is informed by a knowledge of the partner's capabilities at that specific point in time.

Mass customization of partnerships demands one thing above everything else – connectivity in real time. How can that be achieved? Do you frantically construct interfaces between all the (rapidly proliferating) connection points as fast as they arise? As you form new partnerships, do you send in teams of systems analysts to swap systems specifications like children swap Pokémon cards? Not if you want to compete.

The leaders in this field are already talking Business Process Management Language (BPML). BPML offers a universal process language, based on XML. It is an Esperanto for business processes – but, unlike Esperanto, it will become universal because it drives powerful benefits. Once partnerships adopt it, as they are starting to, their ability to mass customize their combined offering will mean that others have to adopt it in order to compete. This can only happen when the technologies talk the same language. BPML makes it seem as if they do.

BPML is a language to connect enterprises with each other and with their customers. Let's say that company A's systems speak French, and company B's German. The only way to connect those systems is to create a French-to-German translation capability – traditionally called an interface. Of course, company A's systems actually speak a score of languages or dialects specific to certain applications, and so do company B's. Now multiply the problem across scores of partnerships and millions of customers operating their own different devices – over which you have no control, because customers own them.

Although initially costly to connect processes, the business case will be made by the savings in non-value adding activities. Connecting customer orders through the supply chain will drive huge savings in the interfaces between firms. The more extensive the reliance upon partnerships, the greater the savings that can be obtained.

Without the foundation of business process management connectivity, interoperability and real-time connectivity cannot be achieved because it is impossible to connect near infinite diversity. To beat the competition to win customers, we will have to be connected to partners; to connect to partners, we will have to use BPM.

Partnerships once created interfaces that were exposed to customers. As station guards shout on the London Underground: 'Mind the gap'. It applies as much to distances between partnerships as to the distance between train and platform. Customer Managed Relationships will force you to change that. Are you ready to mass customize everything?

SUMMARY

1 Reconsider re-engineering from a customer perspective. Consider whether, if you undertook original re-engineering projects, these had a customer cost or value bias, and whether they were successful within your organization.

2 Consider the extent to which you currently mass customize your product or service offering for customers. Disregard any technology or cost constraints, and consider what an ultimate vision of mass customization for your organization would look like. How real could that be in 2010?

3 Consider the extent to which you mass customize process. Do customers drive their connection with you, or do you dictate to them? How could you integrate into your business mechanisms to enable the customer to connect on their own terms?

4 Do you mass customize prices? Consider how flexible real-time pricing models would affect your business and your competitiveness? How realistic are they in your sector? Who is the leader in this in your sector? Who will be the leader?

5 Reflect on the web of partnerships that you currently have within your business. Do customers have to 'mind the gap'? How much does it cost to maintain partnerships? How much to build one? Are partnerships a necessary evil or a nimble feature of your value delivery to customers?

6 Visit www.bpmi.org and think about whether business process management could affect how you compete for customers. If in 2000 you wondered how the world was before the database, so in 2010 you may be wondering how the world was before the 'processbase'.

FURTHER READING

BOOKS

The books mentioned in Chapter 1, on the origins of CRM, make interesting reading. These include:

Michael Porter, *Competitive Advantage: Creating and Sustaining Superior Business Performance*, The Free Press, 1985.

C B Stabell and Ø D Fjeldstad, 'Configuring Value For Competitive Advantage: On Chains, Shops, and Networks', *Strategic Management Journal*, Vol. 19, 1998.

Don Peppers and Martha Rogers, *The One to One Future*, Currency/Doubleday, 1993.

B Joseph Pine II, *Mass Customisation – The New Frontier in Business Competition*, Harvard Business School Press, 1993.

Michael Hammer and James Champy, *Reengineering the Corporation*, Harper Business, 1993.

Michael Hammer, 'Reengineering Work: Don't Automate, Obliterate', *Harvard Business Review*, Jul–Aug 1990.

Frederick Reichheld, *The Loyalty Effect*, Harvard Business School Press, 1996.

Michael Treacy and Fred Wiersema, *The Discipline of Market Leaders*, Addison-Wesley, 1995.

The power of traditional brand marketing is described in:

David Aaker, *Managing Brand Equity*, Free Press, 1991.

Ted Levitt, *The Marketing Imagination*, Free Press, 1986.

UOVP® is described in much more detail in:

Simon Knox and Stan Maklan, *Competing on Value*, Financial Times Management, 1998.

Real options pricing is described simply in:

T Copeland and P Keenan, 'How Much is Flexibility Worth?', *The McKinsey Quarterly*, No. 2, pp. 38–49, 1998.

References for the facts and figures about how CRM is performing in the market:

P Callinan, D Weisman and M Girard, 'CRM Finds Repeat Customers in the Global 3500', *Business Technographics Brief* (Forrester Research Inc.), 2001.

R Chatham, D Weisman, L Orlov, T Nakashima and E Howard, Cambridge, Mass: Forrester Reserach Inc., 2001.

G Olazabal, 'Banking: The IT Paradox', *The McKinsey Quarterly*, Vol. 1, 2002.

David Reed, 'Waiting for the Customer Management Revolution', 2001.

Some of the seminal management works outlining CRM:

D Peppers and M Rogers, *The One to One Future*, Currency/Doubleday, 1993.

M Christopher, A Payne and D Ballantyne, *Relationship Marketing*, Butterworth-Heinemann Ltd., 1991.

J I Pine, D Peppers and M Rogers, 'Do you Want to Keep your Customers Forever?', *Harvard Business Review*, Vol. 73, Mar–Apr, No. 2, pp. 103–114, 1995.

F F Reichheld, *The Loyalty Effect*, Harvard Business School Press, 1996.

Susan Fournier sounded the alarm bells for CRM in the following article:

S Fournier, S Dobscha and D Mick, 'Preventing the Premature Death of Relationship Marketing', *Harvard Business Review*, Vol. 76, Jan–Feb, No. 1, pp. 42–51, 1998.

And for a radical view of CRM, read:

A Mitchell, *Right Side Up* , HarperCollins Business, 2001.